KT-195-668

angles on

psychological research

dedications

To Em   JR
To Tanya   CR

angles on

psychological research

Julia Russell   Craig Roberts

Series Editors: Matt Jarvis Julia Russell

Published in 2001 by:
Nelson Thornes Ltd
Delta Place
27 Bath Road
CHELTENHAM
GL53 7TH
United Kingdom

01 02 03 04 05 / 10 9 8 7 6 5 4 3 2 1

A catalogue record for this book is available from the British Library

ISBN 0 7487 5976 X

Illustrations by Oxford Designers and illustrators, Steve Ballinger
Page make-up by Northern Phototypesetting Co. Ltd

Printed and bound in Great Britain by The Bath Press

contents

acknowledgements

We would like to thank Rick Jackman and Louise Watson whose unceasing efforts and invaluable assistance have once again made this possible. Also thanks to Carolyn Lee; welcome to the team.

I would like to acknowledge the efforts of my past students who have taught me to make research methods fun. Special thanks must go to Anna Naylor whose A-level coursework has contributed to Chapter 14.

Thank you also to my colleagues, Matt and Craig, whose ongoing support I accept with gratitude.

JR

As this is my first 'true' book, I have lots of people to thank. Firstly, a big thank you to Julia and Matt who are simply the best people to work with. Thanks for the many hours of fun at work and while writing and editing my half of the book. We make a great team.

I wish to send my deepest gratitude to my mum Carole, dad Malcolm, sister Vanessa and her husband Stuart, none of whom knew I was writing this book: surprise! Am I still working too hard?

My pillars of support throughout my life, Tanya, Lindsey and Rebekah, how can I thank you enough? You've helped me every step of the way during this book. Tanya, I hope this helps you understand statistics after those many years of you copying my homework two seconds before our maths lesson. I love you all.

Finally, the biggest thanks goes to the person who watched this book develop over the summer of 2000: Señor Javier Garcia Frutos. Thank you for all the support you gave me, all the beer we drank and all the glorious fun we had. 'Dos pintas de cerveza, por favor?' TQM Paper Doll.

PS Em: do we win the bet?

CR

The authors and publishers are grateful to the following for permission to reproduce material:

- *Animal Behaviour* for the diagram redrawn from Seyfarth and Cheney (1986) on p. 29

- Cambridge University Press for the table reproduced from *Simple Statistics* 1st edition by F. Clegg (1982) on p. 274 (table 2)

- Egmont Fleetway Ltd. for survey reproduced from Go Girl on p. 194

- *Journal of Anthrozoos* for questionnaire on p. 55

- Open University Press for tables from *Learning to use statistical tests in psychology* by Judith Greene (1999) on pp. 274–7 (tables 3A–D and table 4)

- *The Independent* for extract on p. 95

- Routledge for photo reproduced from *The Mentality of Apes* by W. Kohler (1925) on p. 206.

Every effort has made to contact copyright holders and we apologise if any have been overlooked.

Photo credits

- The Advertising Archive (pp. 74, 193)

- Bettman/Corbis (p. 187)

- John Birdsall Photography (pp. 40, 88)

- Capilano Suspension Bridge and Park (p. 203)

- Sally & Richard Greenhill (p. 109)

- Angela Hampton Family Life Picture Library (p. 4)

- Robert Harding Picture Library (pp. 80, 115, 162)

- Alexandra Milgram (p. 228)

- Miramax/Buena Vista (courtesy Kobal) (p. 77)

- Paramount (courtesy Kobal) (p. 124)

- University of Wisconsin Primate Library (p. 234)

introduction

People are basically nosy, none more so than psychologists. We're fascinated by the private lives of others and what goes on inside their heads. That's part of the attraction of soap operas, docusoaps and fly-on-the-wall TV programmes. Psychological research gives us an opportunity to pry into the lives and thoughts of others – with due attention to ethical concerns about privacy – so that we can discover just what makes people tick.

So, what makes the practical study of psychology different from the everyday speculation about behaviour that we engage in all the time? Why do people say 'lies, damn lies and statistics'? Why do psychologists bother to replicate other psychologists' work? Why shouldn't we just use our friends and family for experiments? This book will provide you with the necessary understanding to answer these questions and many more about the nature of psychological research.

Much of psychology is surprising, at least to psychologists (because they are the first to encounter evidence that can run counter to our expectations about behaviour). Take the effects of watching violent TV, for example. It seems obvious now that watching violence could make people more aggressive but that's because we are familiar with the findings of research that demonstrates this is the case. Once the evidence from psychological research has been absorbed into the public domain it often seems as though it was just 'common sense' after all. Such an assumption ignores the process of discovery, the way in which psychologists have explored, both theoretically and practically, the ways in which humans and non-human animals behave and think.

The scientific method

Psychologists utilise many different research methods in their work, each of which can be employed within the framework of the scientific method. This is not a single technique for collecting data but an overall approach to tackling a problem. For students of psychology, the focus is on *hypothetico-deductive research*. This approach to the scientific method aims to work from an observation to a testable explanation that can be modified in the light of findings.

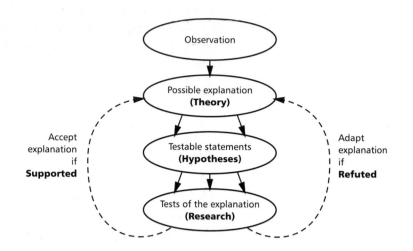

The hypothetico-deductive method

Of course, we need to remember that there are a minority of psychologists who do not see psychology as a science and who do not rely on the scientific method. Once you know enough about scientific research, this is a position you may choose to take. However, don't knock what you haven't tried! You need a good grounding in scientific methodology before you can really appreciate its strengths and weaknesses.

Quantitative or qualitative research?

The research methods used by psychologists may be categorised as qualitative or quantitative but such a distinction is not absolute; they can be considered as opposite ends of a continuum anywhere along which research may fall. Studies that focus on precision, aiming to produce numerical results or data that can in some way be 'counted' (quantified) are described as *quantitative* research. Such studies tend to use large samples of people or animals to gather findings that can be extrapolated to tell us about a population in general. Such methods include experimentation (Chapter 6), correlations (Chapter 7) and surveys (Chapter 4). They are more likely to use data derived from a laboratory setting in which controls can be rigorously employed. The goal of such research, using the hypothetico-deductive method, is to develop general 'laws' of behaviour.

As an alternative to quantitative research, psychologists may investigate a limited numbers of instances studying them in much greater depth, focusing on meanings and generating context-related, detailed, descriptive data. Such approaches, focusing on the qualities of the behaviours observed, are the *qualitative* methods. They include observations (Chapter 3) and case studies (Chapter 5), which are likely to be based in 'real world' settings. Interviews and questionnaires (Chapter 4) can produce either quantitative or qualitative data depending on the phrasing of the questions asked. While quantitative research fits readily into the hypothetico-deductive model, qualitative research does so less easily. Qualitative research may follow the inductive approach, beginning with the collection of data to provide a basis for the formulation of explanations.

Doing your own research

Psychologists are interested in finding out what makes people do the things they do. Research provides a legitimate excuse to find out about other people's behaviour. With the help provided in the following chapters, you can learn how psychologists go about answering questions about the thinking and actions of others. If you are going to begin to explore for yourself what makes people tick, then Chapter 14 will guide you through the process. It covers how to conduct your own research from coming up with an idea, through doing a literature search and planning a study, to collecting data and writing up your coursework.

Navigating through the book

Each chapter begins with a section called *What's ahead*, which tells you what will be covered. Throughout the text we have included *Research method* and *Research issue* boxes. These are summaries of real studies that provide examples of the concepts being discussed. They might also provide you with ideas for your coursework. The sections called *Interactive angles* and *Media watch* provide opportunities for you to explore your understanding as you work through the material in the chapter. Each chapter ends with sections called *Where to now?*, which offers ideas for further reading and *What do you know?*, which is intended to give you the opportunity to test your understanding.

Choosing a statistical test

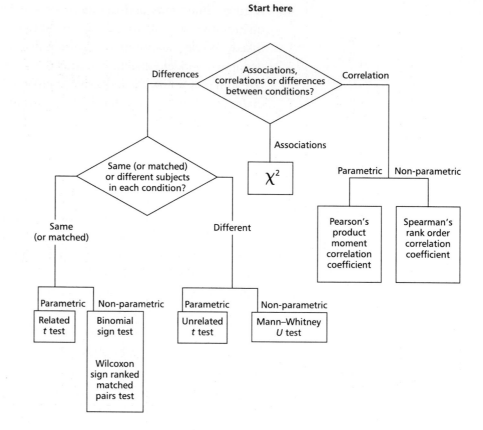

Coverage of examination board specifications

Chapter	Topics covered in the chapter	Edexcel	OCR	AQA A	AQA B
Introduction	Qualitative and quantitative data and methods	Qualitative and quantitative data	Qualitative and quantitative methods		Qualitative and quantitative methods
1 Making Predictions	Aims, hypotheses	Hypotheses: null, experimental/ alternative	Research aims, research hypothesis, null hypothesis	Research question. Aims, hypotheses: experimental/alternative, directional/non-directional, null	Research question. Aims, hypotheses: alternative and null
2 Populations and Samples	Sampling, sampling biases	Sampling: random, systematic, opportunity, quota, volunteer	Population, sample, bias in sampling	Selection of participants, random sampling	Populations and sampling: opportunity, random and stratified
3 Observing Behaviour	Observations, categorising behaviour	Observations	Observations, coding systems, categorising behaviour	Naturalistic observations	Observations: participant and non-participant
4 Questionnaires and Interviews	Questionnaires, interviews, surveys	Questionnaires, interviews	Questionnaires, surveys	Questionnaire surveys, interviews	Questionnaires: open and closed questions. Interviews: structured and unstructured
5 Case Studies, Content Analysis and Simulations	Case studies, content analysis, simulations	Case studies, content analysis	Case studies, content analysis, simulations		Case studies
6 The Experimental Method	Experiments, designs, counterbalancing, operationalisation, Independent Variable (IV), Dependent Variable (DV)	Experiments: designs: repeated measures, independent groups, matched pairs. Counterbalancing. IV and DV. Selection of materials	Experiments: Selection of materials, operationalisation	Laboratory, field and natural experiments. Designs: repeated measures, independent groups, matched participants. IV and DV. pilot studies	Experiments: naturalistic, field and laboratory. Designs: repeated measures, independent groups, matched pairs. Counterbalancing. Pilot studies
7 Correlations	Correlation	Correlational designs	Correlations	Correlations: positive and negative, correlation coefficients	Correlational studies. Positive, negative and zero correlations
8 Descriptive Statistics	Measures of average and measures of dispersion	Levels of measurement. Measures of central tendency, range, standard deviation	Tables. Measures of central tendency. Measures of dispersion	Measures of central tendency and dispersion (median, mode, mean, range, standard deviation)	Tables. Mean, median, mode, range and standard deviation

Chapter	Topics covered in the chapter	Edexcel	OCR	AQA A	AQA B
9 Plotting Your Data	Graphs	Graphs	Visual presentation of data	Graphs and charts: histograms, bar charts, frequency polygons, scattergraphs	Bar charts, histograms, graphs, scattergrams
10 Non-parametric Inferential Statistics	Non-parametric inferential statistics, type I & II errors, probability, level of significance	Mann–Whitney, Wilcoxon, x_2, sign test, Spearman. Critical values, calculated values. Variance.	Probability and significance. x_2, Mann–Whitney, Wilcoxon, Spearman	Levels of significance. x_2, sign test, Mann–Whitney, Wilcoxon, Spearman	Type I & II errors
11 Parametric Inferential Statistics	Parametric inferential statistics, normal distribution	Normal distribution, variance. Related t, unrelated t, Pearson	Normal distribution		
12 Controlling Variables	Validity, reliability, generalisability, controls	Validity, reliability, generalisability, situation and participant variables, controls	Validity, reliability, controls, issue of location, participant reactivity	Validity – internal and external (ecological) – and reliability. Demand characteristics, investigator effects. Order effects, researcher bias, confounding variables	Confounding variables
13 Ethics in Research	Ethical guidelines consent, confidentiality, debriefing, right to withdraw. Non-human animal ethics	BPS Ethical guidelines: consent, confidentiality, debriefing, right to withdraw. Non-human animal ethics	Ethical issues	Ethics: BPS guidelines	Ethical issues and codes of conduct (BPS). ATP guidelines.
14 Coursework	Coursework	Coursework: one piece at AS	Practical folder at AS	Coursework: one piece at A2	Coursework: one piece at AS

1

Making Predictions

what's ahead?

This chapter describes the starting point of psychological research. It introduces the ideas of research questions, aims and hypotheses, explaining how progress is made from one to the next. We consider different types of hypotheses, the role of the alternative hypothesis and the null hypothesis and discuss the difference between directional and non-directional hypotheses.

Aims

The purpose of research in psychology is to answer questions about the behaviour and thinking of people and animals. Each study a psychologist conducts arises from a *research question*. The aim of the study is to answer the research question posed, but where do these questions come from? Questions often originate from either casual or systematic observations, although they may also emerge from ongoing research, when the solution to one problem merely poses another! What sorts of questions do psychologists try to answer?

Some questions that psychologists ask

- How do monkeys raise a predator alarm? (Seyfarth and Cheney, 1986)

- How do pedestrians avoid colliding with one another in the street? (Carey, 1978)

- Does gender affect the nature of play between parents and their children? (Leaper, 2000)

- Do blind children have a more acute sense of smell than sighted children? (Rosenbluth *et al.*, 2000)

- Is there a relationship between religious beliefs and safe sex in young people? (Zaleski and Schiaffino, 2000)

- How does socio-economic status affect early literacy? (Duncan and Seymour, 2000)

Whilst many psychological studies focus on finding out about people or animals, some concentrate on the methods themselves; how to conduct effective research. For example, Hoyt (2000) was trying to answer the question 'what makes observers biased?' (see Chapter 3). Thornton and Lee (2000) investigated the causes of publication bias, the tendency for some findings, particularly positive ones, to reach publication whereas others do not.

inter**active** angles

Look at some of the research methods boxes throughout the book. Using the description of the aims, can you work out what question the researchers were trying to answer?

Having decided upon the question to be answered, this needs to be translated into an *aim*, that is it has to be stated as an achievable goal for a piece of research. For instance, while the question 'Why do we sometimes feel as though we have eyes in the back of our head?' is an interesting one and falls within the domain of psychology, it is not a question that could readily be answered by a single piece of research. However, Colwell *et al.* (2000) translated this question into an achievable aim 'to investigate whether people are able to detect whether someone they cannot see is staring at them' (see page 30).

media
watch

The social psychology of sitting

Perhaps some of the most important social behaviour we engage in involves our work. As students, we attend lectures, tutorials, seminars and lab classes. As employees or employers, we interact with the public, try to sell people things, find out their opinions, persuade colleagues to adopt new ideas or strategies, devise ideas that will promote our company/service/organisation's success, etc.

An interesting question is whether group meetings we engage in are more effective either sitting or standing. On the face of it, this seems an odd, eccentric question. But many American companies insist on stand-up meetings because it saves time without impairing decision-making quality. The rationale for this is that without the comfort of sitting, participants would engage in fewer diversions and keep to the point.

To test this hypothesis, Allen Bluedorn and colleagues from the University of Missouri-Columbia compared the effect of a sitting or standing meeting on the length of the meeting and the quality of the decisions made in it.

The researchers found that although seated meetings were 34 per cent longer (the average time of all meetings was 20 minutes), there was no difference between the two formats in the quality of the decisions made. However, participants expressed greatest satisfaction with the meeting when in the seated condition.

The authors suggest that a standing format may be more effective and appropriate for those whose meetings are similar to those reported in their study.

Bluedorn *et al.* (1999) reported in *The Psychologist*

Questions

1 What is the research question being investigated by Bluedorn *et al.* (1999)?

2 Why was it a useful question to ask?

3 How would you express the aim of their experiment?

Hypotheses

In order to measure the outcome of a piece of research the aim must be expressed as a *hypothesis*, that is, a testable statement. It must be possible to gather evidence that will demonstrate whether the hypothesis has been supported or not. Since our study may either confirm our aims, or contradict them, we need to have two hypotheses, one we accept if the aims of our study are supported, the *alternative hypothesis*, and another we accept if the results are not what we had expected, the *null hypothesis*. Let's look at an example.

research methods

the null hypothesis: goldies for oldies – are dogs good for old people's hearts?

Neer, C.A., Dorn, C.R. and Grayson, I. (1987) Dog interaction with persons receiving institutional geriatric care. *Journal of American Veterinary Medical Association*, 191, 300–04

Aim: To investigate whether geriatric residents would benefit more in terms of health or social variables from attendance at sessions in which they could interact with a dog compared with sessions of an alternative activity.

Method: Sixty-six elderly clients from two residential care facilities were selected by nursing staff on the basis of physical and mental capability, and received an explanation of the study (mean ages 81 and 67 years at the two facilities). Fifty-three clients consented to participate. At each facility, the participants were divided into two groups: one group received the dog activity first and the alternative activity second and the other experienced the activities in the opposite order. Each activity session lasted 45 minutes and were equally scheduled for morning,

afternoon and evening hours. During dog sessions, the participants could groom, pet, feed or play with the dog (a Golden Retriever or Yellow Labrador). During alternative activity sessions, participants were engaged in games, music, arts and crafts and storytelling. One measured outcome was the change in blood pressure, taken before and after every activity, over 12 weekly sessions.

Results: No significant differences were found between the residents' blood pressure measurements between the beginning and end of the activity sessions either with or without the dog.

Conclusion: As the differences between the blood pressure of participants before and after activity sessions did not show a consistent pattern as predicted, the null hypothesis *Any difference between the blood pressure of participants attending dog activity and other activity sessions is due to chance* could be accepted. Alternatively, errors may have occurred in the study that obscured a difference. These might have been caused by factors such as sample size, variability in the measurement of blood pressure, or inadequate time with the dog.

Neer *et al.* (1987) investigated the effect of interacting with a dog on the well-being of geriatric patients. Although some of their findings were as expected, one of their major predictions was not supported; that there would be a difference in blood pressure after sessions of interaction with a dog. The researchers therefore needed a concluding statement that would reflect their evidence; suggesting that interaction with a dog, the factor in question, was not responsible for the variability in participants' blood pressure. This is the function of the null hypothesis.

The alternative hypothesis

The *alternative hypothesis* (H_A or H_1) is a testable statement that proposes the expected outcome of the study. It is a prediction based on the researcher's knowledge from observations, related studies and previous investigations. For example, Neer *et al.* might have predicted that there would be an improvement (i.e. reduction) in the geriatric patients' blood pressure following interaction with the dog. This hypothesis would not have been supported by the evidence and would therefore have been *rejected.*

Experimental hypotheses

In an experimental study, the H_1 proposes that there will be a difference in some measurable outcome between two conditions that are controlled or observed by the experimenter. Neer *et al.* created two conditions by controlling activity sessions for geriatric residents. They proposed a difference between one condition in which the residents could interact with a dog and an alternative condition with activities such as games, music, arts and crafts and storytelling. One measured outcome was the change in blood pressure after 12 weekly sessions.

Hypotheses in correlations

In a correlational study the H_1 proposes that there will be a link between two variables. For example, Dement and Kleitman (1957) correlated time spent in rapid eye movement (REM) sleep with the participants' own estimates of time spent dreaming (see page 127). Although we might feel as though dreams occur in a flash, Dement and Kleitman expected participants to suggest longer times for longer REM periods. Thus a suitable hypothesis would have been *Participants experiencing longer periods of REM will report longer dreams*. Again, the hypothesis must be *operational*, that is it must be expressed in a way whereby the predicted outcome, in this case dream-time, can be measured.

The null hypothesis

In any study, it must be possible for the alternative hypothesis to be contradicted by the findings. When this is the case, the H_1 is rejected but we still need a conclusion. This conclusion must be that our findings are not the consequence of the predicted effect but are instead due to chance. This is the function of the *null hypothesis*. In Neer *et al.* the H_0 could have been *Any difference between the blood pressure of participants attending dog activity and other activity sessions is due to chance.* Note that in this example the null hypothesis does not say that there will be *no* difference. Here, as in all cases, the null hypothesis says that any difference we find is so small that it may have arisen *by chance* rather than having been caused by the variable in question (i.e. the presence or absence of the dog).

It is the null hypothesis that we are actually testing. This makes sense: it is much easier to decide the truth of a negative statement. Consider the statement 'all goldfish are orange'. We have to find only one fish that is black to refute the statement, whereas we could be busy for a long time checking every one. As a consequence, the null hypothesis provides us with a starting point. From here we can use statistical tests, that is employ mathematical principles to help us to decide whether a pattern we can see in our results could have arisen by chance or not (see Chapters 10 and 11). Since the alternative hypothesis is essential to the design of the study but the null hypothesis is used only when analysing the results, it is appropriate to state the alternative but not the null from the outset. Indeed, much published research does not state the null hypothesis at all, it is implicit. However, at this stage you may find that making your hypotheses explicit helps you to understand the process of research (and earn you marks!).

inter**active**
angles

Read the research questions below and write an alternative and null hypothesis for each situation.

1 Are younger people more likely to be helpful than older people?

2 Are scientists less likely to hold religious beliefs than non-scientists?

3 Do dogs learn tricks faster than cats?

4 Do boys and girls differ in their ability at spatial tasks?

5 Are children more likely to imitate their parents than other adults?

6 Does emotional state affect memory?

Predictions about the direction of an effect

Non-directional hypotheses

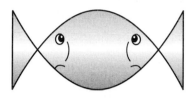

This is a two-tailed hypothofish...can you tell which direction it will go?

In many studies, the researchers are only able to predict that the variable(s) under investigation will affect the outcome rather than being able to make a more precise judgement about *how* the results will be affected. The alternative hypothesis in such instances is described as *non-directional*: it simply states that there will be a difference between conditions in an experiment or a link between variables in a correlation. Non-directional hypotheses are also referred to as *two-tailed*, indicating that the outcome could fall in one of *two* directions. Consider the two-tailed hypothofish opposite.

Directional hypotheses

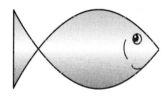

This is a one-tailed hypothofish, it has only one tail...can you tell which way it will go?

It would be expected that Neer's geriatric patients would *benefit* from the presence of the dog, so the H_1 should predict that the blood pressure following a dog activity session would (on average) be lower than that after a non-dog activity session. This kind of prediction is described as directional, that is, it indicates which of the two conditions will result in the greater or more positive change. From these predictions it is possible to generate a *directional hypothesis*, that is an H_1 that states the specific effect ('better' or 'worse') each condition will have on the results. Directional hypotheses are also called *one-tailed* because the prediction indicates that the outcome will fall in *one* direction. Consider the diagram opposite.

It has been argued (e.g. MacRae, 1994) that, in psychology, we can never be sufficiently sure of the possible outcome of a study to use a directional hypothesis. Furthermore, to do so limits our options; if we make a directional prediction and the outcome suggests a difference in the opposite direction than expected, we should accept the null hypothesis. For example, if we predict that *Students who listen to music while doing their homework will perform better than those who work in silence* and find that, in fact, those working in silence perform worse, we would be forced to accept the null hypothesis. This would state that *Any difference in homework performance between students working with music and in silence is due to chance*. This seems unlikely, but perhaps the music helped them to concentrate or relax so they worked harder. We would have been better off with a non-directional hypothesis.

interactive
angles

Decide whether each of the following alternative hypotheses is one- or two-tailed.

1 We can be conditioned to respond to a sound more quickly than we can to a smell.

2 Psychiatric patients are less likely to talk to themselves than psychologists.

3 Eating chocolate affects memory.

4 It is more likely that people will obey a stranger in uniform than one wearing plain clothes.

5 The more positive a person's mood the better they can concentrate.

6 There will be a relationship between fitness and self-esteem.

7 Performance of students who listen to music while doing their homework differs from those who work in silence.

Conclusions

Psychological research progresses from a general research question to testing specific hypotheses. The alternative hypothesis represents a testable statement of our predictions. The null hypothesis provides a basis for subsequent statistical testing.

where to now?

► **Howell, D.C. (1999)** *Fundamental Statistics for the Behavioral Sciences.* **London: International Thompson Publishing** – provides thorough coverage of the role of hypotheses in statistical testing.

what do you know?

1 Define the term 'hypothesis'.

2 Is the following an alternative or null hypothesis: *Any difference between the amount of dreams recalled from REM sleep and non-REM sleep is due to chance.*

3 Differentiate between a directional and non-directional hypothesis.

4 Which of the following are correlational and which are experimental hypotheses?

(a) The longer you stay awake the worse your concentration gets.

(b) Young people are more polite in queues than older people.

(c) More frequent mobile phone use increases forgetting.

(d) Men are more health-conscious than women.

2

Population and Samples

what's
ahead

This chapter introduces you to the methods that psychologists use to obtain participants for their studies. Investigations with different aims may have widely differing requirements in terms of the participants they need, with regard to factors such as gender, socio-economic status, education and prior knowledge. We describe sampling methods including opportunity, random, systematic, stratified and quota sampling and consider the extent to which they are representative of the population from which they derive. We also discuss the advantages of these techniques, the importance of sample size and the factors that may reduce the size of the sample.

Populations

To answer a research question, a psychologist will design a study to be conducted on human participants (or animals). In general, any study has a target *population*, the group to which the results of the study are intended to relate and from which those individuals selected to participate in the study will be drawn. A population can be defined as all of the cases within a given definition from which the sample is selected. In practice this target group may be very narrow, such as 'the shoppers in the precinct' or 'the rabbits in the park' or it may be much broader, such as 'motorists' or 'Internet users'. In addition, the defined population may be highly localised such as 'people attending the local shop', or may be geographically diverse, such as 'depressed people prescribed Prozac'. The task is to identify the most relevant group from which to select potential participants. This should be dictated by the aims of the study (although in practice it may be affected by more pragmatic factors). The population chosen must reflect the objective of the study, thus an experiment exploring attitudes of younger and older people should draw on a group of diverse ages. An investigation into the effects of drugs needs to compare users and non-users (e.g. Wareing *et al.*, 2000, page 102) and research into the consequences of jet lag would require frequent flyers (such as flight attendants, Cho *et al.*, 2000). In Chapter 3 you will encounter studies about the use of dogs to facilitate interaction between residents in care settings. Read through these carefully and decide on the populations being studied.

It is important to remember that the population consists only of those people to whom you potentially have access. If you post an Internet advertisement for participants your population is limited to those people who visit the site, not all Internet users.

interactive
angles

What would the population be in these situations?

- Research into attitudes to health promotion educating people about exposure to the sun and the risk of skin cancer (Jones *et al.*, 2000).

- A study of the relationship between first sexual encounters, safe sex, age and religious beliefs (Zaleski and Schiaffino, 2000).

- An investigation into the effects of fragrance on female arousal and mood across the menstrual cycle (Graham *et al.*, 2000).

- An experiment that assesses the benefits of service dogs for people with ambulatory disabilities (Allen and Blascovich, 1996).

Sometimes it is appropriate, and therefore necessary, to use a narrow rather than a varied population to test a hypothesis. Within the population being considered, a range of other variables is nevertheless the ideal. Rosenbluth *et al.* (2000) investigated the performance of early-blind and sighted children on olfactory tasks (see page 90). They compared 30 sighted and 30 blind children. Thirty-five blind participants were selected from lists of registered blind students obtained from the Department of Visually Impaired Students in the Ministry of Education and from the Jerusalem Home for the Education of the Blind. These lists provided 450 names, approximately 95 per cent of the legally blind children of school age resident in Israel at the time of the study. Of the 35 children selected on the basis of the nature and duration of their blindness and absence of cognitive or motor impairments, 30 agreed to participate. The sighted children were selected from Jerusalem public schools and included a similar range of ages, genders, grades and ethnicity as the sample of blind children.

Rosenbluth *et al.* provide one example of how participants may be obtained. In our discussion of Williamson *et al.* (2000) (see page 15) we describe their use of advertisements in local public places and direct face-to-face approaches to attract participants for their study. In Chapter 3 we describe Leaper's (2000) study of play between parents and their children. In this case, the families were recruited through flyers, enquiries to day centres and using the birth announcements in local newspapers. By using wide-ranging methods of recruitment, researchers aim to obtain access to as large a population as possible. This ensures that those individuals selected can be used as an indicator of the likely responses of the wider group. There are arguments, however, for minimising the sample size in some situations, such as where participation may cause distress and in experiments with animals in which they may suffer pain (see Chapter 13).

Issues that affect the selection of participants, whether by the researcher or by self-selection, may include gender, socio-economic status, payment and prior knowledge. Withdrawal from the study will also affect the nature of the final sample.

research methods

representing the population: factors affecting literacy

Duncan, L.G. and Seymour, P.H.K. (2000) Socio-economic differences in foundation-level literacy. *British Journal of Psychology*, 91, 145–66

Aim: To investigate the effect of socio-economic status (SES) on the acquisition of literacy.

Method: Participants aged four to eight years were selected from two urban areas in Scotland with contrasting socio-economic profiles as indicated by 1991 census data on housing (private or public), unemployment, lone parents and car ownership. This division was reflected by the relative proportions of children in local schools in receipt of free school meals and clothing vouchers. The incidence of ethnic minorities in both areas was small and both schools adopted similar teaching strategies, introducing letter-sound correspondences concurrently with reading scheme vocabulary. At least 20 children from each area, in each school year, from nursery to primary year three were selected. They were tested seven times over a two-month period on the following scales:

- *Measures of foundation literacy*: letter and word knowledge and simple non-word reading (e.g. *zuf* as the name of a dinosaur).

- *Standardised assessments*: British Ability Scales Word Reading Test and a vocabulary test.

- *Metaphonological awareness*: a puppet game where the child was required to find the common sound in non-word pairs (e.g. what sound is the same in /tal/ and /nal/?).

Results: Low SES was associated with impairments relative to chronological age with regard to letter and word knowledge, non-word reading and vocabulary. When the SES groups were equated for reading age the high and low SES performance was indistinguishable. Methodological problems arose because many of the younger low SES children had zero scores and some of the older high SES children reached the highest score, thus obscuring differences between the groups. To overcome this, zero and maximum scores were omitted from the statistical analysis.

Conclusion: The delayed acquisition of literacy skills in low SES children is a consequence of delayed acquisition of letter-sound knowledge. Both groups progressed along the same pattern; the development of the low SES children was not deviant but developmentally constrained. The high SES children were achieving at approximately one academic year above their low SES peers.

Questions

1 Why was it useful to investigate the incidence of free school meals and clothing vouchers in each area?

2 Why was the incidence of ethnic minorities of importance?

3 Why was it important that the schools employed a similar approach to reading instruction?

4 If a control group of children were required for a study, would it be more important to match them for SES, age or reading ability? Why?

A population may be defined by a particular experience of its individuals, such as crash survivors, by a personality characteristic, such as claustrophobia or by any other shared characteristic. Furthermore, a population might not be composed of people but of animals, such as squirrels in a park, lions in the Serengeti or primates housed in zoos. Alternatively, the target populations may not composed of individuals at all but of discrete items such as television programmes or books which could be the focus of a content analysis.

interactive angles

What were the populations in the following studies?

- Seyfarth and Cheney (1986) page 29
- Ireland (1990) page 39
- Metzler *et al.* (2000) page 83
- MacDonald *et al.* (2000) page 100

Sampling

Once the target group has been identified, selection of those individuals who will participate, the *sample*, presents a further range of questions relating to how these individuals will be chosen. A sample can be described as the part of a population that is studied so that the researcher can make generalisations about the whole of the original population. We generally take samples because populations are simply too large to test everyone. We aim to make samples as similar to the parent population as possible, in order to make our generalisations valid. For example, if you conduct a survey on attitudes to mobile phones by calling mobile phone users you are unlikely to get a cross section of opinion. Similarly, if you placed an advertisement for participation in a sex survey in 'top shelf' magazines, the resulting biased sample would invalidate the results of the study.

In most cases, those individuals who participate in a study do so voluntarily, so they thus constitute a *volunteer sample*. As we discuss in Chapter 13 on ethics, it is generally unacceptable to conduct research on people who are unaware that they are being studied. An exception to this would be in the observation of people in public places where they expect to be seen. Here, participants may be unaware of their involvement in the research so cannot volunteer.

Non-representative sampling

Opportunity sample

An *opportunity sample* selects a group of participants based on the section of the population available at a given time. This is a non-representative sampling technique because there is no guarantee that the full range of diversity that exists within the population will be accessed when a sample is obtained on the basis of availability. Those individuals who are unavailable may share an important criterion that will, as a consequence, be under-represented in the sample. For example, conducting a survey when it is cloudy may mean that participants who dislike rain are not available to be interviewed. This may not matter if you are investigating attitudes to mobile phones but if you are assessing the incidence of seasonal affective disorder (depression related to low light levels in winter) this sampling error could be serious. The key implication is that, if the sample fails to accurately represent its parent group, then it is inappropriate to generalise from that sample.

interactive
angles

Consider the following examples; what are the risks associated with the opportunity sample in each case?

- A researcher investigating attitudes to disability places himself upstairs in a shopping mall so he is not a nuisance.

- In a study on memory for nonsense 'facts', a student asks the first people she sees leaving the Sociology Department at her college to participate.

- An experiment is designed to test whether there is a difference in locus of control between employed and unemployed people. It is conducted between 9 and 11 a.m. each weekday.

In practice, the sample used in much psychological research consists simply of those people who are readily accessible to the researcher. By default, these are often university students. The generalisability of such a sample would be questionable in some cases (for instance in studies where the outcome being measured is dependent on age or education) but is otherwise acceptable. Many recent studies have relied wholly or partly on the student population for their participants, for example Morrison and Ellis (2000), University of York, Wright *et al.* (2000), University of Bristol and the University of the West of England, Deręgowski *et al.* (2000), University of Aberdeen, Féry and Vom Hofe (2000), University René Descartes, and Rosenblum *et al.* (2000), University of California. In Chapter 3 (page 30) we describe Jacob and McClintock's (2000) study which used staff and students from the University of Chicago.

research
methods

opportunity sample: thinking of buying a car?

Williamson, J. Raynard, R. and Cuthbert, L. (2000) A conversation-based process tracing method for use with naturalistic decisions: An evaluation study. *British Journal of Psychology*, 91, 203–21

Aim: To test the Active Information Search (AIS) method used to investigate decision making. Specifically, to apply it to the naturalistic setting of consumer behaviour and to enable respondents to reply verbally, within a conversation, rather than to think into 'empty space'.

Method: An opportunity sample of 96 paid participants was recruited through advertisements in local public places and direct face-to-face approaches. Full-time students and those with no experience of using credit were not selected since part of the study required such prior knowledge. A range of socio-economic and employment groups was represented in the sample, including manual, semi-skilled and professional occupations. There were 42 males and 54 females, in the following age categories: 18–24 years (5), 25–44 years (57), 45–64 years (32), 65+ years (2). Respondents were briefed about the nature of the research, the task and their right to withdraw. They were assured of their anonymity, invited to ask questions and permission was sought to tape-record the protocols.

The participants' task was to make a consumer decision about the purchase of either a car or a washing machine. Interviewers were briefed to answer questions asked by the respondents in order to enable them to make decisions (orally providing facts such as the price of the item). There were several variations:

- *Conversational AIS* – interviewers prompted after 60 seconds of silence with comments such as 'Don't forget you can ask me anything you like'.

- *Conversational think aloud* – interviewers asked respondents to 'think out loud' and the interviewers responded conversationally (but without interrupting) during the respondents' monologues. This avoided the 'empty space' problem, the difficulty we experience in the absence of a recipient for our speech, such as when talking to an answerphone.

- *Post-decision interviews* were either *non-directive* cued only by the open-ended questions 'Can you say in your own words how you made each of your decisions?' and 'Anything else?' or *interactive* in which the non-directive summary was followed by probe questions intended to elicit evaluative information and reasons for particular decisions.

Each participant undertook both the car or washing machine task in one of these conditions. Some participants received the car task, others the washing machine task, first. After completing all the tasks, the participants were debriefed, given the opportunity to ask questions about the study and thanked for their participation.

Results: Thinking aloud did not affect the number of questions asked by participants nor their post-decision summaries. One 'think aloud' protocol for the car task was recorded as follows:

I: The Tipo is £2390 after your trade-in.
R: £2390. And H registration is that? What year is that?
I: 1990.
R: 1990 and K is?
I: 1992.
R: Alright 1992. 34,000 miles. So that's quite low then really.
I mean I wouldn't go for the Rover personally because they're sort of family cars.
The old man sort of cars…I would go for the VW if I had a large disposable,
A large disposable income? cos VWs are known for expense
and high insurance and things like that.
So a 1600 engine would just be more expensive basically to insure for myself.
So Fiat Tipo is like more of a sensible choice for me.
I: Okay.
R: A bit small, they're pretty reliable, fairly cheap on insurance,
and easy, cheaper to get parts for, the parts are cheaper,
so I would probably opt for the Tipo considering the rust and all that business.

Conclusion: Thinking aloud did not appear to interfere with participants' decision-making processes. This suggests that when 'think aloud' is experienced in a conversational context rather than an 'empty space' it is a valuable tool in tracing the decision-making process. It enables the researcher to understand more about the thought processes without interfering with them significantly.

Questions

1 Why were full-time students excluded?

2 Why was it important to get a range of representation of different socio-economic groups and occupations?

Since an opportunity sample may be limited in terms of access to participants, it is sometimes advantageous to expand the recruitment base by asking existing participants to ask other people if they would consider participating; the *snowball effect*. This has two advantages: firstly, it increases the absolute number of participants and, secondly, it may provide a means to recruit from within otherwise inaccessible groups such as people with disabilities or criminals. This technique was used by Wareing *et al.* (2000) to obtain additional participants in their study on drug-users (see page 102).

for and against

non-representative sampling

+ Large numbers of participants can be obtained relatively quickly and easily using opportunity sampling.

− An opportunity sample may not contain sufficiently varied participants to allow generalisation to the parent population.

Representative sampling

Representative sampling is a method of selecting a group of participants that contains all the important characteristics of the parent population. Such a sample may be taken in a variety of different ways.

Random sample

A *random sample* is one in which each member of the population has an equal chance of being selected. Thus it is inappropriate to say that the researcher approached random individuals in the street. To do this we would have to be equally likely to ask all individuals; this is patently not the case. We would be unlikely to invade the privacy of a couple engaged in conversation, to ask a lone parent struggling with children, bags and a pushchair or to approach someone who was apparently drunk. We therefore select certain types of individuals for inclusion in the sample and deselect others thus excluding some groups within the population.

In order to ensure that we are selecting on a random basis, we need access to the entire population being investigated. This is often problematic. In practice, access is limited to lists such as birth records, school enrolments and the electoral role. Even resources such as these provide a complete population only of those registered; for instance the electoral role does not provide a complete list of all over 17-year-olds in a ward, only those who have *registered* to vote. In addition, access to records may be limited; for example school and doctor's surgery lists contain confidential information. Having obtained a list from which to work, a random sample cannot be taken by selecting, say, every fifth name. Clearly in such a system every individual does not have an equal chance of selection. Individuals must be chosen using a randomised system, for instance by allocating every individual a number and using a random number generator or random number tables. For small groups it is possible simply to write each participant's number on a piece of paper, jumble them together and draw out the sample. If this method is to provide a truly random sample the container must be large enough to mix them effectively (hats are probably too small for this purpose!), the slips should be of equal size, should be folded in the same way and should not be visible during selection.

interactive angles

For each of the following situations, decide whether the sampling described is randomised or not. Justify your decisions.

- Selecting companies to ask about their attitude to equal opportunities by taking every other name in the Thompson Directory.

- Allocating each adult on the electoral role a number, then using digits from the Yellow Pages to select a sample to participate in a study on extrasensory perception (ESP).

- Giving each individual in the population a two-digit code, then selecting the codes using a random number generator on a computer to decide who will be invited to participate in an investigation into belief in UFO.

- Allocating each member of a school a number and asking only those students whose numbers contain a zero to participate in an experiment on the quality of school food.

research methods

random sampling: healthy ageing

Perrig-Chiello, P., Perrig, W.J. and Stähelin, H.B. (1999) Health control beliefs in old age – relationship with subjective and objective health, and health behaviour. *Psychology, Health and Medicine*, 4, 83–94

Aim: To examine the health control beliefs (internality, powerful others, chance) in elderly people and to explore whether these beliefs are related to actual or perceived health or to health-related behaviour.

Method: Participants were recruited for an interdisciplinary study begun in Switzerland in 1960 with 6400 healthy persons. By 1993, the pool still comprised 3768 people. A sample of 65–94-year-olds (309 males and 133 females) was selected. When the second set of tests was conducted in 1995, 332 participants remained (227 men and 105 women). On each of the two sessions, the following tests were conducted.

- *Measure of health control beliefs*: This was measured as a response to statements such as physical diseases are part of the destiny of old people; physical diseases in old age cannot be avoided by regular medical visits; my health depends mainly on myself; health is a gift, a grace.

- *Objective health index*: This score gave an approximate index of actual physical health which included blood pressure, blood tests (e.g. cholesterol, iron, blood sugar) and heart monitoring.

- *Subjective health rating*: Participants rated their health on matters such as impaired vision, headaches, heart troubles and respiratory difficulties.

- *Health behaviour*: Participants were asked whether they performed any strenuous exercise and if so how often, and rated their use of psychiatric drugs.

Results: Chance factors affecting health were believed to be more important than internality or powerful others. Objectively sick or healthy people did not differ in their health control beliefs but participants reporting the most self-appraised complaints (subjectively sick) had lower internality scores and higher chance scores than the other participants. This group also differed in their health-related behaviour; they engaged in less sport and took more psychiatric medication.

Conclusion: Successful ageing may depend on the acceptance of the inevitability of disease and frailty with age. Personal responsibility can allow an elderly person to actively approach these issues by seeking the assistance of powerful others if necessary, thus maintaining a belief in internal control. The findings relating to perceived health suggest that the elderly person's subjective experience of their own health may be a valuable diagnostic tool.

Questions

1 What were the attrition rates (percentage loss of participants) for males, females and overall between 1993 and 1995? What might the reasons have been?

2 Why was it better to take a random sample from the over 65s in the original group of 6400 people than to use sources such as residential care homes for the elderly?

Systematic sample

In order to achieve a sample that is representative of the population, a researcher may use *systematic sampling* to select the participants so that those chosen illustrate the variety of characteristics exhibited within the population. The basis of systematic sampling is very simple: we select every *n*th person on a list. By dividing the total population by the size of the sample we require we find the basis for sampling. For example, if we have a population of 100 and wish to select a sample of 20, we would include every fifth person (100/20 = 5, hence every fifth). However, this technique does not necessarily result in a representative sample. In the map opposite, every other household might either produce a sample containing only people from large houses with a rural view or only people from small houses surrounded by other properties.

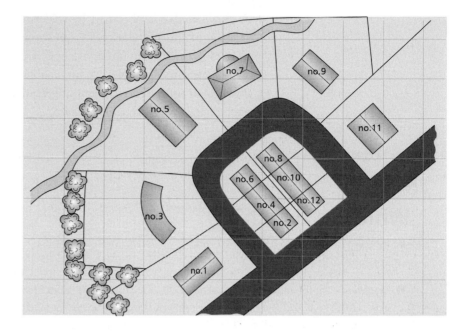

Systematic sampling doesn't always result in a representative sample

Stratified sample

Stratified sampling is a method in which individuals are taken to represent each major strata or layer within the population. Such subdivisions might include socio-economic groups, ages, geographical locations and racial origin. For example, a study conducted in a school to investigate the incidence of bullying should ensure that children from each academic year are selected to participate. Similarly, in an area with an ethnic minority, it would be appropriate to ensure that each of the racial groups is represented. Duncan and Seymour (2000) obtained a sample of school children stratified by age (see page 12).

In *proportionate strata sampling* individuals from the different strata are selected according to the incidence of that subgroup within the population. For example, in a town that has a high proportion of retired residents, it may be appropriate to select a sample that has an equally skewed representation of elderly participants. Similarly, in an area with high unemployment or many resident students, it would be appropriate to ensure that these groups appear in the sample with the same frequency as they do in the parent population.

In *disproportionate strata sampling* the relative incidence of subgroups is not reflected in the sample. This may be deliberate in order to ensure that there is some representation for particularly 'rare' groups or unequal weighting may be given to subgroups that are known to be more variable.

Quota sample

This is essentially a proportionate strata sample obtained by opportunity. It is, as a consequence, less rigorously representative than a strata sample.

A *quota sample* is obtained by selecting participants from each chosen stratum of the population by questioning any available individuals. As time progresses, individuals are encountered who fulfil the requirements. When the target sample size for a subgroup has been met, further similar individuals are rejected. Sampling continues until sufficient numbers in each category have been obtained.

interactive
angles

Which is which?

- A sample that is obtained by asking every tenth person in a car park queue about their opinions on road rage.

- To select their sample, a student finds out that 60 per cent of her fellow students are in their first year at college, 35 per cent in their second year and 5 per cent have been there for three years or more. She intends to take a sample of 20 participants. As students walk through the canteen, she asks them which year they are in and whether they will participate in her study. The first 12 year one students, the first 7 year two students and the first fourth year who agree to participate become her sample.

- From the population of a large town a researcher is keen to know whether more people with stress-related disorders live in the centre. She divides a map of the town into 81 squares and selects all of those in the central nine squares followed by one from each of the remaining blocks of nine.

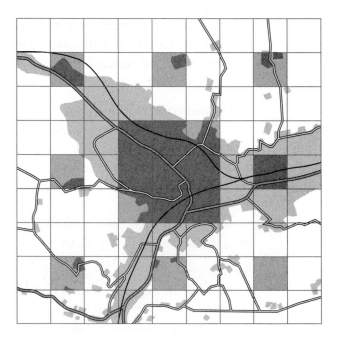

- To investigate the use of child-care by different families a sample is taken from a city population. The proportions of each level of socio-economic status and of lone parent families are known and their representation in the sample is in the same proportions.

for and against

representative sampling

+ A representative sample allows the researcher to generalise confidently from the sample to the parent population.

– Obtaining details of a population from which to select is often difficult.

– The appropriate criteria upon which to select participants for a stratified or quota sample may be hard to determine.

Sample size

The size of a sample for a study will depend on several factors:

- *Size of the target population* – a larger population will require a larger sample in order to be representative. Where the population is very small it may be appropriate to invite all members of the population to participate and not take a sample at all. This might arise in research on uncommon neural disorders or Siamese twins.

- *Nature of the research* – if the study is likely to have an impact on policy making, such as investigations into adoptions by gay couples or the impact of cigarette advertising on children's smoking habits then the sample needs to be larger than for, say, a student project.

- *Statistical analysis* – tests that judge the statistical significance of the findings of a study generally have minimum sample sizes. These may depend on the number of participants or the number of scores in each condition. Chi-squared, for example, is invalid unless at least 80 per cent of the cell values are over five (see page 151).

- *Practicalities* – access to participants will ultimately be limited by your time and resources.

- *Ethics* – a researcher conducting a study in which animals suffer pain should try to minimise the number of animals used (see Chapter 13).

inter**active**
angles

Here are some brief descriptions of studies and their sample sizes. Why do you think they vary?

- Rosenbluth *et al.* (2000) were looking for differences in sense of smell between blind and sighted children, they used 60 participants (30 sighted and 30 blind children).

- Graham *et al.* (2000) tested the effects of fragrance on female arousal in a study that involved the use of a vaginal probe. Their sample size was 28.

- Millings Monk (1999) investigated the effects of financial stress, coursework and emotional difficulties on student mental health. She used 40 students in her pilot study and a further 120 in the main investigation.

Attrition and ineligibility

Once the population has been identified and accessed and potential participants have been approached, not all of those individuals who accept may become part of the sample. Some of those people who are willing to be participants may, in fact, be ineligible; they may not fulfil the requirements for participation. For example, Graham *et al.* (2000) recruited 69 potential participants for their study but nine, when contacted by telephone, were found to be ineligible. In Chapter 1 we discussed a study in which the eligibility of elderly people in residential care is decided by their nursing staff (Neer *et al.*, 1987).

Of those participants who begin a study, not all may finish it. Graham *et al.* paid their participants $40 for completing their first session and a further $60 for the second; despite this, not all of the sample completed both sessions. This loss of participants during the study is the *drop-out* or *attrition rate*. It is expressed as the percentage retention of those who complete the study. For example, Perrig-Chiello *et al.* (1999) used a sample which, in 1960 consisted of 6400 participants and by 1993 had fallen to 3768. Using the formula:

$$\frac{\text{Total initial number of participants} - \text{remaining number of participants}}{\text{Total initial number of participants}} \times 100$$

these figures give us: $\frac{6400 - 3768}{6400} \times 100 = 41\%$

So the attrition from 1960 to 1993 is 41 per cent. For their study, Perrig-Chiello *et al.* found only 442 willing and eligible participants, during the two years of their study this had fallen to 332. Again this drop-out can be expressed as a percentage:

$$\frac{442 - 332}{442} \times 100 = 25\%$$

research
methods

attrition rates: is scent sexy?

Graham, C.A., Janssen, E. and Sanders, S.A. (2000) Effects of fragrance on female arousal and mood across the menstrual cycle. *Psychophysiology*, 37, 76–84

Aim: To investigate the effects of male and female fragrances on women's mood and sexual arousal over the menstrual cycle.

Method: Potential participants were recruited through advertisements in the student newspaper and family campus newsletter at Indiana University. The eligibility requirements of the women who responded were: at least 18 years of age, not using birth control pills or other hormonal medication, regular menstrual cycles (21–35 days), sexually attracted to men, not using any psychotropic medication, non-smoker, no known allergies to fragrances, no breathing problems or asthma, no known medical conditions that affect sense of smell. Of the 69 women who were screened, 20 decided not to take part and 9 were ineligible. Of the 40 women who began the study, only 28 completed both tests. There were three fragrance conditions (male, female and a control) and during exposure to each of these, participants' reactions to both erotic films and sexual fantasy were evaluated. Prior to each recording, baseline measures were taken while participants watched a neutral film about cats. These tests were conducted twice, following menstruation and ovulation. Some participants saw the film first, others saw it second and some were tested on the first occasion following menstruation, for the remainder the first test followed ovulation. The fragrances had been previously rated in a pilot study using different participants to select the most masculine and feminine odours. Sexual arousal was measured using reports from the participants and a vaginal photoplesythmograph, which detects changes in blood volume in vaginal tissue.

Results: The self-report data indicated greater sexual arousal following ovulation than following menstruation. Following menstruation the male fragrance produced a positive effect on genital arousal but not subjective arousal.

Conclusion: While fragrance does have some effect on sexual arousal this is limited in terms of occurrence during the menstrual cycle and the effect does not appear to be mediated by mood. This suggests that fragrances may act directly on olfactory areas of the brain or indirectly by eliciting memories of previous sexual encounters. However, conclusions must be treated with caution as the value of generalisations may be limited. Participants who volunteer for studies about sex are not representative of the population as a whole as they tend to be more liberal and positive in their views regarding sexuality and more sexually active than non-participants.

Questions

1 Why do you think the advertisement used 'sense of smell' rather than referring to fragrances or not mentioning this aspect at all?

2 What percentage of the original respondents was ineligible?

3 Using the initial number of women who were interviewed, the number starting the experiment and the number completing it, calculate the percentage attrition at the interview and experimental stages.

4 What was the purpose of the measurements taken during the film about cats?

In questionnaire-based studies, the opposite of attrition rate is reported. The number of questionnaires returned, expressed as a percentage of the total number sent or given out is the *response* or *return rate*. Many factors affect the likelihood of participants returning their questionnaires. Lund and Gram (1998) used several versions of a questionnaire of different lengths with different titles. The titles, rather than the number of pages seemed to have the greater effect on return rate (see page 62).

Conclusions

A researcher must take care to select their sample so as to ensure that they can generalise from that sample back to the parent population. Representative sampling is more likely to provide participants that truly represent the diversity of a population although it is more difficult to conduct than non-representative sampling. The size of a sample is affected by the researcher's needs, such as statistical testing or generalisability, and practicalities such as availability of participants and their willingness to participate.

where to now?

▶ **Robson, C. (1993)** *Real World Research*. **Oxford: Blackwell**

▶ **Clark-Carter, D. (1997)** *Doing Quantitative Research*. **Hove: Psychology Press** – both texts describe a wider range of sampling techniques used in the social sciences than are discussed in this chapter.

what do you know?

1 What population would you select for your study if you were attempting to research each of the following questions?

(a) What are the problems surrounding racial prejudice in inner cities?

(b) How can bulimia be treated?

(c) Which antidepressant drug is most effective in treating depressed young people?

2 If you wanted to investigate people's attitudes to the use of parking spaces for disabled badgeholders, you might choose to take a stratified sample of the population.

(a) What is meant by a stratified sample?

(b) Why would this type of sampling be preferable to opportunity sampling in this instance?

(c) What groups within the population might you want to represent in the sample?

3 (a) What are the advantages of using university students as participants?

(b) What disadvantages might there be to such a sample?

3

Observing Behaviour

what's
ahead?

This chapter introduces the use of observation as a research design in itself and as a tool in experimentation. Observations often form the starting point for any research in psychology; we need to observe that people forget before we can study forgetting, we might watch children at play before embarking on research into the purpose of their play. We describe how initial, casual observations can lead to rigorous investigations that use other techniques, including more structured observation, to collect data to test hypotheses.

We shall see how observations can constitute a primary research method producing detailed, descriptive data and how they can be used to measure the dependent variable in an experimental design. We will look at naturalistic observations and field experiments as ways to collect data outside the laboratory. Finally, we describe how reliability in observations can be improved by using operational definitions, employing strategies to raise inter-observer reliability and by formalising and limiting behavioural recording using observational techniques such as time sampling.

Observation as a research method

In this section we consider observations as a basis for an exploratory studies, either investigating an entirely new area of interest or tackling an old problem from a new perspective. For example, early investigations into antipredator vocalisations in vervet monkeys (Seyfarth and Cheney, 1986) took the form of observations, followed later by experimental work. Initial observations tend to be relatively non-focused; the aim is to observe the range of behaviours displayed whereas subsequent observations are focused on particular events. Alternatively, observations may follow, or be conducted alongside, other research techniques. There had, for example, been many studies of autism prior to the observations of Baron-Cohen *et al.* (1985) which took the field in a different direction, focusing on the theory of mind. In addition, observations may be used to validate or corroborate an existing research programme. Russell (1990) conducted experimental studies of captive ferrets to elucidate the role of play with objects in the acquisition of hunting behaviour in carnivores. To supplement this, she observed a range of zoo-housed animals to demonstrate a common pattern of predation-related play activities across species.

In *naturalistic observations* the researcher gathers data by watching participants (people or non-human animals) in their normal environment (this is not necessarily their 'natural' situation). For people, this may be at home, school, work, at the shops or in the street. For animals, this may be the home in the case of pets, parks, zoos, farms or in the wild. Such studies could also be described as *field studies* as they take place outside the laboratory.

research methods

naturalistic observations: alarmed monkeys

Seyfarth, R.M. and Cheney, D.L. (1986) Vocal development in vervet monkeys.
Animal Behaviour, 34, 1640–58

Aim: As a prelude to later experiments, the researchers needed to observe and record the behaviours and vocalisations of vervet monkeys in response to predators.

Method: Typically, two researchers spent 2.5 hours observing each of three groups of monkeys each day. Vocalisations were audio taped from a distance of 1.5–3 metres and the behaviour preceding and following each new vocalisation was recorded. One observer attempted to identify the predator species or other cause for the alarm to be raised while the second observer recorded the identity of the first and subsequent individuals to vocalise.

Results: The audio tape data suggest that vervet monkeys use a different call for different classes of predator (birds, snakes and big cats). The data from different individuals suggest that the monkeys become more accurate in their calling as they get older.

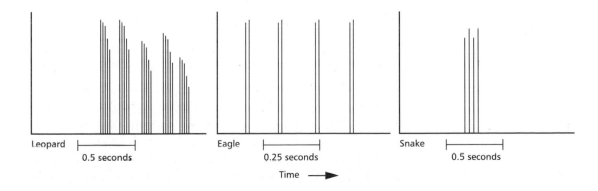

29

Conclusion: The results showed trends that formed the basis for subsequent field experiments using pre-recorded alarm calls. These tested whether the audible differences in calls produced differing responses in the recipients and whether maturation or experience improved the accuracy of alarm calling by juveniles.

The presence of observer(s) can affect the behaviour of the observed so it is necessary to control for this potential influence. Consider how much effect a doting grandmother has on the misbehaviour of her grandchildren. The mere belief that one might be visible to others can affect our behaviour; think about the way you respond if you believe someone behind you has their eyes trained on the back of your head. Surprisingly, according to Colwell *et al.* (2000) we are able to detect such an influence.

research
methods

observation: do we have eyes in the back of our head?

Colwell, J., Schroder, S. and Sladen, D. (2000) The ability to detect unseen staring: a literature review and empirical tests. *British Journal of Psychology*, 91, 71–85

Aim: To investigate whether people are able to detect when someone they cannot see is staring at them.

Method: The experiment compared the ability of participants to detect the presence of an unseen person. In the two conditions this person either did or did not stare at the participant.

Results: When the participants were not being stared at they were unable to detect the presence of a person behind them. In the 'staring' condition, however, participants scored better than they would have if they were just making chance guesses at detecting the observer.

Conclusion: Whilst this suggests that participants can detect the presence of someone they cannot see, the researchers identified some uncontrolled variables such as the effect of participants employing implicitly learned non-random response patterns which may have resulted in their apparent ability.

Non-participant observation requires that the observer does not interact, so that the participant's behaviour cannot be affected by the observer's presence. This might be achieved by being a long way away, or by the observer being hidden, for example watching children in a nursery though a one-way glass screen.

research methods

non-participant observation: how do pedestrians avoid collisions?

Carey, M. (1978) Does civil inattention exist in pedestrian passing? *Journal of Personality and Social Psychology*, 36, 1185–93

Aim: To confirm the rule of 'civil inattention', that is that as pedestrians approach each other in the street, they look at one another until they are approximately 2.5 metres apart and then avert their gaze.

Method: Observers covertly photographed pairs of approaching pedestrians from windows above the street. These were later coded for variables which indicated eye contact such as whether their heads and eyelids were lowered or level and whether gaze was directed towards or away from the approaching pedestrian.

Results: The findings showed that pedestrians do indeed initially make eye contact and then avert their gaze as they approach.

Conclusion: The rule of civil inattention was confirmed.

Participant observation also ensures that the participants are unaware of the presence of an observer, by disguising them as a legitimate member of the situation. The justification for this is twofold. Firstly, if permission were sought in some situations it would be denied, thus observations would be impossible. Secondly, knowledge about the presence of the observer may affect the behaviour of the observed individuals. There are clear ethical objections to this reasoning; deliberate deception is unacceptable. In general, therefore, the observer's role is made clear to the participants. Nevertheless, covert observations may be conducted of public behaviour in public places, of children with the informed consent of a parent or guardian or with consent to be observed but where the true purpose of the observation is masked. For example, someone who appears to be a school helper may conduct an observation in a playground and observations of shoplifting may be conducted by would-be shoppers.

research
methods

participant observation: the career of a football hooligan

Marsh, P., Rosser, E. and Harre, R. (1978) *The Rules of Disorder*. London: Routledge, Kegan Paul

Aim: The researchers were interested in the differing 'roles' football fans occupy as their status as a supporter changes.

Method: This study was a naturalistic observation of the behaviour of football crowds using participant observation (Marsh himself was a supporter of Oxford United FC). Following a video-taped pilot investigation of the behaviour of fans at the London Road End of Oxford United's ground, Marsh *et al.* were able to make detailed observations of the fans' behaviour from their involvement as supporters on the terraces.

Results: From their observations, Marsh *et al.* were able to describe the 'careers' of football fans through changing roles within their group of fellow supporters.

Conclusion: Marsh *et al.* note that participant observation should be exactly that; the experiential aspect of a social situation comes from an attempt to *share* rather than merely *record* the emotions of the observed. This is acknowledged as not particularly 'scientific'; such experiences may not provide quantifiable data but they do allow the researcher to gain an insight that will enable them to understand the social context.

The task for the participant observer is to achieve a balance between being a convincing participant and an objective observer. They must on the one hand reduce the potentially confounding effects of demand characteristics by taking on the role of participant, yet maintain sufficient objectivity to maximise the reliability and validity of their observations.

There may also be questions surrounding the physical or ethical costs to the observers and participants. Infiltration of a criminal group (such as Patrick, 1973, and Parker, 1974) or of a cult threatening mass suicide may put the observer at risk. Studies using concealed observations can invade the privacy of the observed and involve unacceptable deceit, such as Humphreys' (1970) study of homosexual activity. Although Humphreys attempted to protect the unwitting participants in his study by avoiding the disclosure of the location of his research, his procedure did not respect the privacy of the people being observed (see page 223). Humphreys contrived a covert participant observation under the guise of a 'gay voyeur', someone who derives sexual pleasure from watching actual encounters between gay people. This deception was in Humphreys' view necessary because he was aware that homosexuality (then a crime in the USA) resulted in the formation of a suspicious subculture. While a small number of those being observed were aware of Humphreys' motive for watching them, the majority was unaware that their behaviour was being scrutinised for the purposes of research.

We have assumed thus far that all observations are covert, that is, that the observers themselves, or their purpose, are hidden from the observed. This is not necessarily the case. In Parker's (1974) study of thieving in Liverpool, the observer's role was known to 'The Boys'; this was an overt participant observation. Similarly in Leaper (2000) and Fick (1993) the observers were non-participant yet the participants were aware that they were being observed.

for and against

+ Participant observation allows researchers to limit demand characteristics caused by knowledge about being observed.

+ A participant observer gains insight into the social context.

+ Validity of a participant observer's records can be increased by improving integration into the group through consideration of characteristics such as appearance, age, gender, social class and ethnic group.

− Being a participant in a social situation can colour the observer's view.

− To be effective, participant observation may require the observers to deceive the observed.

− As a participant, it is difficult to record observations immediately, thus introducing errors into the data.

+ Participant observations tend to generate qualitative data, the participant observer being able to provide detailed accounts of their observations.

+ Non-participant observations can generate quantitative data which can be analysed statistically

Exam tip

Try writing yourself a mnemonic (like 'Richard of York gave battle in vain') to help you to remember that, as a generalisation, PArticipant observations tend to produce QuaLitative data and rely on DEscriptive statistics. Whereas NOnparticipant observations generate QuanTitative data so can use Inferential Statistics. Two letters of each key term have been highlighted. See if you can make up a mnemonic or story to help you to recall them.

Structured observations

Non-focused observations can only generate qualitative data, descriptions of the events observed. In many cases, however, we wish to generate numerical data from our observations. This can be achieved through a *structured observation* in which behaviours are categorised, selected and defined prior to observation.

Categorising, selecting and defining behaviours

In order to decide what will be observed and how, a researcher wishing to conduct a structured observation may begin by conducting non-focused observations. This provides an opportunity to decide what behaviours are occurring and which to observe, i.e. to select and define the behaviours to be recorded – in other words to develop a *coding scheme*. This step is essential as behaviours often occur too rapidly to record everything and, in general, only some of the activities are relevant to the hypothesis in question. Observations in the exploratory stage of a study may be followed by supportive observational research, aiming to collect more data to validate initial findings. Alternatively, observations may be supplementary, serving to validate conclusions reached by approaching a research question from other directions.

Coding schemes

In order to record systematically, behaviours to be observed must be operationally defined and measurable, that is, the observers must be able to recognise the behaviours from the definitions and it must be possible for them to accurately record the behaviours exhibited. The following are some guidelines for developing a coding scheme:

- *Focus:* Concentrate on behaviours that are relevant to your hypothesis.

- *Utility:* Consider whether, having recorded the information, it will be possible to use it. If not, either change your scheme if the item is essential or leave it out if not.

- *Operational definition:* Ensure that it is possible from your definition to decide which behaviours do, and do not, fall into the category.

- *Objectivity:* Your definition should not require the observer to make inferences about the participant, the behaviour should be explicit; code actions rather than states.

- *Context independence:* Where possible, behavioural codes should be *consistent* over different contexts.

> - *Exhaustive:* Codes should cover all possible behaviours, this may necessitate a 'not recorded' or 'waste basket' category.
>
> - *Mutually exclusive:* At any time the recording of one code should preclude the need to record another simultaneously. This may however be impractical or inappropriate in some situations.

research methods

coding schemes: talk about dogs

Fick, K.M. (1993) The influence of an animal on social interactions of nursing home residents in a group setting. *American Journal of Occupational Therapy*, 47, 529–34

Aim: To determine the effect of a dog on the frequency and nature of social interactions of nursing home residents.

Method: This study used point sampling, a technique similar to time sampling which allows the observer to record the behaviour of each member of a group in each time interval. The group of 36 residents was observed during 30 minute socialisation sessions where they sat in a circle. The observers sat away from the group and systematically scanned behaviour at 40-second intervals during 10-minute observation periods at the beginning and end of each session. The coding system used was as follows:

- *Non-attentive behaviour* – The participant was observed sleeping or initiating other solitary activities, such as reading a magazine or leaving the group to engage in another activity in a separate part of the room.

- *Attentive listening* – The participant was observed to have eyes open and to maintain eye contact with the group leader or other residents addressing the total group

- *Verbal interaction with another person* – The participant was observed initiating or responding in a verbal manner with another person.

- *Non-verbal interaction with another person* – The participant was observed touching, gesturing, smiling or nodding to another person.

- *Verbal interaction with the animal* – The participant was observed verbalising or making sounds directed to the animal.

- *Non-verbal interaction with the animal* – The participant was observed touching, reaching, or gesturing toward the animal.

There were four 10-minute observation periods, so that the presence of the dog in the first or second half of the 30-minute session was controlled for. The dog was introduced to the group either at the beginning of the session, or after the first 15 minutes by a volunteer from the

Humane Society, who frequently brought animals to this facility. This was not unusual and the investigator explained that the dog was being trained for nursing home use and needed exposure to group settings. Observations began two minutes after the introduction of the dog.

Results: A significant difference was found between the 'verbal interaction with another person' score with, compared to without, the dog present. No significant differences were found on any other person-to-person measure.

Conclusion: The presence of the dog appeared to facilitate social interaction between individuals. This supports the role of animal-assisted therapy programmes as an effective medium for enhancing socialisation among residents in long-term care establishments.

Categorising behaviours and responses

Behaviour is a continuous stream upon which we, as observers, must impose divisions, separating it into actions that we can categorise and record. With observational methods such as note-taking and diary-keeping the data obtained may be so complex and unstructured that they cannot be readily organised to extract what is useful. It is preferable therefore to formalise observations to make the data more valid and reliable, even when we may have less informative data as a consequence.

Selecting behaviours and responses

Observers cannot record everything. Even with a video recorder we can only record events occurring in the direction of the lens and there may be other factors impinging on the situation from other directions. Thankfully, not all behaviours will be relevant to the hypothesis being investigated; those that *are* can be ascertained during a pilot study. During the pilot, observations will be *non-focused*, that is, all behaviours may be recorded with a view to narrowing the range to those which are appropriate.

One danger with observation is the tendency to record not only *behaviours*, which can be seen, but also *states,* which cannot. If you watch a small child or a pet for a while and describe it, you are likely to include 'observations' such as 'it was having fun' or 'it was surprised'. However, such records are not of actions but of the emotional condition which, strictly speaking, cannot be observed. At best we can only observe *indicators* of state or arousal, such as facial expression or posture.

interactive
angles

Watch an episode of a soap, and if possible ask other people to watch the same episode but separately. Identify each of the main individuals present. List 20 *behaviours* in which the individuals engage. In addition, identify and justify three *states* such as '*annoyed*' or '*content*' displayed by these characters, noting when they occurred. What differences do you find when you compare your observations? It is generally quite difficult to break the sequence of behaviour into individual events. You will probably find even greater variation in your descriptions of states. This is because you are making *inferences* rather than just recording direct observations.

Operational definitions

The operationalisation of variables serves several functions. Its aim is to put a variable into *operation*, that is, make it useable. It is a description that identifies variables by factors that can be manipulated or measured, for instance because they are observable. It provides a framework for improving reliability both within and between observers. One individual is more likely to be consistent if they have a clear definition in their head about the nature of the variable being recorded. Similarly, multiple observers are more likely to record accurately if they are all working to the same definition. This is a measure of *inter-observer, or inter-rater, reliability*, the extent to which different individuals generate the same records when they observe the same sequence of behaviour. By correlating the scores of observers we can measure inter-observer reliability; individuals (or groups) with highly correlated scores are demonstrating good inter-observer reliability.

Hoyt (2000) identifies observer bias as a substantial source of error in psychological research. So, what can we do to increase the reliability of observers? In addition to the use of operational definitions, giving observers practice, for instance by asking them all to record the events in a videotape sequence and allowing them to discuss how they arrived at their decisions, also improves inter-observer reliability. Hoyt suggests some additional measures to reduce bias:

- *Avoid linked observations* – if possible, each observer should only record one of two linked variables.

- *Use multiple observers* – where a score is derived from multiple records, it is preferable if several observers rate the same target behaviour.

- *Counterbalance observers across targets* – although it may be better to have multiple observers, this is only the case in correlations if each observer rates every target. Smaller numbers of well-trained observers may therefore be more desirable.

interactive angles

Repeat the activity on page 37 but agree operational definitions for just five behaviours in two individuals. Your inter-observer reliability should improve.

for and against

+ Naturalistic observation has high ecological validity.

+ Compared with interviews or questionnaires, it is more difficult for participants in observations to misrepresent themselves, for instance by lying.

+ Participants in naturalistic observations are relatively unaffected by demand characteristics.

– It is difficult to control variables in naturalistic observations.

– High inter-observer reliability is hard to achieve in observations.

+ Naturalistic observations are an equally effective way to study both humans and non-human animals.

Recording behaviour in observations

When making a record of behaviour by hand or using an event recorder, such as a computer, it is not possible to describe every action in detail. To make the task possible researchers can limit either the number of behaviours they observe or the amount of detail they record. The following techniques are commonly used in observational studies to organise the way in which observations are made. They are all *focused* observations, that is, the technique directs the observer's attention to a limited number of behavioural events.

Formalised observations generate data that are more easily interpreted than those from relatively unstructured information gathering. While open-ended observations such as note-taking and diary-keeping provide rich, complete data, such observations are difficult to synthesise and analyse. Formal observations are therefore preferable as the losses in terms of complexity and completeness are balanced by gains in reliability, validity and ease of organising the data.

The recording of events may be triggered by the actions themselves, as in checklisting and event sampling or by time, as in time sampling. In any system the behaviours recorded may or may not be mutually exclusive. Where they are, observations are simplified but less informative. Each technique has advantages and disadvantages.

Checklist

This is a simple list of all the behaviours being recorded. On every occurrence of a behaviour on the list, a single tally is recorded. At the end of the observation period, the observer has a record of the number of occurrences of each of the behaviours being investigated. A 'checklist' might be recorded automatically, for instance by an electronic device. Ireland (1990) used a radio-tracking device to detect the movement of a wild female mink in and out of her den while she was feeding her young. Ireland was able to keep a 24-hour record of the mink's presence or absence.

Checklist

Williams *et al.* (1976) used the following checklist to ascertain the level of disability in a community sample of males.

- Cannot use bus or train unaccompanied.   ☐
- Does not use transport unaccompanied.   ☐
- Does not walk out of doors unaccompanied.   ☐
- Cannot dress without help.   ☐
- Cannot wash without help.   ☐
- Cannot undress without help.   ☐
- Cannot sit and stand without help.   ☐
- Cannot use W.C. or commode without help.   ☐
- Does not get out of bed.   ☐
- Cannot eat without personal help.   ☐

Time sampling

This technique enables the observer to record some information about when behaviours occurred. Each technique provides only indications of the frequency and duration of behaviours and does not record the sequential relationship between behaviours. The observation period is divided into predetermined intervals and records of behaviours are related to these. Leaper (2000) used 5-second time intervals to record play behaviours in parent–child interactions over 8-minute sampling periods. There are three different ways in which the time intervals can be used, as described below.

- One-zero sampling (1/0). During each time interval, a record is made if the chosen behaviour occurs at all. No further record is made if that behaviour occurs again within that interval.

- Instantaneous scan sampling (I/S). No records are made until the end of the time interval. At this *instant* a record is made of any behaviours that are occurring.

- Predominant activity sampling (P/A). Observation is continuous and an estimate is made in relation to the activity that occupied most of the preceding time interval.

Time sampling schedules

One-zero sampling

A 2-minute observation of a child in a sand pit

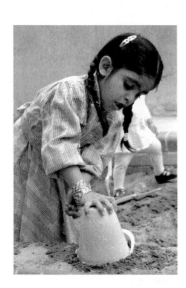

	Time (seconds)											
	10	20	30	40	50	60	70	80	90	100	110	120
Digging		x	x			x	x					x
Pouring				x					x			
Patting					x					x	x	
Other activity	x								x			

Instantaneous scan sampling

A 5-minute observation of a hedgehog in a garden

	Time (seconds)									
	0	30	60	90	120	180	210	240	270	300
Walking	x	x							x	x
Eating				x	x		x			
Nose in the air			x			x		x		
Curled in ball										
Other activity										

Predominant activity sampling

A 1-minute observation of a sparrow at a bird table

	Time (seconds)											
	5	10	15	20	25	30	35	40	45	50	55	60
Head up	x		x		x			x			x	x
Feeding		x		x			x	x		x		
Other activity					x							

Time sampling enables us to record the key behaviours occurring during a stream of behaviour.

interactive angles

If the following problems arose in the use of the coding schemes opposite, what amendments would you make? You can use the guidelines in the box on page 39 to help.

- How would you classify the behaviour of a child who was scraping at the sand with her hand?

- How would you code the behaviour of a child who was tapping the top of a bucket with his spade?

- Generate operational definitions for *digging* and *patting* that will solve these issues.

- What problem arises if *sitting* is recorded in addition to *digging*, *pouring* and *patting*?

- What other behaviours might a child exhibit in a sandpit? Try to produce operational definitions for these.

- Why is the hedgehog behaviour described as *nose in the air* rather than *sniffing*?

- Why do you think the time intervals and numbers of coded behaviours differ between the three observations?

research methods

time sampling: parents and children at play

Leaper, C. (2000) Gender, affiliation, assertion, and the interactive context of parent–child play. *Developmental Psychology,* 36, 381–93

Aim: To search for systematic gender differences in the play of children with their parents.

Method: Ninety-eight children (49 sons and 49 daughters) were observed during play with their mothers and fathers. The children were aged 26–65 months (mean 47.5). Other factors recorded about the families included ethnicity, siblings' ages, age of parents and parental employment and education. Families were recruited through flyers distributed at day-care centres and pre-schools and names and addresses obtained from birth announcements in local newspapers and a purchased mailing list. Letters to the families described the study as an investigation into normal children's play and language development. Each family received a children's book or a $10 gift voucher for their participation.

Observations were conducted in the family's home, typically in the living room. Mother–child and father–child interactions were observed on separate occasions, 1–2 weeks apart, equal numbers of visits began with mother or father observations. Three 8-minute sessions were recorded onto videotape, each with a different toy, provided by the researcher. The first toy presented was a gender-neutral Playmobil Zoo, used as a warm-up session to acclimatise the parent and child to playing together while being videotaped. The following two toys were presented in a counter-balanced order within each family: a feminine-stereotyped Playskool kitchen toy, with food, pots and place settings, and a masculine-stereotyped Little Tikes track to be assembled with a tunnel, station and cars.

Behaviours were coded on 7-point ordinal scales for affiliation and assertion, each participant being rated on each scale every 5 seconds; thus 384 records were made in total per 8-minute session. To increase inter-observer reliability, the observers were trained for 6–8 weeks prior to the study and were retrained every 2–3 months over the two years of data collection. Spearman rank correlations between observers were $r = 0.59$ and $r = 0.66$ respectively for affiliation and assertion. These were significant at $p < 0.001$ (see page 143).

Results: Mother–child dyads were higher in mean affiliation ratings and lower in mean assertion ratings than father–child dyads. Mothers were demonstrating higher levels of affiliation while fathers were more assertive. However, there was no significant effect of the *child's* gender on affiliation or assertive behaviour; parents were no more likely to exhibit affiliation with daughters or assertion with sons. There was, however, a difference between gender-stereotyped settings; boys were more assertive than girls in the masculine setting. The toy food situation was associated with higher rates of affiliation and assertion. Mothers, fathers and daughters, but not sons, tended to show higher affiliation in the toy food setting. No effects were found for affiliation in relation to cross-gender play.

Conclusion: Parental behaviour during play may reinforce stereotypes of affiliative females and assertive males. As the children were, in general, more assertive than their mothers but not their fathers, a stereotyped view that women are less powerful and can be more easily influenced may inadvertently be reinforced. The findings have implications for the equality of parents as role models.

Questions

1 What was the sampling technique being used in this study?

2 As behaviour was videotaped, what choices were available for subsequent analysis of the events?

3 What efforts were made to ensure the reliability of the recordings?

Event sampling

Observation, timing and recording are continuous. The onset and end of each behavioural event is recorded along a single time base. Russell

(1990) studied the response of juvenile captive ferrets directed towards a remote-controlled car covered in fur as a measure of predatory behaviour. The ferrets could pursue, pounce on and bite the 'remote rat' as they would a prey animal.

Event sampling

behaviour	onset / offset times
chase	
pounce	
bite	
other	

time (seconds) 0   5   10   15   20   25   30   35   40

key: onset: ⌐
offset: ⌐

for and against

− Every event cannot readily be recorded.

+ Operational definitions and the opportunity to practise improve inter-observer reliability.

+ Checklists provide an easy way to record a wide range of activities.

+ Time sampling focuses on specific behaviours and improves reliability over a checklist.

− If time intervals are longer than the shortest possible duration for a behaviour data may be distorted (entire behaviours may be omitted from the record).

+ Event sampling provides detailed information about the frequency, duration and sequence of behaviours

Observations as a tool in experiments

Field experiments are studies with an experimental design (they are looking for differences and have an independent variable, IV, and a dependent variable, DV) that take place using participants in their normal surroundings. For example, McNicholas and Collis (2000) observed the attention an individual received from passers-by when they did or did not have a dog with them. Field experiments such as this are described as *contrived*, since the levels of the IV are created by the researcher.

research
methods

field experiment: dogs as social catalysts

McNicholas, J. and Collis, G.M. (2000) Dogs as catalysts for social interactions: robustness of the effect. *British Journal of Psychology*, 91, 61–70

Aim: Dogs being walked by their owners are known to act as social catalysts, encouraging people to interact. This study aimed to find out whether the response of passers-by would still arise if the dog itself did not solicit attention, for instance by approaching passers-by and to test the effect across a range of situations other than dog walking.

Method: In this study, the researchers observed the attention an individual (the handler) received from passers-by when they did or did not have a dog with them. The dog was highly trained so that it did not introduce uncontrolled variables by attracting attention. In addition, the handlers were observed in a range of daily activities, rather than only when walking their dog and when dressed in smart or scruffy clothes.

Results: The handlers were more likely to be approached by passing people when they had a dog than when they were alone in all activities, not just when walking the dog. The presence or absence of the dog had a bigger effect on the likelihood of being approached than the way the handler was dressed.

Conclusion: They concluded that pet dogs can act as effective social catalysts for human interaction across a range of situations.

An alternative to a contrived design is a quasi-experiment, in which the experimenter does not have control over the allocation of participants to levels of the IV. For example, in a study comparing the foraging habits of red and grey squirrels the researcher could not control which individuals were 'red' or 'grey' since they are different species: this would therefore be a quasi-experiment. If this were conducted in the natural habitat, i.e. a woodland, it would also be a field experiment. You will find a further discussion of quasi-experiments in Chapter 6, pages 89–91. Similarly, comparisons of males and females are quasi-experiments, for instance Jacob and McClintock (2000) tested the effect on mood of steroidal compounds believed to be human pheromones. They found that the two compounds ($\Delta 4,16$-androstadien-3-one and $1,3,5(10)16$-estratetraen-3-ol) increased positive mood state in women but decreased it in men.

media watch

It's the pits

Never mind letting your heart rule your head – if recent research is anything to go by, it's your nose that rules when you're out on the pull. Scientists now want us to believe the smell of male sweat is a turn on and that ugly blokes become more attractive by letting their natural body odour shine through! In tests carried out at the Northumbria University, women rated men far more attractive when secretly exposed to pheromones – the chemicals found in male sweat ... So, if you end up with a face like a monkey's bum this summer, at least you know it's only because he smells. Bonus.

Company, July 2000

How would you test the effects of human pheromones on attractiveness using a quasi-experiment?

Observations can also be used as a means to measure the DV in laboratory experiments. The observer may be non-participant, such as in Leaper (2000) who videotaped parent–child interactions during play or Bandura's studies of children where the observer was hidden by a one-way screen.

research methods

non-participant observation: will children copy violent behaviour?

Bandura, A., Ross, D. and Ross, S.A. (1961) Transmission of aggression through imitation of aggressive models. *Journal of Abnormal and Social Psychology*, 63, 575–82

Aim: To investigate whether aggression learned through observation of the aggressive acts of others would generalise to new settings where the model was not present and to investigate the effect of gender on such modelling.

Method: Children aged three to six years (36 boys and 36 girls) were first scored for initial level of aggressiveness, being rated by a teacher and an experimenter for physical aggression, verbal aggression and aggression towards objects. The children were divided into groups matched for initial behaviour; a control group that did not see a model and two groups that were exposed to adult models who behaved in either aggressive or non-aggressive ways. Half of each group saw a same-sex model, the others an opposite-sex model. The children were then tested in different situations to ascertain the extent to which they would imitate the aggressive acts of the model. The experimenter took each child to a playroom, meeting an adult (the model) who was invited to 'join in the game'. The child sat at a table offering potato printing and coloured stickers to play with while the model sat at another with Tinkertoys, a mallet and a 5-foot high inflated Bobo doll. In the non-aggressive condition, the model assembled the Tinkertoys for 10 minutes, in the aggressive condition this lasted only one minute after which the model attacked the Bobo doll. The sequence of behaviour was identical each time: Bobo was lain on its side, sat upon, punched on the nose, picked up and hit on the head with the mallet. It was then thrown up in the air and kicked about the room. This sequence was performed three times over nine minutes accompanied by aggressive comments such as 'kick him' and 'pow'.

After exposure to the model, all participants were put in a situation designed to frustrate them, to increase the likelihood of aggression being displayed. They were taken to a room containing attractive toys such as a fire engine and a doll with a wardrobe (remember, this is the 1960s). After a short opportunity to play the children were told that these toys were for other children and were moved to another room. This final stage offered non-aggressive toys such as crayons, dolls, a ball, cars, a tea set and plastic farm animals and aggressive toys including a Bobo doll, a mallet and dart guns. The children were allowed to play here for 20 minutes and were observed by the experimenters using a one-way mirror. Records were made of aggressive acts that replicated the model's behaviour (both physical and verbal), other aggression with the mallet and non-aggressive behaviour. These were then compared.

Results: Children exposed to violent models imitated both physical and verbal aggression and were more aggressive than those children who did not receive aggressive modelling. Boys imitated more aggression, especially from a same-sex model but girls were more likely to imitate verbal aggression.

Conclusion: The findings demonstrated that observation and imitation can account for the learning of specific acts without reinforcement of either the models or observers. Same-sex modelling may have been more effective for boys than for girls because male aggression is more culturally typical so carries the weight of social acceptability.

Questions

1 The researchers used a one-way mirror: what type of observation was this?

2 Why was the sequence of the adult's behaviour with the Bobo doll identical each time?

Conclusions

Observations are problematic in ensuring adequate controls and reliability but offer a unique way to collect information about behaviour in a natural setting. Studies with both people and non-human animals have shown that it is possible to gain reliable and worthwhile data from naturalistic observations. These can be both a source of information in themselves and provide a platform from which experimental studies can develop.

where to now?

▶ **Marsh, P., Rosser, E. and Harre, R. (1978)** *The Rules of Disorder*. **London: Routledge, Kegan, Paul** – this provides a fascinating account of a study based in part on participant observation

▶ **Robson, C. (1993)** *Real World Research*. **Oxford: Blackwell** – this covers many of the research methods well but is unusual in offering good coverage of the observational method

▶ **White, M. (2000)** *Studying animal behaviour in Zoos. Ringtailed lemurs: recording and scoring selected behaviours*. **Association for the Study of Animal Behaviour** (video pack).

what do you know?

1 How does a naturalistic observation differ from a field experiment?

2 What is inter-observer reliability and how can it be improved in an observational study?

3 Describe two advantages of event sampling over other methods of observational recording.

4

Questionnaires and Interviews

This chapter introduces the research methods of questionnaires and interviews used in psychological research. The questionnaire research method is the most widely used in social science research and there are a number of techniques that can be utilised to aid data collection. We will look at these techniques and show you how best to use them when creating a questionnaire. From this, we will introduce interviewing methods and illustrate how questionnaires may be of use when interviewing participants in research. We will also examine factors that may affect the return of questionnaires and debate whether questionnaires or interviews are the best method for data collection in psychology. Throughout this chapter we will introduce you to research that has used questionnaires, interviews or both.

Questionnaires: an introduction

Questionnaires, as a research method, could be said to have a 'rough deal'. Why is this? Well, most people perceive questionnaires as an easy option and believe that they are simple to create and use. They learn rather quickly that this is not the case. The perception of questionnaires is usually that you ask a few questions then look at the responses and before you know it you have a conclusion and you can go home! Sadly this is far from the truth. Questionnaires take time to create and throughout this chapter we will introduce you to the methods that can be used to write a good questionnaire.

Fife-Shaw (1995) noted that '…designing the perfect questionnaire is probably impossible…' (p. 175). This may well be true. However, you can gain a great deal of information from a well-designed questionnaire or a well-conducted interview that cannot be obtained through other research methods.

As will become apparent, the entire procedure for creating, testing and using a questionnaire or interview is a long process but one that is fulfilling and rewarding when you are drawing firm conclusions from something you have designed.

Techniques and methods for successful questionnaire design

There are a variety of techniques that can be used to gain information through questionnaires. We are going to look at *Likert scales*, *Thurstone method*, *semantic differentials*, *open-ended questions* and *closed questions*. This should cover all techniques necessary to be successful at designing and implementing questionnaires in data collection.

Likert scales (Likert, 1932)

These scales are used to measure attitudes to certain ideas. You are probably familiar with these scales without realising it. These are the scales that allow you to strongly agree, agree, strongly disagree, etc., with a variety of statements. To design and implement a Likert-type questionnaire, follow the procedure outlined below:

- Choose an *attitude object*. This is the area of research that you want to gain an attitude about from participants. Examples could be 'attitudes to pet ownership' or 'attitudes towards college'. You can make this as general or specific as you like depending on what you are intending to measure.

- Generate as many 'statements' as possible that you feel measure the attitude object. The statements are not questions but merely a sentence that can generate a response in your participants. An example could be 'owning a pet gives support and happiness' or 'college is a fun place to be'. The more statements the better (20+ is a good benchmark).

- Once you have generated as many items as possible you must now decide what a *high score on your questionnaire indicates*. For example, a 'high score could indicate a favourable attitude to pet ownership' or a 'high score could indicate a favourable attitude towards college'.

- Make sure you have *roughly equal amounts of positive and negative statements*. A *positive statement* is a statement that agrees with what a high score indicates. A *negative statement* is a statement that does not agree with what a high score indicates. So, in other words it agrees with what a low score indicates. You may have to switch some statements from positive to negative or negative to positive to gain roughly equal amounts. Below are three statements for the 'pet ownership' and 'college' attitude objects.

inter**active**
angles

For each one, write down whether you feel it is a positive statement or a negative statement:

Item	Positive or negative?
Owning a pet can decrease lonely feelings	
Pets have parasites that can cause disease in humans	
Pets are expensive to keep	
College is a fun place to be	
The only good thing about college is the bus ride home	
I learn a great deal from my teacher in psychology	

I hope you remembered to state what a high score was first before making a decision on the statements!

- *Randomise* the statements so that there is a good mixture of positive and negative statements throughout the questionnaire. This will hopefully stop the participant from getting bored by answering all statements the same!

- Under each item/statement give the participant a choice of responses – this usually takes the form of a 5-point scale: *strongly agree, agree, don't know, disagree, strongly disagree.* An odd number of choices (5 or 7) is optimal as it enables the participant to choose 'don't know' if they truly have no view on the matter! A 4-point scale could force a participant to agree or disagree with a statement when in reality they have no opinion.

- Create two master copies of the questionnaire. Leave one blank so you have a spare to photocopy and on the other choose how to score each individual item. This involves writing a number by each response for every item/statement. For example:

Owning a pet gives support and happiness.

Strongly agree	Agree	Don't know	Disagree	Strongly disagree
5	4	3	2	1

Pets are expensive to keep.

Strongly agree	Agree	Don't know	Disagree	Strongly disagree
5	2	3	4	5

- To rationalise your initial questionnaire (that is, to get rid items that are not measuring your attitude object) you can perform an *items analysis*. You need to get between 10 and 20 people to complete your questionnaire. Each participant receives a *total score* by adding up each individual item score based on their responses.

- *Rank order* the total scores from all of the participants and choose the top three and the bottom three scores. You must now analyse each item individually to see if it is a good *discriminator* between high and low scorers.

- Write down the responses to question 1 for the three people in the high-scoring group and the three people in the low-scoring group:

High-scoring group   Low-scoring group
SA, SA, A   SD, SD, SD

This item should be *accepted* for the questionnaire, as the responses from the two groups are distinctly different.

High-scoring group   Low-scoring group
A, DK, SD   A, A, D

This item should be *rejected* for the questionnaire, as the responses are not distinctly different between the two groups.

- The items that are *accepted* form the basis for your questionnaire. You can now use this questionnaire to gain the data for your piece of research but you cannot use the same people who you used for your items analysis.

- Create two master copies of the questionnaire as you did before conducting the items analysis.

for and against

the Likert scale

+ Ideal for measuring attitudes.

+ Easy to swap positive to negative statements (and vice versa).

− Items analysis is rather subjective. You choose whether to accept or reject an item.

− It can be difficult to create enough initial statements without repetition.

− You may be left with no items after items analysis.

− Repetitious with the same responses for each statement.

+ Easy to score and add up a final total.

+ A reliable measure after the items analysis.

media watch

The Sugar drink and drugs survey

Wanna have your say about drink and drugs? Fill out this *totally* confidential survey, send it to *Sugar* and you could win a Single Use cameras, worth £4.99. These colour cameras are easy to use and you can take 'em anywhere!

1. Do you smoke

- occasionally ☐
- frequently ☐
- excessively ☐
- never ☐

2. If you do smoke, or have smoked, at what age did you start?

- 11 ☐
- 12 ☐
- 13 ☐
- 14 ☐
- 15 ☐
- other *(please state)* [＿＿＿＿＿]

3. What do you think is the biggest danger of smoking?

- getting caught ☐
- putting boys off you ☐
- ruining your skin ☐
- getting a cough ☐
- getting lung cancer ☐
- getting thrombosis ☐
- other *(please specify)*

[＿＿＿＿＿＿＿＿＿＿]

4. If you don't smoke, what do you think about people who do?

(you can tick more than one box)

- they look cool ☐
- they stink ☐
- they're poisoning people with 'passive smoking' ☐
- they have ash-tray breath ☐
- they're just another drug addict ☐
- they're sad ☐

5. Do you drink alcohol?

- occasionally ☐
- frequently ☐
- excessively ☐
- never ☐

6. If you never (or rarely) drink alcohol, what do you think of people who drink?

- they're cool ☐
- they look stupid ☐
- they're irresponsible ☐
- it's said that they can't have a good time without alcohol ☐

Adapted from *Sugar* magazine

How would you analyse the responses to each question?

The Thurstone method (Thurstone, 1931)

Initially, this method applies the principle of the *Likert scale* to create a questionnaire. However, Thurstone believed in using 'expert judges' to rate each item on how important it was at measuring the attitude object. The basic procedure is:

- Choose an *attitude object*.

- Create as many statements as you can that you feel measures the attitude object. Again, try to create a good mix of positive and negative statements.

- Engage a panel of 'expert judges of your attitude object' (at least 8–10) to rate each item on a scale from 0 (highly negative on this issue) to 10 (highly positive on this issue). Urge the panel to try to use the full range of scores (0–10) when rating the items.

- For each item, calculate the *mean score* by adding up the values each judge gave that item and dividing this figure by the number of judges.

- The figure you have calculated now becomes the *score a participant receives if they tick that item.*

- *Randomise* the list of items so that the low-scoring items or the high-scoring items are not clustered together. Next to each statement provide a box for the participant to tick if they *agree with the statement.*

- Create two master copies of the questionnaire. Leave one blank so you have a spare to photocopy and on the second one write the mean values by each of the items.

- Now you can get participants to fill in the questionnaire. To *score* the questionnaire, simply add up the values of each item that the participant has ticked.

for and against

the Thurstone method

+ Do not have to swap negative to positive items (and vice versa).

− Can be difficult to find an expert panel!

− Should not really use the mean as the average. (What should it use?)

− It is a long process for the panel if you have lots of items to rate.

+ Easy to administer.

+ Easy to add up and create a total score.

+ Reliable as you have used an expert panel.

Semantic differentials (Osgood *et al.*, 1957)

This type of scale allows you to assess the feelings and thoughts about a description or a picture that people may have. These are supposed to help you build up a picture of what a 'typical' person is thought to be (e.g. pet-owner, dog-trainer). To create a semantic differential scale you must follow this procedure:

- Choose the person or people that you want your participants to rate. These can be in the form of a description of a person or an actual picture for them to rate.

- Choose as many *bi-polar adjectives* that you can think of which assess the description or picture. Some examples are strong–weak, hot–cold, clean–dirty, pleasant–unpleasant and introvert–extravert.

- Similar to the procedure for a Likert scale, you must decide what a *high score indicates*.

- After you have decided what a high score indicates, *randomise* the list of bi-polar adjectives so that not all of the 'good' traits are on the left-hand side and all the 'bad' traits are on the right-hand side, as below:

good	—	—	—	—	—	—	bad
weak	—	—	—	—	—	—	strong
active	—	—	—	—	—	—	passive

- As with the Likert scale procedure, have either five or seven response spaces for people to rate their responses (above is an example of seven spaces).

- Create two master copies of the questionnaire. Leave one blank so you have a spare to photocopy and on the other choose how to score each item (based on what you have chosen as a high-score indicator). Rate each item individually from 1 to 5 or 1 to 7 depending on how many choices you are giving per item.

- To *rationalise* your questionnaire you can execute an *items analysis* as described under the *Likert scale procedure*.

- Create two master copies of the questionnaire as you did before the items analysis.

research methods

semantic differentials: are alligators cute?

Baenninger, R., Dengelmaier, R., Navarette, J. and Sezov, D. (2000) What's in a name? Uncovering connotative meanings of animal names. *Anthrozoös*, 13 (2), 113–17

Aim: To examine whether certain animal names elicited distinct characteristics, for example, lions are perceived as being fierce.

Method: The research team created a *semantic differential* questionnaire that examined each animal name on 19 criteria. A copy of the questionnaire is shown below:

EAGLE

Good — — — — — — —	Bad
Awful — — — — — — —	Nice
Beautiful — — — — — — —	Ugly
Dirty — — — — — — —	Clean
Pleasant — — — — — — —	Unpleasant
Dislike — — — — — — —	Like
Strong — — — — — — —	Weak
Small — — — — — — —	Large
Heavy — — — — — — —	Light
Delicate — — — — — — —	Rugged
Brave — — — — — — —	Cowardly
Thick — — — — — — —	Thin
Old — — — — — — —	Young
Kind — — — — — — —	Cruel
Passive — — — — — — —	Active
Fast — — — — — — —	Slow
Calm — — — — — — —	Agitated
Ferocious — — — — — — —	Peaceful
Relaxed — — — — — — —	Tense

Baenniger *et al.* (2000)

How would you rate these animals on a semantic differential scale?

Each of the 12 animals that were assessed (alligator, bullfrog, canary, deer, eagle, fox, goldfish, hamster, lion, lizard, shark and turtle) appeared at the top of the questionnaire. All 100 participants had to fill in the questionnaire for *each* animal. The animals were presented in a random order for each participant.

Results: There was a large consensus across the sample as to how each animal was perceived. The profiles for canary and alligator were 'mirror images' of each other. For example, the canary was seen as being beautiful, cowardly and peaceful, whereas the alligator was seen as being ugly, brave and ferocious.

Conclusion: It would appear that for this sample of people, there were large similarities as to how the 12 species were perceived on the 19 chosen criteria.

inter**active** angles

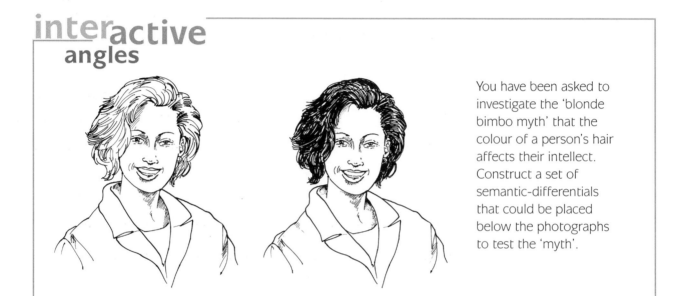

You have been asked to investigate the 'blonde bimbo myth' that the colour of a person's hair affects their intellect. Construct a set of semantic-differentials that could be placed below the photographs to test the 'myth'.

for and **against**

semantic differentials

+ An effective technique for direct comparison between two pictures, or other stimulus material.

− Items analysis is subjective.

− Can be difficult to find two comparable pictures (e.g. one picture may be smiling and the other sulking!).

+ Easy to calculate a total score.

− Cannot be sure it is just the picture or other stimulus material that is causing the responses given by the participant.

− Can be difficult to create enough bi-polar adjectives.

+ Good for assessing emotional responses in people, which can be very difficult when using the Likert scale or Thurstone method.

Open and closed (fixed-choice) questions

An open-ended question gives us *qualitative data* based on the 'richness of the responses'. These types of question ask a participant to respond to a set question but leave a blank underneath the question so the participant can answer in whatever style they choose. These are usually used to assess emotional aspects and reasons why people choose to do certain things. However, you should restrict the space used to answer the question or you could be analysing essays as answers. Also, in a restricted 'answering space' the participant is likely to give the crux of their feelings straight away.

Closed, or fixed-choice, questions give the answers to the participant and they have to choose the most appropriate for them. This allows it to be easier to analyse the questionnaire quantitatively.

Example

Say we are interested in why a person owns a pet. We can ask them about their motives in an open-ended style or a fixed-choice style as follows:

Open-ended: Please state the main factors affecting your decision to keep a pet at present.

....

....

Fixed-choice: Please tick the main factors as to why you own a pet at present.

Companionship	☐
Security	☐
'I have always owned animals'	☐
Affection	☐
Stress reliever	☐
It was a stray	☐
Other (please state below)	

interactive angles

Create a series of open-ended and fixed-choice answers as to what qualities people like to see in their friends.

Some examples of questionnaires that use the techniques described in this chapter:

General Health Questionnaire (extract from GHQ-12, available from NFER-Nelson, Windsor)

Have you recently…

1. been able to concentrate on whatever you're doing	Better than usual	Same as usual	Less than usual	Much less than usual
2. lost much sleep over worry?	Not at all	No more than usual	Rather more than usual	Much more than usual
3. felt that you are playing a useful part in things?	More so than usual	Same as usual	Less useful than usual	Much less than usual

Short Form Social Support Questionnaire (extract from SSQ6, available from NFER-Nelson, Windsor)

(1) Whom can you really count on to distract you from your worries when you feel under stress?

(a) No one   3)   6)   9)
    1)   4)   7)
    2)   5)   8)

(b) How satisfied?   6   5   4   3   2   1

(2) Whom can you really count on to help you feel more relaxed when you are under pressure or tense?

(a) No one   3)   6)   9)
    1)   4)   7)
    2)   5)   8)

(b) How satisfied?   6   5   4   3   2   1

(3) Who accepts you totally, including both your worst and best points?

(a) No one   3)   6)   9)
    1)   4)   7)
    2)   5)   8)

(b) How satisfied?   6   5   4   3   2   1

for and against

questionnaires

+ Good for research that can involve socially sensitive matters (e.g. sexuality, drug-taking).

− Can be expensive to produce long questionnaires.

− People may give socially desirable answers.

+ People may disclose more on a questionnaire as it does not involve talking to another person.

− Questions have to be carefully worded to avoid bias.

Factors affecting the questionnaire research method

Make the questionnaire specific

It may appear that this would be one of the first things you would think about when using questionnaires. However, if you are attempting to measure a range of things (e.g. anxiety, depression) there may be questionnaires that measure both on the same scale or there may be separate questionnaires that measure each separately. A research example of this comes from McCann *et al.* (1999) who were interested in estimation of alcohol consumption using three different measures. One was specifically for alcohol consumption, while the other two had alcohol 'sections' among other consumption measures. Although the specific alcohol questionnaire was the best given the aims of the research, the two other questionnaires produced the same rank order of consumption across the participants.

research methods

questionnaire length: don't ask so many questions!

McCann, S.E., Marshall, J.R., Trevisan, M., Russell, M., Muti, P., Markovic, N., Chan, A.W. and Freudenheim, J.L. (1999) Recent alcohol intake as estimated by the Health Habits and History Questionnaire, the Harvard Semiquantitative Food Frequency Questionnaire and a more detailed alcohol intake questionnaires. *American Journal of Epidemiology*, 150 (4), 334–40

Aim: To examine how estimation of alcohol intake varies between Food Frequency Questionnaires (FFQs) that have limited questions on alcohol and on other measures. McCann *et al.* had noted how FFQs had been used in previous research but were concerned about the conclusions drawn from them due to limited assessment of alcohol intake on the FFQs.

Method: One hundred and thirty-three healthy American participants completed three separate questionnaires (the Health Habits and History Questionnaire, the Harvard Semiquantitative FFQ and the Drinking Patterns Questionnaire). The questionnaires had a different amount of questions pertaining to alcohol consumption. The questionnaires were completed with interviewer-administered computer-assisted interviews over a two-week period in 1995.

Results: Each participant was rated via the three questionnaires on alcohol consumption (each type of drink was noted and multiplied depending on the amount of alcohol in the drink; for example, vodka has more alcohol in it than a glass of wine, so intake would be adjusted accordingly). Estimates of total alcohol consumed and spirits consumed tended to be higher in the Drinking Patterns Questionnaire than in the FFQs. Beer and wine estimation was not significantly affected by questionnaire type.

Conclusions: The results suggest that the Drinking Patterns Questionnaire produced higher estimates of alcohol consumption compared to the two other FFQs. However, both FFQs agreed with the Drinking Patterns Questionnaire on the rank order of consumption across the 133 participants. It could therefore be argued, depending on the aim of the specific research, that any of the questionnaires could be used for estimation of alcohol intake. However, if the research is specifically about over-drinking, it may be more useful to use the Drinking Patterns Questionnaire as this overestimates alcohol consumption and may therefore limit or reduce actual alcohol consumption on a detoxification programme.

Questions

1 Why do you think McCann *et al.* obtained the results they did where there was a higher estimation of alcohol intake on the Drinking Patterns Questionnaire compared to the FFQs?

2 Create some questions you think would be on the Drinking Patterns Questionnaire.

3 Create some questions you think would be on the FFQs.

4 Do you think questionnaires would be useful to assess alcohol consumption in over-drinkers? Justify your answer.

The best questionnaires are not necessarily those with the most items. Research conducted by Angbratt and Moller (1999) shows how a short version of a questionnaire that had only eight key questions about calcium intake gleaned enough information for diagnosing a risk for osteoporosis than a questionnaire comprising 52 questions. The latter added no more information that could be utilised for risk diagnosis than the former questionnaire. Again, the more specific questionnaire had more usage and would obviously reduce completion time so many more people can be assessed.

research methods

questionnaire reliability: untrustworthy questionnaires? – a Swedish investigation

Angbratt, M. and Moller, M. (1999) Questionnaire about calcium intake: Can we trust the answers? *Osteoporosis International*, 9 (3), 220–5

Aim: As estimating calcium intake is very important in evaluating risk of osteoporosis, Angbratt and Moller devised two questionnaires to see which one (or both) gave reliable answers.

Method: Questionnaire A contained eight questions about consumption of dairy foods (from which a large amount of calcium is consumed in the Swedish diet). Questionnaire B contained 52 questions (including the eight from Questionnaire A) about the consumption of calcium-rich dishes. A random sample of 467 Swedish women received Questionnaire A to complete. Women identified with a 'low-calcium intake' from this questionnaire were then sent Questionnaire B. In an attempt to validate the smaller questionnaire further, a sample of the women was interviewed with their dietary history known.

Results: A total of 363 Questionnaires A were returned of which 118 were identified with low calcium intake. A total of 96 women completed Questionnaire B and 22 were then interviewed. Statistical analysis showed no significant difference between responses to the same questions that appeared on Questionnaire A and Questionnaire B.

Conclusions: The much shorter Questionnaire A provided reliable information about the women who did not have adequate calcium intake. The much longer Questionnaire B provided no more information than Questionnaire A. Therefore, the shorter questionnaire can be used as a quick and efficient measure of women on low calcium diets who may be at risk from osteoporosis.

Questions

1 What types of questions do you think appeared on the eight-item Questionnaire A?

2 How could Angbratt and Moller draw a random sample of females to take part?

3 What percentage of women was identified with a low calcium intake?

Title and length of questionnaire

Many people complain that the length of a questionnaire puts them off completing and returning it. However, is this truly the case? In a rather innovative piece of research, Lund and Gram (1998) sent out five questionnaires of varying length but also with different titles. The questionnaires included a two-page questionnaire entitled either 'Women and Cancer' or 'Oral Contraceptives and Cancer', a four-page questionnaire entitled either 'Women and Cancer' or 'Women, Lifestyles and Health', or a six-page questionnaire entitled 'Women and Cancer'. The two-page questionnaires were otherwise exactly the same, as were the two four-page questionnaires. The six-page questionnaire asked more probing questions than the two- and four-paged questionnaires, so it would give a more thorough analysis of the topic area. Intriguingly, the length of questionnaire had no real effect in response rates and the six-page questionnaire had the second highest return rate. However, the title of questionnaire significantly affected the return rates. The simpler title that told the respondent exactly what the questionnaire was about ('Women and Cancer') had the highest return rate by far, so much so that these questionnaires filled the top three ranked positions based on percentage returns!

research methods

questionnaire length and questionnaire title: the title and length of questionnaire affects response rate

Lund, E. and Gram, I.T. (1998) Response rate according to title and length of questionnaire. *Scandinavian Journal of Social Medicine*, 26 (2), 154–60

Aim: To investigate how the response rates to a postal questionnaire were affected by the title and length of the questionnaire.

Method: Over 5000 randomly sampled Norwegian women, aged 35–49 years, were sent one of five questionnaires: either a two-, four- or six-page questionnaire entitled 'Women and Cancer', a two-page questionnaire (the same as the other two-page questionnaire) but given the title 'Oral Contraceptives and Cancer', or the same four-page questionnaire as above but entitled 'Women, Lifestyle and Health'.

Results: Over 3000 questionnaires were returned (overall return rate = 62.1%). The rank order of returned questionnaires by percentage were:

1. Two-page questionnaire – 'Women and Cancer'	70.2%
2. Six-page questionnaire – 'Women and Cancer'	63.3%
3. Four-page questionnaire – 'Women and Cancer'	62.8%
4. Two-page questionnaire – 'Oral Contraceptives and Cancer'	60.7%
5. Four-page questionnaire – 'Women, Lifestyle and Health'	57.1%

Conclusions: In this Norwegian sample it is clear to see that the title of the questionnaire affected the response rate: the simpler title filled the top three places. The length of questionnaire did not have a great deal of influence on the response rate as the more comprehensive six-page questionnaire gained the second highest response rate, while the Oral Contraceptive two-page questionnaire had a relatively low response rate. Also, the study suggests that the benefits of increased information from a longer, more comprehensive questionnaire outweigh the potential non-responder bias brought about by a lower response rate. Therefore, keep the title of the questionnaire short and snappy!

Questions

1 How could Lund and Gram have drawn a random sample of Norwegian women?

2 What questions do you think could have featured on the questionnaire (think of four or five)?

interactive angles

Try to find some questionnaires that you have received through the post or been handed to you in the street. How does the title affect the likelihood you will complete it?

Interviews

An introduction

There are many types of interview that utilise the questionnaire research method. The two broad categories of interview are *structured* and *unstructured*. Structured interviews are those that have previously decided questions answered in a particular order. The responses may be fixed as in the Likert scale, or fixed-choice answers provided on a questionnaire and the interviewee picks the closest answer. An unstructured interview has a number of topic areas to be covered but it is not as prescriptive as a structured interview. That is, fixed questions and fixed-choice answers are not provided or elicited, so the whole procedure is much more open-ended.

Factors affecting the interview research method

Structure of the questions

Breakwell (1995) noted six areas where questions can be poorly formulated and then used in a questionnaire or interview. This can lead to difficult interpretation of the answers given. The six areas are as follows:

1 Questions should not be double-barrelled. For example, 'do you think that cats and dogs are good pets?' A 'no' answer could be interpreted as being no to cats only, no to dogs only or no to both!

2 Do not introduce an assumption into the question that could affect the respondent's answer. For example, 'do you think genetically modified crops are bad because they are harmful to the environment or bad for us?'

3 Do not include jargon or complicated terms. For example, 'do you agree with the neo-Freudian notion of the lesser significance of a maternal figure on cognitive-emotive development?' At this point the interviewee may leave!

4 Do not use leading questions. For example, 'do you think Ibuprofen is more harmful than aspirin?'

5 Do not use double negatives. For example, 'do you feel it is not true that not all children need a stable maternal figure in early years for sound development?' How would you interpret a 'yes' answer to that question?

6 Do not use 'catch-all' questions. For example, 'tell me all you know about HIV and how it has influenced your sexual behaviour?' It will be difficult for the interviewee to continue talking without further prompts or a more structured series of questions. They may simply omit crucial facts, as there is so much to get across to you.

interactive angles

The website http://www.hoaxkill.com dispelled a myth, started on the Internet, that the use of underarm antiperspirant caused breast cancer. What questions might you ask people to investigate their attitude to such a rumour?

Face-to-face or not?

Breakwell (1995) stated that 'telephone interviewing seems to yield similar data to face-to-face interviews' (p. 235). This appears to be a rather erroneous conclusion as recent research has shown a vast difference between the techniques, even when a computer-assisted interview package is employed.

Donovan *et al.* (1997) compared face-to-face interviews with telephone interviews used to assess a health foundation in Perth, Australia. In the telephone interview group, people were more likely to describe lower levels of smoking and unsafe alcohol consumption compared to the face-to-face group.

research methods

interview technique: face-to-face or on the telephone – which is best for measuring health?

Donovan, R.J., Holman, C.D., Corti, B. and Jalleh, G. (1997) Face-to-face household interviews versus telephone interviews for health surveys. *Australian and New Zealand Journal of Public Health*, 21 (2), 134–40

Aim: To compare the response rates on a health survey given via face-to-face interviews or telephone interviews.

Method: Two samples of people were drawn from Perth, Australia: a face-to-face interview group (*n* = 1000) and a telephone interview group (*n* = 222). A stratified-type sample (see Chapter 2) was drawn for both groups as part of a three-yearly assessment of a health foundation.

Results: There was a significantly lower reporting of smoking behaviour and unsafe alcohol consumption in the telephone interview group. There was also a significantly higher recall of 'health messages' in the telephone interview group.

Conclusions: Donovan *et al.* concluded that 'health researchers should treat comparisons between different survey modes with caution, and should be aware that campaign evaluations using telephone surveys and household surveys may yield substantially different results' (p. 134).

Questions

1 What types of questions could Donovan *et al.* have asked participants?

2 From this study, which method appears more accurate: face-to-face or the telephone?

Furthermore, to counteract the statement by Breakwell (1995), Hayashi *et al.* (1999) discovered a much higher response rate from a telephone interview compared with a face-to-face interview when questioning a sample of Japanese people on their sexual behaviour. It should also be noted that in this research the questionnaire response rate and the telephone interview response rate were exactly the same.

research
methods

questionnaire response rates: sex and the questionnaire – a Japanese perspective

Hayashi, M., Iwanaga, T., Mitoku, K. and Minowa, M. (1999) Getting a high response rate of sexual behaviour survey among the general population in Japan: three different methods of survey on sexual behaviour. *Journal of Epidemiology*, 9 (2), 107–13

Aim: To investigate which of three techniques (postal questionnaire, telephone interview or face-to-face interview) had the highest response rate when questioning people about sexual behaviour.

Method: A random sample of 360 Japanese people aged 20–49 years drawn from two geographically different areas were randomly assigned to the three techniques noted above. Gender was balanced between the two geographic areas. The survey was conducted between October 1995 and February 1996.

Results: The percentage response rates per technique were:
1. Postal questionnaire   69.2%
1. Telephone interview   69.2%
3. Face-to-face interview   55.8%

Conclusion: Hayashi *et al.* state that it is difficult to determine the best method through response rates alone, but for cost-efficiency (money and labour hours) the postal questionnaire was deemed cheapest and the best research method for a national sex behaviour survey.

Questions

1 How could the participants have been randomly assigned to the three techniques? Was it a good idea to do this?

2 Why do you think the face-to-face interview had the lowest response rate?

Kissinger *et al.* (1999) reported that women were more likely to give socially desirable answers in a face-to-face than a computer-assisted interview when questioned on sexual health. Certain socially undesirable behaviours, such as infrequent condom usage, were reported less often in a face-to-face interview compared to a self-administered computer interview. All participants had taken the face-to-face interview *and* the computer interview.

research
methods

computer interviews: computers – a sure way to safe sex?

Kissinger, P., Rice, J., Farley, T., Trim, S., Jewitt, K., Margavio, V. and Martin, D.H. (1999) Application of computer-assisted interviews to sexual behaviour research. *American Journal of Epidemiology*, 149 (10), 950–54

Aim: To compare the responses from video-enhanced computer-assisted self-administered interviews (V CASI) and face-to-face interviews (FTFI) on sensitive sexual behaviour matters. Also, to see if interviewer bias is reduced in the V-CASI approach.

Method: A total of 280 women attending a clinic for sexually transmitted diseases or attending a family planning clinic with diagnosed *Chlamydia trachomitis* completed an eight-question closed response behavioural questionnaire (four socially undesirable, two socially desirable and two neutral questions) using the V-CASI and FTFI methods.

Results: There was good reliability between the two methods but women tended to admit to more socially undesirable behaviours on the V-CASI method compared to FTFI. Thirty per cent of the sample gave more socially desirable answers on the FTFI compared to the V-CASI technique. Furthermore, women who reported a socially undesirable behaviour on the V-CASI (e.g. more than two sexual partners and infrequent condom usage) were more likely to not report them on the FTFI.

Conclusions: The V-CASI technique can reduce socially desirable answers and improve the validity in this area of sexual health research. Again, it shows that differing techniques can produce different results in socially sensitive research matters like sexual behaviour and health.

Questions

1 Which technique produced more socially desirable answers? Why do you think this happened?

2 In what ways could there be interview bias in the FTFI approach?

Finally, a recent piece of research by Canterino *et al.* (1999) examined whether it would be more effective using a questionnaire, interview or both when examining domestic abuse. The latter appeared the most effective.

research
methods

interviews versus questionnaires: an example examining domestic abuse

Canterino, J.C., VanHorn, L.G., Harrigan, J.T., Ananth, C.V. and Vintzileos, A.M. (1999) Domestic abuse in pregnancy: A comparison of a self-completed domestic abuse questionnaire with a directed interview. *American Journal of Obstetric Gynecology*, 181 (5, pt 1), 1049–51

Aim: To compare the results of a self-completed questionnaire and an interview in identifying pregnant women who were victims of domestic abuse.

Method: All patients who attended a prenatal visit between March and September 1997 were asked to complete a domestic abuse questionnaire. This was then followed with an interview that reviewed what had been completed on the questionnaire. Canterino *et al.* classified domestic abuse as any positive response to an item on the domestic abuse questionnaire *or* the interview. Participants were also rated if they responded 'positively' in both questionnaire *and* interview conditions.

Results: Of the 224 patients evaluated, 80 (36 per cent) reported domestic abuse via either the questionnaire or the interview. The domestic abuse questionnaire alone identified 85 per cent of these patients while the interview alone identified only 60 per cent (this was statistically significant, $p = 0.03$). The use of the domestic abuse questionnaire and the interview together identified a further 15 per cent of abuse victims not picked up by each instrument alone.

Conclusions: The domestic abuse questionnaire appears to be superior at detecting abuse compared with the interview when used independently. However, when both are used in conjunction, the number of patients identified as being abused rose further. Therefore, it may be easier for patients to complete a questionnaire when the subject matter is sensitive and then be interviewed about the responses. A combination of questionnaire and interview worked best for domestic abuse victims.

Questions

1 What sort of questions do you think featured on the questionnaire?

2 How many people did the domestic questionnaire identify as being abused?

3 How many people did the interview alone identify as being abused?

where to now?

> **Oppenheim, A.N. (1992)** *Questionnaire design, interviewing and attitude measurement.* **London: Pinter Publishers** – a very thorough account for designing questionnaires and interviews and how to analyse them.

what do you know?

1 List factors that affect the responses from a questionnaire and/or an interview.

2 What is meant by a Likert scale?

3 Distinguish between a structured and an unstructured interview.

4 What are meant by the following terms linked to questionnaires: (a) closed questions; (b) semantic differential; (c) attitude object?

5

Case Studies, Content Analysis and Simulations

This chapter will tackle three separate research methods that are used quite often in psychological research. Case studies are usually used in clinical settings in an attempt to understand psychopathological conditions. However, they are used in a variety of contexts and are not just a focus on an 'individual'. A family or a work unit may be analysed in depth and form a 'case study'.

Content analysis has been used for several decades, but recently it has begun to 'bloom' in the social science research sector. This research method refers to the analysis of the content of literature, speech patterns, television shows, newspaper articles (to name but a few) to look for trends in presentation, tone, length of article, portrayal of characters or anything the researcher thinks is relevant. Conclusions are drawn from the analysis about how people may perceive the literature they read or television shows they watch.

Simulations are any contrived event that attempts to mimic a 'real-life' situation. They may be used to investigate situations that cannot be studied directly owing to ethical or practical limitations.

The case study

According to Shaughnessy and Zechmeister (1997), a case study is 'an intensive description and analysis of a single individual' (p. 308). As with correlations, case studies are not a unique research method; they simply utilise other research methods in a quest for drawing a conclusion (e.g. naturalistic observation, interviews or questionnaires). Variables are not systematically controlled or altered as in single case experimental designs. Case studies are just in-depth detailed analyses of individuals or close-knit groups of people as in a family unit.

Lukoff *et al.* (1998) defend the use of case studies as useful tools in research. They argue that this research method does provide useful data even if it is a single person case study. They compared the case study with the more 'scientifically regarded' randomised trial research, for example with drug trials where half of the participants receive the true drug and half a placebo, and believe that the latter method is not really ideal or feasible for assessing unconventional treatments in the health field. Lukoff *et al.* state that with so many factors uncontrolled in randomised trials (e.g. health belief of participant, patient/practitioner interactions plus multiple treatment and multi-symptom cases), the case study allows for the true exploration of these areas.

Sometimes case studies form longitudinal studies. These types of study are ones that extend over a period of time. That is, the researcher studies the same individual or unit of individuals for a fixed amount of time, for example, over five years. It allows an analysis of the development of behaviour over a time period. Of course, longitudinal studies do not have to be exclusively about one person or unit of individuals. They can involve following a cohort (group) of people for the purposes of analysing the development of behaviour. As shall be noted later in this chapter, researchers can conduct a 'longitudinal' study via content analysis, too.

research methods

case study: feeling legless?

Halligan, P.W., Athwal, B.S., Oakley, D.A. and Frackowiak, R.S. (2000) Imaging hypnotic paralysis: implications for conversion hysteria. *The Lancet,* 355, 18 March, 986–87

Aim: To investigate if hypnosis and conversion hysteria (where people claim paralysis even though there is no organic cause, e.g. brain damage) share common neuropsychological mechanisms.

Method: The participant was hypnotised to believe that their left leg was paralysed. A series of trials to attempt to move the leg were performed alongside trials where the right leg had to be moved. The participant was told which trial was next (e.g. whether it was the turn of the left leg or the right leg to move). On some trials the leg had to move in time with a metronome, while on other trials the leg was only to be moved when tapped with a pen. Positron Emission Tomography (PET) scans were recorded for each trial to deduce which areas of the brain were activated.

Results: The left leg never moved during any of the trials (as detected by electrodes on the leg), but the *right anterior cingulate* and the *right medial orbitofrontal cortex* were activated, which probably indicates the inhibition of movement in the left leg. The brain was stopping the limb from moving!

Conclusion: In comparison to brain scans of a conversion hysteric, the same brain areas were activated. Therefore, even though the research is based on the comparison of two case studies, it appears that hypnotic paralysis and conversion hysteria could share common neuropsychological mechanisms. This could help understand and treat people suffering from conversion hysteria.

Questions

1 Do you think you can generalise the results of this research to all people who have conversion hysteria?

2 How would you set up an experiment to assess the aim of this case study?

for and against

case studies

+ They are a rich source of data.

– You can overlook certain factors you feel are unimportant (e.g. the relationship between two siblings), which could be causing the behaviour you are assessing.

– Difficult to generalise to other people.

+ A good way of studying atypical behaviour.

– Can be time consuming.

– Can lose objectivity through getting to know the participant.

Content analysis

Content analysis in psychology and the social sciences has been used for the best part of a century. However, only recently have many studies been published that examine the role of certain publications, television shows and even music videos on our behaviour or our perception of certain activities. Content analysis is a quantitative research method in that it can be used to examine the number of certain key words or the language used in a variety of media.

A recent example of the use of content analysis is given below.

research methods

content analysis of television advertisements: food behaviour and content analysis – a study of food advertising around children's programmes

Lewis, M.K. and Hill, A.J. (1998) Food advertising on British children's television: a content analysis and experimental study with nine-year olds. *International Journal of Obesity and Related Metabolic Disorders,* 22 (3), 206–14

Aim: The content analysis section of this research examined the content of food advertisements shown in between children's television shows.

Method: Ninety-one hours of children's television shown on four terrestrial channels were analysed. Lewis and Hill produced a detailed record of advertisement style and content of advertisement.

Results: The following key results were reported:

- 50 per cent of advertisements were for food products.

- 60 per cent of these advertisements were for cereals or confectionery.

- Food advertisements used significantly more animation to sell products than other types of advertisements.

- Food advertisements also used more story-telling, humour and the promotion of fun or happiness or mood alteration to sell products compared to other types of advertisement.

Conclusions: Advertisements are dominated by those for foods that have 'dubious' nutritional value. Also, they are portrayed in such a way to engage attention and produce an emotional response after watching. This may have an effect on the audience to which the advertisement is aimed. (It should be noted that in the experimental section of this research, Lewis and Hill found that overweight children who watched food-product advertisements were more influenced by them negatively with regard to healthy behaviour as rated by the perceived health of product and appetite for sweets. That is, they rated these products as being more healthy.)

Questions

1 Lewis and Hill examined the content of food advertisements between children's TV shows. How do you think they categorised the advertisements?

2 How do you think you could measure the emotional response an advertisement might produce?

3 Do you think the results would be the same if the sample of advertisements analysed was just before Christmas? Explain your answer.

Which do you see more often?

As can be seen from the above example, content analysis can be time consuming but is very useful for examining the role of things like the media on subsequent behaviour in the viewer or reader. So, how do we conduct a content analysis study?

Robson (1993) identified six main steps to execute a content analysis:

1 **Start with a research question.** As with the example above (Lewis and Hill, 1998), the specific question posed was 'what type of advertisements are shown in between children's television shows?' Research has posed questions such as 'what do children produce when asked to draw how an alien would get to Earth?' (Roberts *et al.*, in press) and 'is there evidence that alcohol consumption and tobacco usage is featured in music videos?' (DuRant *et al.*, 1997). Try to make the question as specific as possible to make the next five steps easier.

2 **Decide on a sampling strategy.** For example, do you take a random sample of television shows over a one-week period, or articles

featured in a specific newspaper? The sample is usually dictated by the question posed. As with the above example (Lewis and Hill, 1998), the sample was of 91 hours of terrestrially transmitted advertisements before or after children's television shows.

3   **Define the recording unit.** By this, Robson (1993) means under what criteria you are recording the data. He states that the most common recording unit in content analysis of the written word is a single word. That is, you would record the number of occurrences of that single word (but beware the choice of words: some words have more than one meaning, for example 'mean' or 'mode'). However, you do not have to limit yourself to single words, you may choose themes, paragraphs or whole items as your recording unit. It may also be useful to record the context of the use of a word, just in case you are using a broad inference for its inclusion in the analysis (e.g. whether it is a favourable, neutral or unfavourable use of the word). Again, the more precise and thorough recording unit you choose, the more reliable and valid your analysis will become.

4   **Construct categories for analysis.** It is better to choose categories that do not overlap so that each category is separate and therefore easier to rate. For example, in the research of Roberts *et al.* (in press), the researchers categorised shape of craft into categories such as 'flat bottomed disc', 'domed-disc', 'irregular curvilinear' and 'zooloid' (animal-shaped). The more specific the categories, the easier it will be to content-analyse whatever you are researching. Similarly you could even rate on a numerical scale to say how favourable an article is towards homosexuality, where 1 = very unfavourable article up to 10 = very favourable article.

5   **Test the coding on samples of 'text' (or whatever is being content analysed) and assess reliability.** This will ensure that your categories are self-explanatory and can be used in the research. It also enhances reliability among those doing the rating if you have a team of researchers. For example, in the research of Roberts *et al.* (in press), 10 pictures were chosen for reliability purposes on shape and aggressive nature of picture with a concordance of 100 per cent. Any other strange shapes that cropped up in the sample of pictures were rated by all three researchers to keep high reliability. (Other categories such as dominant colour, or number of 'aliens' were not subject to reliability measuring.)

6   **Carry out the analysis.** Simply use the recording units and categories chosen to analyse the sample you have selected. The whole procedure can be very rewarding if definite trends become evident quickly (but remember not to let that make you interpret the subsequent articles in a biased light: remain objective).

Examples of pictures that were content-analysed by Roberts *et al.* (in press)

An example of a simple content analysis with far-reaching consequences is given below.

research methods

content analysis of journal articles: sexuality examined by content analysis

Clark, W.M. and Serovich, J.M. (1997) Twenty years and still in the dark? Content analysis of articles pertaining to gay, lesbian and bisexual issues in marriage and family therapy journals. *Journal of Marriage and Family Therapy*, 23 (3), 239–53

Aim: Clark and Serovich asked the question 'To what extent do marriage and family therapy journals address gay, lesbian and bisexual issues?' (p. 239).

Method: The recording unit was either the single words 'gay', 'lesbian' or 'bisexual', or the phrase 'sexual orientation'. Issues of the *Journal of Marriage and Family Therapy* were the sample strategy with the specific date range of 1975 to 1995.

Results: A total of 13217 articles were content-analysed and 77 were found to have the recording unit within it (this represents 0.006 per cent of all articles published).

Conclusions: This research was used to fuel the debate that gay, lesbian and bisexual issues were not being tackled by marriage and family researchers.

Questions

1 Can you think of any other recording units that Clark and Serovich could have used in this research?

2 What implications do these results have for family psychologists?

There has been a vast range of research questions tackled by content analysts, including women and smoking in Hollywood movies (Escamilla *et al.*, 2000), guidelines on handling requests for euthanasia in the Netherlands (Haverkate *et al.*, 2000), educational media about menstruation (Havens and Swenson, 1989), smoking issues in Irish journals (Howell, 1996) and how dogs are perceived in feature films (e.g. *Beethoven*) and TV shows (e.g. *The Simpsons*) (Rajecki *et al.*, 2000).

Escamilla *et al.* (2000) content-analysed Hollywood movies for scenes of women smoking

interactive angles

Conduct a content analysis on TV advertisements to see if they gender stereotype. That is, do females advertise cooking and washing products whereas males advertise beer and cars?

for and against

content analysis

+ It is unobtrusive. The researcher can observe things without actually using the observational research method.

− The material used in the analysis may not have been written for the purposes of being content-analysed. They could have been written for something completely different from what is being investigated.

− Documentation may be limited for analysis.

+ As the documents used are 'permanent' (e.g. videos, newspapers), other researchers can replicate the analysis increasing reliability.

− Cause or effect? Are the documents a reflection of our social world or are they causing it?

+ As documents are archived (e.g. newspapers, Internet, TV shows), it is a cheap way of conducting a longitudinal study (and you do not have to wait years to conduct it).

− There could be experimenter effects due to the subjective nature of the analysis, unless you conduct strict inter-rater reliability tasks.

Simulations

Using many of the research methods covered so far, researchers attempt to apply findings to the real world. Simulations, however, attempt to bring elements of a real-world setting into a laboratory or other controlled environment. It is hoped that this imitation can 'shed light' on the process under investigation.

According to Robson (1993), a good example of a simulation involves the use of juries. It is impossible for an investigator to observe the real situation to study group dynamics, or minority–majority influence in decision making for instance. However, a simulated jury procedure may allow an observation of such processes. Following are two examples of simulated jury procedures.

research methods

simulation: eyewitness v. earwitness

Hollien, H., Bennett, G. and Gelfer, M.P. (1983) Criminal identification comparison: aural versus visual identifications resulting from a simulated crime. *Journal of Forensic Science*, 28 (1), 208–21

Aim: To examine whether aural (listening) or visual identification is more accurate at identifying a criminal from a simulated crime.

Method: The witnesses were 61 students of a law class. They all watched a simulated crime. The students were split into four groups. Group A had to make identifications of the criminal one day, one week and then one month after the 'crime' via photographs and a tape recording of the criminal. Group B saw the photographs and heard the tape only once. This was one week after the 'crime'. Group C saw the photographs and heard the tape only once, too. However, this was two weeks after the 'crime'. The final group, D, followed the same schedule as group A *but* were presented with foils – these were of similar appearance and/or sounded the same as the true 'criminal'. The student witnesses had to rate their confidence with respect to correctly identifying the 'criminal'.

Results: The visual identification (via photographs) was quite accurate although it was not consistently good. The latency period (one day, one week or one month) between the 'crime' and identification did not seem to have an effect on accuracy. However, aural identification (via the tape recordings) was poor. Confidence did not appear to be linked to accuracy. That is, whether the student reported high or low confidence, they were equally likely to choose the correct 'criminal'. Finally, the foil was more likely to be chosen the longer the latency period between the 'crime' and identification.

Conclusion: Eyewitness testimony is not faultless so can be accurate sometimes while earwitness testimony is not reliable in the large majority of cases. Juries should be aware of these findings when assigning weight to this type of evidence in trials. However, some people are good eyewitnesses and/or earwitnesses!

Questions

1 Why do you think eyewitnesses were better than earwitnesses in this study?

2 Do you think this simulation has any ecological validity?

research methods

simulation: harsh justice from hostile jurors

Ackerman, A.M., McMahon, P.M. and Fehr, L.A. (1984) Mock trial jury as a function of adolescent juror guilt and hostility. *Journal of Genetic Psychology*, 144 (2), 195–201

Aim: To examine whether certain personality characteristics (e.g. hostility) and/or age of jurors affect sentence length in trials.

Method: A total of 277 male adolescent jurors were presented with a fictitious child abuse case. They were asked to sentence the abuser. All participants completed the Mosher Hostility Guilt Scale and the Siegel Manifest Hostility Scale to measure personality.

Results: The older participant jurors attributed more of the blame on the defendant and therefore administered less severe sentences than the younger participant jurors. Those participants who scored high on the Guilt Scale tended to give shorter sentences. Those participants who scored high on the Manifest Hostility Scale tended to give longer sentences.

Conclusion: Certain personality traits can affect sentence length given by jurors. There appear to be age effects, too.

Questions

1 Create some items that could have been on the Hostility Guilt Scale.

2 Do you think it was good to use only male participants? Do you feel females would have responded in the same way?

3 Do you think this simulation has any ecological validity?

Do simulations of the courtroom in psychology research mirror real-life courtrooms?

interactive
angles

We would be unlikely to record people's reaction to an actual murder. However, if participants were invited to take part in a study on biorhythms and vigilance in which they were required to monitor closed circuit TV from a room, alone, at night, we could observe their response to a simulated murder apparently caught by the CCTV system. How would you design such a study?

for and
against

simulations

— Artificial situations may affect behaviour (low ecological validity).

+ Allows you to set up a situation where naturalistic observations are difficult or impossible (e.g. criminal trials, prisons).

where to now?

 Robson, C. (1993) *Real World Research*. **Oxford: Blackwell** – a great introduction to case studies and the procedures for content analysis. Some good examples used throughout.

what do you know?

1 Describe **one** strength and **one** weakness of using case studies in psychological research.

2 In content analysis, why is the inter-rater reliability exercise useful?

3 What are simulations and why are they useful in psychological research?

4 How would you conduct a content analysis on whether students are perceived unfavourably in newspapers?

6

The Experimental Method

what's
ahead?

This chapter introduces the ways in which psychologists use experimentation. We discuss the importance of experimental variables and how experiments can be conducted in the laboratory and in the real world. Finally we consider how to select materials and plan for experimental studies.

The experimental method

When we use the word 'experiment' in day-to-day life we mean we 'try something out'; *'I thought I'd try canoeing for an experiment'*, *'I experimented with some new ingredients in the kitchen'*. We engage in these activities in the hope of discovering something we did not know before. In psychology, the same is true, the experiment serves to find out whether a *causal relationship* exists, i.e. we are trying to see if one factor affects another.

So, the purpose of an *experiment* is to systematically vary one factor, the *independent variable* (IV), while observing the effect of that change on another factor, the *dependent variable* (DV). The IV is the factor that is manipulated by the experimenter. By controlling either the nature of the participants, their experiences or the way data are selected for analysis, the experimenter generates levels of the IV. These levels or 'conditions' are used to compare the effects of the variable under investigation. For example, an experiment might be designed to test the effects of reading science fiction on the incidence of nightmares, in which case the IV would be the type of reading material and the levels would be science fiction or a control such as historical novels. In a study conducted by Hemmings *et al.* (2000) the IV under investigation was *sports massage*, and the levels of the IV experienced by participants were either *massage* or *rest* (following a boxing exercise).

The DV is the measurable outcome in the experiment. It is called the *dependent* variable because we predict that any changes in this variable are caused by (i.e. are dependent upon) changes in the IV. So, in the science fiction example, the DV would be nightmares, which could be measured by counting the number of bad dreams occurring or by rating their unpleasantness. Hemmings *et al.* (2000) measured the DV of the effectiveness of the massage in several ways; by observing changes in the boxers' heart rate, by asking the boxers to rate their perception of their own recovery and by comparing their performance to a second set of exercises.

research methods

independent and dependent variables: safe sex, social skills and STDs

Metzler, C.W., Biglan, A., Noell, J., Ary, D.V. and Ochs, L. (2000) A randomised controlled trial of a behavioural intervention to reduce high-risk sexual behaviour among adolescents in STD clinics. *Behavior Therapy,* 31, 27–54

Aims: To investigate the effectiveness of an intervention programme on the incidence of risky sexual behaviour by adolescents.

Method: 339 adolescents aged 15 to 19 years were recruited from sexually transmitted disease (STD) clinics and were randomly assigned to receive either the experimental intervention or usual care. The intervention programme targeted decision making about safer sex, social skills for handling difficult sexual situations and acceptance of negative thoughts and feelings about changing sexual behaviour. Participants in the intervention programme attended five weekly sessions lasting 60–90 minutes. All participants were given baseline, 6-month and 12-month follow-up assessments.

Results: At the 6-month follow-up, the intervention group reported fewer sexual partners, fewer non-monogamous partners, fewer sexual contacts with strangers in the previous three months and less use of marijuana before or during sex than the control group. The intervention group also performed better on a taped situations test of skill in coping with difficult sexual situations.

Conclusion: Raising adolescents' awareness of the importance of monogamy and abstinence to sexual health in risky situations and providing them with the knowledge and social skills to handle such situations reduce the occurrence of high-risk sexual behaviour.

Questions

1 What is the independent variable in this study?

2 What is the dependent variable in this study?

3 Write a suitable one-tailed hypothesis.

So, in an experiment, we create two or more conditions by altering the independent variable. We then look to see how this alters the dependent variable, which we can measure. In addition, other factors that might affect the dependent variable should be controlled, that is kept constant across different conditions of the independent variable. This ensures that any difference in the dependent variable between conditions *is* the result of the IV and is not due to other, chance, variations. The control of variables is discussed at length in Chapter 12.

interactive
angles

identifying the independent and dependent variables

In each of the situations below, identify the independent variable including each of the manipulated levels and the dependent variable, stating how this might be measured.

- Bartholomew *et al.* (1991) investigated whether people who were highly fantasy-prone were more likely to report UFO sightings.

- Morrongiello and Dawber (2000) compared the likelihood of mothers to intervene in the play of boys and girls when there was a risk of injury.

- Low and Durkin (2000) tested children's ability to recall information from television programmes when the story was presented in either a jumbled or logical order.

- Williamon and Valentine (2000) investigated the differences between the quality and quantity of practice employed by experienced and novice musicians who were asked to learn a new piece.

- Wareing *et al.* (2000) studied memory deficits, anxiety and arousal in current and previous users of MDMA ('Ecstasy').

In an experiment, the effect of the IV on the DV is a causal one; thus the hypothesis must predict a difference between the levels of the IV in terms of the outcome, that is, a change in the DV. So, if we return to the science fiction example, a hypothesis could read 'there will be a difference between the number of nightmares experienced after reading science fiction and historical novels'. This could also be expressed as a directional hypothesis 'sleepers will have more nightmares after reading science fiction than after reading historical novels'. In each case we are suggesting that the IV of reading a particular type of book will affect the DV, namely the occurrence of nightmares. Hemmings *et al.* (2000) investigated the effect of massage (the IV) on sports performance (the DV). They were anticipating that massage would improve performance, so a directional hypothesis would be appropriate, such as 'boxers will make a faster recovery after massage than after rest'.

interactive
angles

writing hypotheses for experiments

For each of the pairs of independent and dependent variables below, write either a directional or non-directional alternative hypothesis and a null hypothesis.

1 Research question: does watching TV during revision affect exam performance?
IV: watching the TV
DV: exam results

2 Research question: can a UFO researcher tell the difference between a real report of a UFO sighting and a simulated one produced under hypnosis?
IV: hypnotically induced or genuine report of UFO sighting
DV: apparent genuineness

3 Research question: does alcohol increase the likelihood of night-club violence?
IV: consumption of alcohol
DV: extent of violence

4 Research question: do food additives increase aggression in children?
IV: food additives
DV: aggressive behaviour

Laboratory experiments

A *laboratory experiment* is conducted in a laboratory or other contrived setting away from the participants' normal environment. In this situation the researcher can manipulate the levels of the independent variable and accurately record changes in the dependent variable. In addition, considerable control can be exercised over potential confounding variables. It is this aspect that represents the most significant advantage of laboratory studies over other techniques. A researcher in a laboratory can be more confident than their counterpart in the field that the changes they are observing in the DV *are* attributable to the IV rather than being the consequence of some uncontrolled aspect of the situation. The IV may be manipulated to create two or more experimental conditions (such as eating white, milk, plain and mint chocolate) or to compare an experimental condition with a control (chocolate and no chocolate).

The control condition

In some situations the researcher does not want to compare two levels of the IV but instead wishes to observe the effect of the presence or absence of some factor. In this instance there is an experimental condition and a *control condition*, the latter being a situation in which the variable under consideration is absent. In some cases this can simply be achieved by removing the variable in question. In many cases, however, the control condition is also manipulated in order to ensure that it is *only* the IV that differs between the two conditions. For example, if we are investigating the effect of music on concentration we need to be sure that we are testing the effect of *music* as opposed to sound. Participants in our control condition must hear white noise at the same volume through the same apparatus (such as headphones) as our control participants hear music.

We are all familiar with the term *placebo*, an inert substance administered in place of a drug to 'blind' participants, that is, ones who are unaware that they are not receiving a real drug. The placebo is thus a control. You may have conducted studies on human participants or *Daphnia* (water fleas) using coffee or caffeine. With *Daphnia* in a Petri dish you can vary the amount of pure caffeine in the water, i.e. set up experimental levels of the IV with different concentrations of caffeine and a control condition of pure water. For human participants it is more practical to provide standard measures of coffee, either ordinary (the experimental condition) or decaffeinated (the control condition).

research
methods

the control condition: mice with the munchies

Fride *et al.* (2000) reported in *New Scientist*, 8 July 2000, 9

Aim: To investigate the effect of cannabinoids, the active ingredient in cannabis, on feeding. The property of cannabis to stimulate eating is used to help cancer and AIDS patients by increasing appetite. Cannabinoids have been detected in human milk and may play a role in the early development of newborns.

Method: Newborn mice were injected with a cannabinoid antagonist, a drug that blocks the natural effect of cannabis-like substance in the body. The mice were then injected with the active component in cannabis, in a dose sufficient to swamp the receptors and counter the effect of the antagonist.

Results: None of the mice treated with the antagonist fed from their mothers. Some died within a week and if they survived, they developed slowly. Following treatment with cannabis derivative the mice fed and grew normally.

Conclusion: The findings suggest that the effects of the antagonist are not due to its toxicity but a direct consequence of its effect on the action of cannabis-like chemicals in the mouse brain. Endogenous cannabinoids seem to trigger ingestion of food.

Questions

1 Which treatment is the control condition, the administration of the active component in cannabis or its antagonist?

2 Why was it necessary to follow one condition with the other?

Field experiments

As we discussed in Chapter 3, *field experiments* are studies with an experimental design (they have an IV and DV), which take place using participants in their normal surroundings. Look back at McNicholas and Collis's (2000) observation of the attention received from passers-by when the accomplice of the experimenter did or did not have a dog with them (page 44). Can you identify the IV and DV in this study? Field experiments such as this are described as *contrived*, since the researcher creates the levels of the IV.

research methods

field experiment: sorted – student rubbish

Matthies, E. and Krömker, D. (2000) Participatory planning – a heuristic for adjusting interventions to the context. *Journal of Environmental Psychology*, 20, 1–10

Aims: To investigate ways to improve the sorting of rubbish for recycling by university students.

Method: Sorting of rubbish for recycling was measured at the start of the experiment in two student residences. Participants in one residence were contacted and helped to set up an action group. This group implemented measures designed to encourage better sorting of rubbish such as information about the sorting system, providing signs and having larger containers. They also sent all students a bogus letter threatening that their residency costs would rise unless sorting improved. A final measure of recycling was taken in both locations.

Results: By the end of the study the amount of unsorted rubbish had fallen from 69 per cent to 53 per cent in the experimental residence but had risen from 64 per cent to 74 per cent in the control area.

Conclusion: The students' involvement with the intervention improved their participation in the recycling of rubbish.

Questions

1 Why is this a field experiment?

2 What is the IV in this study and how did the researchers create the experimental and control conditions?

3 What is the DV in this study and how was it measured?

What makes people recycle their rubbish?

How could you investigate people's motives for recycling and use this information to test ways to improve motivation for sorting rubbish?

Atmosphere essentials

You love the smell of your scented candles but did you know you can use essential oils to influence people and treat stress?

Living space	Desired effect	Essential oils
Living room	Calming	Geranium relieves anxiety
		Vanilla relaxes and soothes
Bedroom	Soothing	Camomile helps with insomnia
		Ylang ylang and jasmine act as aphrodisiacs
Bathroom	Relaxing	Lavender calms and relaxes
		Rosemary and pine act as nerve tonics
Office space	Energising	Basil clears the mind, helping indecision
		Neroli heightens mental activity
Dining room	Entertaining	Jasmine combats shyness
		Sandalwood opens the mind to new ideas
Kitchen	Uplifting	Peppermint lifts the spirits
		Coffee and cocoa make food taste better

Cosmopolitan, May 2000

Design a field experiment to test whether one of the essential oils listed above really does have the effect described. Carefully consider the advantages of using a field study over a laboratory experiment in this situation.

Natural experiments

As we discussed in Chapter 3, *quasi-experiments* are those in which the experimenter does not have control over the allocation of participants to levels of the IV. Suppose a cinema was piloting a new style advertisement for a product on sale in the intermission. While experimenters testing the effect of the advertisement on purchasing could control when it was or was not shown, they could not dictate which participants would happen to be in the cinema at the time. In this case, participants in the opportunity sample could not be randomly allocated to experimental groups. People who watched films on different days of the week or different times of the day might have differed from one another in some patterned way which could affect their purchasing irrespective of their exposure to the advertisements.

research
methods

quasi-experiments: you don't have to see it to smell it

Rosenbluth, R., Grossman, E.S. and Kaitz, M. (2000) Performance of early-blind and sighted children on olfactory tasks. *Perception*, 29, 101–10

Aim: To find out whether blind children outperform sighted children on olfactory (smell) based tasks.

Method: Thirty sighted and 30 blind children were compared. Thirty-five blind participants were selected from lists of registered blind students. Ninety per cent of those selected had been blind from birth, the remainder had been blind from age three years. Eighty-three per cent were totally blind, the others had only light (not form) perception. None had cognitive impairments. Of those selected, 30 agreed to participate. The sighted children were selected from local schools and matched to each blind child by age, sex, grade and ethnicity (it was not possible to match one of the blind children for grade or two for ethnicity). All were native Hebrew speakers. Consent was obtained from each child's parents. They were informed that the purpose of the study was to investigate the development of olfaction in blind and sighted children but they were not told the predictions being tested.

Initially, children were questioned (in Hebrew) about whether any family members smoked. They were then given an olfactory threshold test that consisted of determining the minimum level of *N*-butyl alcohol they could detect by comparing 13 dilutions with a 'blank' stimulus of deionised water. The order of presentation of the target and blank source on each trial was randomised and each paired test was separated by one minute during which the child played with games provided.

To test the children's ability to label familiar odours, each child (blind or sighted) wore a blindfold and smelled the contents of a jar containing a cotton wool pad soaked in the source. The 25 sources included chocolate, ketchup, peanut butter, orange peel, cola, coffee, cinnamon, mint, vinegar, vanilla, toothpaste, bleach, glue, cigarette butts and rubber. The order of presentation of the sources was randomised.

Results: Although the children did not differ significantly in their threshold for detection of an odour, the blind children were significantly more accurate at labelling smells: they scored 12.1/25 compared with 10.4/25 achieved by the sighted children. The blind children were significantly better than the sighted children at detecting some smells in particular: vanilla, glue, cola, toothpaste and chocolate. There were no targets for which the sighted children surpassed the blind children.

Conclusion: Blind children appear to be better at self-generating and retrieving labels for odours. As the blind children out-performed the sighted children at labelling smells but not in terms of absolute detection, they must have an enhanced cognitive ability rather than increased sensitivity with regard to odour detection.

In one class of quasi-experiment, the *natural experiment*, the researcher cannot control the IV at all, the levels are derived from pre-existing and naturally occurring differences. For example, a study looking at the effect of weather on mood would require the selection of participants when conditions were sunny or cloudy. There would be no reason to suppose that the participants available on one occasion would differ from those on another, although they might do so. This would be a quasi-experiment because individuals could not be allocated to 'sunny' or 'cloudy' levels of the independent variable. In this case the quasi-experiment would be classed as having 'non-equivalent groups'. Here, the researcher can neither control allocation of participants to conditions nor when or how those conditions arise.

research methods

natural experiment: desertion and delinquency

Bowlby, J. (1946) *Forty four juvenile thieves.* London: Balliere, Tindall and Cox

Aims: Bowlby believed that prolonged separation from the primary carer during the first two or three years of life could cause permanent emotional damage. One way in which this damage manifests itself is affectionless psychopathy. Bowlby aimed in this study to see whether teenage criminals who displayed affectionless psychopathy were more likely to have had an early separation than those who had not.

Method: Forty-four of the teenagers referred to the Child Guidance Clinic where Bowlby worked were selected on the basis that they were involved in criminal activity and that they were living with their biological parents. Bowlby interviewed the teenagers in order to assess whether they exhibited signs of affectionless psychopathy. This was identified by lack of affection to others, lack of guilt or shame at their actions and lack of empathy for their victims. Bowlby also interviewed the families of the delinquents in order to establish whether the children had had prolonged early separations from their primary carers in their first two years. Bowlby then matched those young people who had been classified as affectionless psychopaths with those who had had prolonged maternal deprivation in the first two years. A control group of non-delinquent young people was established in order to provide a comparison to see how commonly maternal deprivation occurred in the non-delinquent population.

Results: The results were striking. Of the 14 children identified as affectionless psychopaths, 12 had experienced prolonged separation from their mothers in the first two years. By contrast, only 5 of the 30 delinquent children not classified as affectionless psychopaths had experienced similar separations. Of the 44 people in the non-delinquent control group, 2 had experienced prolonged separations.

Conclusions: The young criminals who had a prolonged separation in their first two years were several times more likely to exhibit affectionless psychopathy than those who had no such separation. This provides strong support for Bowlby's maternal deprivation hypothesis (see *Angles on Child Psychology*, Jarvis and Chandler, 2001).

Questions

1 This study would be called a naturalistic experiment. What is a naturalistic experiment and why does this study fall into that classification?

2 Suggest a suitable alternative hypothesis for this study.

3 Identify the independent and dependent variables in the study.

4 Why would it be important for Bowlby to ask all the young people the same questions when assessing them for affectionless psychopathy?

5 A flaw in Bowlby's design is that he conducted the interviews with the young people and their families himself. What is a double-blind design and how would it have helped in this case?

interactive angles

Looking back at the situations and experiments described in the boxes on pages 6 and 84, try to decide which would be most effectively studied as laboratory, field or natural (quasi) experiments. Remember, it may be possible to answer some questions using several alternative methods, for others there will only be one choice.

for and against

+ Experiments enable us to determine cause and effect.

+ Laboratory experiments allow for rigorous control of extraneous variables and can therefore be replicated.

– Laboratory experiments can lack ecological validity.

+ Natural experiments can have high ecological validity.

– In natural experiments extraneous variables are harder to control so they may lack reliability.

– By focusing on specific variables, experiments designs may overlook important effects.

Formal designs in experiments

The aim of an experiment is to evaluate whether the IV produces a change in the DV. We therefore either need to compare the effects of the IV for participants in different conditions or to observe differences in the DV for the same participants experiencing each of the different levels of the IV. These alternatives are essentially the different formal designs used in experiments. Sometimes it is impossible for the same people to participate in both levels of the IV, such as in natural experiments. In a test of the role of culture in expectations about parenting, participants can represent only one cultural group. The same would apply to comparisons between males and females or different species of animal. On other occasions it is preferable that, while participants physically *could* participate in both conditions, they do not. For example, in the study described earlier, testing the effects of reading science fiction before bed, participation in both conditions could result in participants still recalling the science fiction even when they have moved on to reading historical novels. If they had nightmares as a consequence these would be mistakenly attributed to the historical novels, obscuring the experimental effect.

Repeated measures

In an experiment with a *repeated measures design*, each individual participates in every level of the IV, that is, the levels of the IV are compared by each participant *repeating* their performance under different conditions. This is also referred to as a *within-subjects* or *related design*, since comparisons are being made *within* one group rather than across participant groups and each score in one condition *relates* directly to that person's score in the other condition(s). For example, Chawarski and Sternberg (1993) tested the effects of priming. The participants read stories that provided a context, which was to act as a prime. They were then asked to identify words on a list as having been in the story or not. The words were either: *irrelevant, relevant but not from the story* or *relevant and from the story* (i.e. primed). All participants were tested on all types of words.

Example of a Story Used by Chawarski and Sternberg (1993)

The airplane glided in over the trees with a whisper, the propeller spinning silently as the wheels touched the grass. After rolling a few yards, it turned and taxied toward a group of people chattering outside a tiny hangar. A hand-painted sign proclaimed 'Airplane Rides $2.' I stood straddling my bike in a clump of trees near the runway. I'd never been so close to a real airplane before. I'd been riding northeast of Tampa, Florida, looking for a promising spot for large-mouth bass, when the airplane swooped just overhead. After following the noise to the airstrip, I hid among the pines and watched. The pilot helped a passenger into the front seat and climbed in the back. With a

---

low purr the airplane spun around and pulled onto the runway. The tail wheel rose, and the buttercup-coloured aircraft rolled along perched on its front wheels. Then, in a fluid motion that thrilled me to no end, it rose slowly and climbed out of sight. I leaned the bike against a tree and sat down. Ten minutes later, the airplane reappeared in a gentle descent. There was no engine noise, just the whoosh of air through the struts as the plane settled into a perfect landing. I sat there enthralled for the rest of the afternoon, wishing for all the world I had two dollars.

Words to be identified included *plane, airport, pilot, dollars.*

research methods

repeated measures design: mobiles boost your brain power

Koivisto, M., Revonsuo, A., Krause, C., Haarala, C., Sillanmaki, L., Laine, M. and Hamalainen, H. (2000) Effects of 902 MHz electromagnetic field emitted by cellular telephones on response times in humans. *Neuroreport*, 11, 413–15

Aims: To investigate whether mobile phones can enhance cognitive functioning.

Method: Participants were tested on a range of cognitive tasks including subtraction, vigilance and reaction time tasks. Their performance was compared with and without exposure to a 902-MHz electromagnetic field (as emitted by cellular phones).

Results: Performance in mental arithmetic, vigilance and reaction time was significantly enhanced with exposure to the 902-MHz field, the participants were faster and no less accurate.

Conclusion: The electromagnetic field emitted by mobile phones improved performance on cognitive tasks. These tasks required sustained attention and are typical of frontal lobe functions so the effect may be mediated by increasing the temperature of brain tissue in this area.

Questions

1 Why might a repeated measures design have been chosen for this study?

2 If the effects of mobile phone use are long term, why might an independent measures design have been preferable?

Keeping in touch: what cost?

Does your mobile phone fry your brain or feed it? How could you test whether it was actually an increase in frontal lobe temperature which was responsible for the improvement in cognitive function demonstrated by Koivisto *et al.* (2000)?

media watch

Male intelligence is an annual outbreak

IN SPRING, a young man's fancy turns not only to thoughts of love, but to higher things.

According to researchers, men are more intelligent in spring than autumn because seasonal changes in the production of testosterone can alter their mental performance.

Professor Doreen Kimura of the University of Western Ontario in Canada and the author of the report *Sex and Cognition* said: 'In Europe and North America, men have higher testosterone levels in autumn than in spring and we have found that they perform spatial tasks better in the spring. Men also do better at mathematical reasoning, and both are components of intelligence.'

Professor Kimura, who is one of the world's leading experts on sexual differences in the human brain, is currently involved in a study measuring mathematical ability and testosterone levels. She said that just why male hormone levels change seasonally is still not fully understood.

'One evolutionary reason why they may increase in the autumn is that among our early ancestors it was probably an advantage to have children conceived then and born in the summer. Most people do associate high testosterone levels with spring, but it may be that while a young man's thoughts do turn to love in the spring, they turn to sex in the autumn', she said.

article by Roger Dobson, *The Independent*, 10 January 2000

Using the information in the text above, answer the following questions:

1 How do you think the original data about spatial task performance and mathematical skill was obtained? What sort of experiment would this be?

2 Design a laboratory study using animals to test the theory that testosterone affects spatial ability. What factors would you control that cannot be controlled when studying humans?

Independent groups

In an experiment with an *independent measures design* separate groups of individuals participate in the different levels of the IV, that is the data sets relating to each level of the IV are *independent* of each other. This is also referred to as a *between subjects* or *unrelated design* since comparisons are being made *between* groups rather than within them and the data points in one level of the IV are *unrelated* in any specific way to the data points for other levels.

research
methods

independent groups design: don't describe your decisions

Schooler, J.W., Ohlsson, S. and Brooks, K. (1993) Thoughts beyond words: when language overshadows insight. *Journal of Experimental Psychology: General*, 122, 166–83

Aims: To examine whether verbalisation disrupts insight problem solving.

Method: Eighty-six participants were randomly assigned to one of two conditions, either verbalisation or unrelated interruption. There were six different insight problems presented in written form. Two minutes after starting each problem the participant was interrupted for 1.5 minutes. Those in the *verbalisation* group were given the following instruction 'please stop working on the problem now and write down, in as much detail as possible, everything you can remember about how you have been trying to solve the problem. Give information about your approach, strategies, any solutions you tried, and so on.' Participants in the *unrelated interruption* group worked on a crossword puzzle. They were then allowed a further five minutes to solve the original problem. Four participants who, when asked, said that they were already familiar with the problems used were eliminated from the study.

Nine pigs are kept in a square pen. Build two more square enclosures that would put each pig in a pen by itself.

Solution

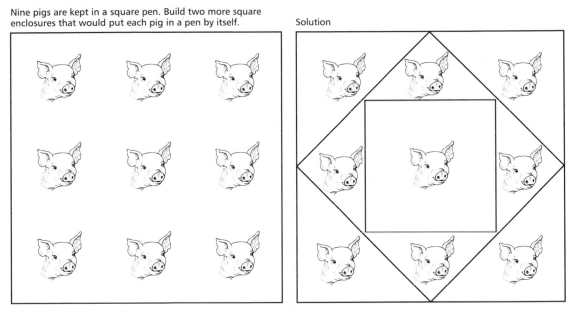

'Pigs in a pen' problem: one of the insight problems used

Results: The DV of accuracy was measured as the total number of problems solved in the allotted time. Participants in the *verbalisation* condition solved 35.6 per cent whereas those in the control condition solved significantly more (45.8 per cent).

Conclusion: In the experimental group, verbalisation interrupted the cognitive processes being employed by the participants to solve insight problems and resulted in poorer scores compared with those who were interrupted by an irrelevant activity.

Questions

1 Write a directional hypothesis for this study.

2 Why was it necessary that this experiment used an independent groups design?

3 What was the purpose of the crossword puzzle?

4 What was the attrition rate for this study?

Describing your thought processes disrupts your thinking

Design an experiment to test whether it is the writing down of the thought processes which is disrupting or merely interrupting oneself and thinking back over the process in detail which has the detrimental effect on subsequent problem solving.

Matched pairs

The matched pairs design is, in some ways, a compromise between repeated measures and independent groups, maintaining the significant advantages of each arrangement. In a *matched pairs design*, the scores are obtained for each level of the IV from different participants (as in an independent groups design). However, for each member of one group there exists in the other group an individual with certain characteristics in common. The groups are created by ensuring that every participant is part of a *matched pair*; two individuals who have been selected because they share features of importance to the experiment. Look back to Rosenbluth *et al.* (2000) on page 90, a study that compared the sense of smell in blind and sighted children. Their aim in constructing experimental groups was to match each blind child to a sighted child of the same age, sex, grade and ethnic group and native language. These criteria were deemed to be relevant to the experiment.

interactive
angles

Working as a group, imagine you are about to conduct a study on animal phobias. You might decide to match male and female participants on criteria such as childhood pet ownership, holiday experiences on farms, in zoos and parental fears. Can you find suitable pairs?

for and against

+ Repeated measures minimises the effects of participant variables.

− Independent groups design reduces the impact of demand characteristics compared with repeated measures.

+ Matched pairs design avoids both the problems of exposure to potential demand characteristics in a repeated measures design and limits the confounding effects of participant variables between groups in an independent measures design.

− Appropriate criteria on which to match participants may be difficult to identify and matching participants may be hard to find.

Planning an experiment

Operationalising variables

One of the key benefits of experimentation is that the rigour with which experiments can be conducted allows for *replication*, that is a repetition of the experiment to verify the findings. One reason for this being possible is the extent to which the variables within the experimental setting can be controlled. In order to replicate a study accurately, the manipulations of the IV and the mechanisms for measuring the DV must be the same as in the original study.

You must be able to describe the variables that you are manipulating or measuring in a way that makes them operational. An *operational definition* is a description that identifies a variable by factors that can be measured or manipulated. Take a study investigating the effects of mobile phone use on hearing for example. The IV of *phone use* could be operationalised by establishing three groups: *non-users* who do not have or use a mobile phone; *occasional users* who use a mobile for less than ten minutes per month; and *frequent users* who spend more than an hour a week calling from their mobile phone. If the outcome was hearing loss, it could be measured as the lowest audible volume (in dB), thus operationalising the DV.

Harrell *et al.* (2000) investigated the differences in the way students assisted the way-finding of (hypothetical) visitors around their university campus. The independent variables were the sex of the participant and the nature of the visitor. Since the visitors were hypothetical (the students were given a brief description of the visitor before giving their directions) this was easy to manipulate. The experimenters controlled the following features relating to the visitors:

- *destination* (near or distant);
- *gender* (male or female);

- *age* (25 or 75 years);

- *familiarity with the campus* (unfamiliar – new to the campus and did not know his or her way around – or familiar – had formerly attended the university but had not been on campus recently).

The dependent variable was the participants' proficiency at directing the visitors, measured as the accuracy of their estimate of the time it would take the visitor to reach their destination and the completeness of a map they were asked to draw. The maps were analysed for the inclusion of the following:

- *buildings and landmarks* (one mark for each, such as university buildings, trees, doors, stairways and paths);

- *cardinal indicators* (whether north or south was marked on the map and if it was correct);

- *directional arrows* (showing the route the visitor should take);

- *supplemental directions* (additional words to guide the visitor).

Harrell *et al.* (2000) found that male students produced more complete maps but were no more likely to include landmarks or labelled buildings. The males were also more likely to take into account the characteristics of the visitors, including more detail for older or unfamiliar visitors or those attempting to navigate complex routes.

research methods

does alcohol affect young people's condom use?

MacDonald, T.K., Fong, G.T., Zanna, M.P. and Martineau, A.M. (2000) Alcohol myopia and condom use: can alcohol intoxication be associated with more prudent behaviour? *Journal of Personality and Social Psychology*, 78, 605–19

Aims: To investigate whether alcohol intoxication results in more or less sexually risky behaviour and whether this can be moderated by provision of cues to behaviour.

Method: Three separate studies measured the likelihood of risky sexual behaviour using a questionnaire following a description or video of a situation in which a man and woman were likely to have sex without a condom. In the *laboratory experiment* there were three conditions; sober, placebo and intoxicated. The placebo group believed they were consuming alcohol since the rims of the glasses they were drinking from had been dipped in alcohol. The blood alcohol level of participants in the experimental (intoxicated) group was raised to 0.08 per cent (i.e. 80 mg per litre, the legal limit for driving in Britain). After viewing a video which ended with the potential for unsafe sex, the participants answered questions either in an *inhibiting* condition, where reference was made to 'sexual intercourse **without a condom**' or in an *impelling* condition where reference was simply made to 'sexual intercourse'. In the *field experiment* a blood alcohol level was not manipulated by the experimenters, participants were instead recruited in bars and their blood alcohol levels were measured using a portable breathalyser. They then read a description of a situation and answered the same questionnaire as above. In the *second field experiment* 'safe sex' cues were manipulated. Again using patrons in bars, three conditions were established in addition to blood alcohol. These were achieved using hand stamps like those used in clubs, as illustrated:

On each day, only one of the stamps was used. Again participants read a passage then responded to the statement 'If I were in this situation, I would have sex' on a nine-point scale.

Results: The *laboratory experiment* showed that alcohol heightened the participants' responses to the impelling and inhibiting cues. Intoxicated participants exposed to the standard video and questions demonstrated clear intentions to have sex without a condom but those who read the text containing the '**without a condom**' cue were less likely than the sober participants to engage in unsafe sex. This was supported by the findings of the first *field experiment*. In the *second field experiment* the SAFE SEX stamp was not effective but with the AIDS KILLS stamp the intoxicated participants were less likely to report the intention to have unprotected sex than the sober participants in the SMILEY FACE condition.

Conclusion: These results support the theory of alcohol myopia, that is, that intoxication narrows the range of stimuli to which a person attends. The intoxicated participants focused on the cues provided ('**without a condom**' or AIDS KILLS). Their responses, to increase or reduce the likelihood of risking unprotected sex, were more extreme than those of the sober participants. The findings have implications for health interventions, suggesting that getting safe sex messages to the place where risky decisions may be made under the influence of alcohol could effectively inhibit sexually unsafe behaviour.

Questions

1 The IV in the first two experiments was the blood alcohol level. Describe how this varied and use this to justify the *research method* used in each of the three studies, what *type* of experiments were they?

2 Identify the DV in each experiment and describe how it was measured.

3 In the third study there were two independent variables: what were they?

4 The third study was a quasi-experiment: why?

Selecting materials

Having decided definitions for the variables, the next stage in planning an experiment is to select appropriate materials. These may be necessary to create an appropriate environment, for experimental stimuli or as a distracter. Location also matters to the success of a study; consider how different the results of a survey on healthy eating might be if conducted in a doctor's surgery or a confectioner's, even if the same participants were used. For some experiments it may be necessary to prepare the environment, such as covering windows of a room to be used to test participants who may object to being observed perhaps during hypnosis or while conducting a demanding task. In addition, some experiments require a particular setting, such as for tests of context-dependent memory or staged scenes for eyewitness testimony.

Many studies also require specific materials such as questionnaires or stimuli. The preparation of these will require searching for appropriate sources such as word frequency lists, stories, illustrations or other materials. If these are not available it may be essential to create them yourself. In this way matched stimuli can be devised, such as stories with the same plot but of differing complexities or sets of nonsense syllables which are more or less nonsensical. Look back at MacDonald *et al.* (2000), page 100: what materials did they need to prepare?

interactive
angles

Find the following studies reported elsewhere in the text and pair up each study with the materials used.

- Wareing, Fisk and Murphy (2000)
- Chawarski and Sternberg (1993)
- Neer, Dorn and Grayson (1987)
- Schooler, Ohlsson and Brooks (1993)
- Duncan and Seymour (2000)

1 Socio-economic status based on housing (private or public), unemployment, lone parents and car ownership; tests were conducted on letter and sound knowledge, reading of words and non-words.

2 Dog presence or absence; blood pressure.

3 Current, past and non-MDMA users; tests of cognitive functioning including information processing speed (a task involving classifying sequences of letters) and a self-report questionnaire on anxiety and arousal.

4 Word lists (relevant- primed or unprimed, irrelevant); stories.

5 Crosswords, insight problems.

Finally, you will need to prepare an appropriate brief, standardised instructions and debrief. There may need to be different versions for participants experiencing different levels of the IV. Details about these can be found in Chapters 13 and 14 on ethics and writing coursework reports.

Pilot study

In order to ensure that the method being employed in an experiment will work according to plan it is sometimes important to run through the protocol with a small number of participants so that amendments can be made. These might be aspects such as the volume at which to present an auditory stimulus, the number of items needed in order to be able to discriminate high, low and mid-range scores on a test or simply to establish how long the procedure will take. This process is called a *pilot study* and is a scaled-down pre-run of the experiment used to test the method and identify any uncontrolled variables. The results obtained from these participants do not contribute to the final analysis. For example, Schooler *et al.* (1993) used data from previous studies to select six from the ten available insight problems. Those chosen had a mean pilot performance of approximately 50 per cent.

Conclusions

Experimentation provides a means to investigate the effects of a single variable (or small number of variables) while controlling other factors in the situation. The findings of experiments can thus be readily replicated and validated. The experimental method allows for studies to be conducted both within and outside the laboratory environment offering a range of research opportunities.

where to now?

▶ **Hayes, N. (2000)** *Doing Psychological Research*. **Buckingham: Open University Press** – provides excellent and understandable detail on all aspects of experimental design

▶ **Nunn, J. (Ed.) (1998)** *Laboratory Psychology, A Beginner's Guide*. **Hove: Psychology Press** – discusses the advantages and disadvantages of different formal designs as well as covering basic experimental design issues.

what do you know?

1 Can you define independent variable and dependent variable?

2 What are the advantages and disadvantages of repeated measures and independent groups designs?

3 What was the formal design of Kissinger *et al.* (1999) reported on page 67?

4 What was the formal design used by Dutton and Aron (1974) reported on page 202?

7

Correlations

what's
ahead?

Correlations do not constitute a separate 'research method' as such because other research methods are used to gain the data. Correlational 'designs' look for relationships between the measures collected from other research methods, for example, questionnaires or observations. Correlations can be defined as the relationship between two measured variables. In this chapter we will examine the different types of correlation that research can generate (e.g. positive, negative correlation) to show the wide range of areas in psychology that use this type of research method.

Types of correlation

There are three broad categories that results of correlational studies can fall into: *positive*, *negative* or *no* correlation. A *positive correlation* takes the form that if one measured variable increases, the second variable is also likely to increase. For example, there may be a positive correlation between a person's height and their shoe size. That is, we expect that a taller person will have larger feet. As one variable increases, so does the other.

A *negative correlation* takes the form that if one measured variable increases, the other measured variable decreases. For example, there may be a negative correlation between the number of therapy sessions a person has and the number of depressive symptoms they exhibit. That is, we expect as the number of therapy sessions increase, the number of depressive symptoms exhibited decreases. As one variable increases, the other decreases.

No correlation refers to the situation where no definite trend occurs and the two measured variables do not appear to be related to each other. For example, if we attempted to correlate the circumference of the head of a person and then rated them on a 'big-headedness scale' (e.g. how much they liked to talk about their achievements and boost their ego!) we would probably find no correlation. (One of the authors has tried this many times and no correlation tends to occur, although once there was a rather strong positive correlation!)

interactive
angles

Using your class or friends and family as participants, measure each of the following pairs of variables:

- Foot length and forearm length (from elbow to beginning of hand).

- Width of tongue and how talkative a person is on a scale from 0 to 10.

- Height and the number of strides it takes to cross the room.

What type of correlations do you think you will get for each of these?

How do we know if we have a correlation?

On pages 165 and 184 you will find details about the inferential statistical tests that help you conclude whether you have found a correlation or not. For the purposes of this chapter all you need to know is that correlations are measured via *correlation coefficients* (represented by '*r*'). These coefficients range from −1 to +1. A correlation that has a minus sign as part of its correlation coefficient is a negative correlation (minus = − = negative). A correlation that has a plus sign as part of its correlation coefficient is a positive correlation (plus = '+' = positive). A correlation with a coefficient around 0 represents no correlation. The larger the number of the coefficient, the stronger the correlation.

Example

A correlation that has a coefficient of +0.83 represents a stronger positive correlation than one with a coefficient of +0.33. Furthermore, a correlation that has a coefficient of −0.77 represents a stronger negative correlation than one with a coefficient of −0.29.

Below is a chart that will help you understand the strength of a correlation:

What do correlation coefficients mean?

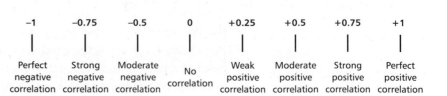

−1	−0.75	−0.5	0	+0.25	+0.5	+0.75	+1
Perfect negative correlation	Strong negative correlation	Moderate negative correlation	No correlation	Weak positive correlation	Moderate positive correlation	Strong positive correlation	Perfect positive correlation

Representing correlations on a graph

Correlations are always represented on a scatterplot (sometimes called a scattergram or scattergraph) and it is usual that you can spot the type of correlation from it. Below are some examples, showing different correlations and their estimated coefficient values.

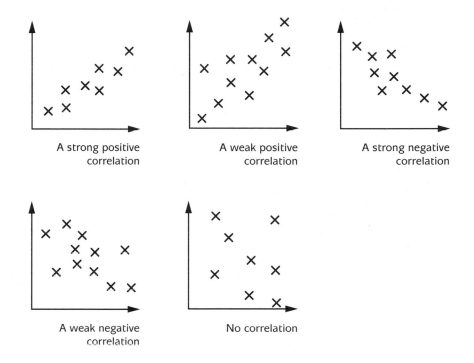

| A strong positive correlation | A weak positive correlation | A strong negative correlation |

| A weak negative correlation | No correlation |

Below is a series of examples highlighting how correlations are used in psychological research. Bjork *et al.* (1997) were interested in examining the relationship between how depressed a person feels and how aggressive they actually are.

research
methods

positive correlations: a relationship between depression and aggression?

Bjork, J.M., Dougherty, D.M. and Moeller, F.G. (1997) A positive correlation between self-ratings of depression and laboratory measured aggression. *Psychiatry Research,* 69 (1), 33–8

Aim: To see if there was a correlation between self-ratings of depression and laboratory measured aggression.

Method: Sixty-five people self-completed the Beck Depression Inventory (BDI) and were assessed on the Point Subtraction Aggression Paradigm (PSAP) for aggression. There were 42 women and 23 men in the sample.

Results: There was a significant positive correlation between the BDI symptom score and level of aggressive responding in the PSAP in women ($r = +0.442$) but not in men ($r = +0.064$).

Conclusions: This study provides some evidence of a link between aggressive behaviour and depressive symptoms possibly due to a common neurochemical cause.

Questions

1 Can you think of any reasons why Bjork *et al.* found a stronger correlation for women compared to men?

2 Note two limitations of this research.

Chantome *et al.* (1999) examined if there was a correlation between a person's hippocampal volume and explicit memory (which requires a conscious effort to recall material that has been learned previously).

research methods

negative correlation: can you remember if you have a big brain?

Chantome, M., Perruchet, P., Hasboun, D., Dormont, D., Sahel, M., Sourour, N., Zouaoui, A., Marsault, C. and Duyme, M. (1999) Is there a negative correlation between explicit memory and hippocampal volume? *Neuroimage*, 10(5), 589–95

Aim: To study the relationship between explicit memory and hippocampal volume.

Method: Seventy healthy adults were given one implicit memory test and one explicit memory test. Afterwards, all participants underwent a magnetic resonance imaging brain scan.

Results: Chantome *et al.* discovered that there was a significant negative correlation between the explicit memory test and the hippocampus/brain volume ratio in the left hemisphere ($r = -0.25$) and right hemisphere ($r = -0.27$).

Conclusions: The findings are consistent with research that has consistently noted a relationship between decrease in memory performance and hippocampal damage.

Questions

1 How did Chantome *et al.* know they had a negative correlation?

2 What do you think the next stage of this research should be?

Are bad eating habits learned or are they genetic?

research methods

correlation: sisters are dieting for themselves!

Vachon, C.M., Sellers, T.A., Kushi, L.H. and Folsom, A.R. (1998) Familial correlations of dietary intakes among postmenopausal women. *Genetic Epidemiology*, 15 (6), 553–63

Aim: As a positive family history is a main risk factor in many chronic diseases, Vachon *et al.* examined if eating habits were familial and if they could influence family-history diseases.

Method: Food frequency data was collected from 3515 participants in Iowa, USA, consisting of post-menopausal women. They examined whether dietary intake (via energy consumption) in sisters was more similar than in unrelated individuals.

Results: The main significant correlations (because the sample size was so large, small correlations become significant) between sisters were vitamin D intake ($r = +0.16$), dietary fibre ($r = +0.15$), calcium ($r = +0.14$), vegetable fat ($r = +0.13$) and animal fat ($r = +0.12$).

Conclusions: Even Vachon *et al.* admit that the correlations were modest, but note that 'these correlations may be high enough to influence familial clustering of complex diseases that are attributed, in part, to diet' (p. 553).

Questions

1 Which intake had the highest correlation between sisters?

2 Which intake had the lowest correlation between sisters?

3 Do you think the results could be generalised to other countries?

In a series of studies, Kerry Jang and colleagues have investigated correlations of personality traits and atypical disorders in twins (monozygotic = identical; dizygotic = non-identical) and the general population. Below are some examples of her work:

research
methods

correlation: personality and SAD

Jang, K.L., Lam, R.W., Harris, J.A., Vernon, P.A. and Livesley, W.J. (1998) Seasonal mood change and personality: an investigation of genetic co-morbidity. *Psychiatry Research*, 78, 1–7

Aim: To examine whether there are any genetic links between Seasonal Affective Disorder (SAD) and personality.

Method: One hundred and sixty-three monozygotic pairs of twins and 134 dizygotic pairs of twins completed a battery of questionnaires measuring levels of SAD and levels of personality.

Results: There were large correlations between SAD scores and neurotic scores ($r = +0.52$), anxiousness scores ($r = +0.37$) and stimulus-seeking scores ($r = +0.45$) in monozygotic twins.

Conclusion: The results provide some evidence to suggest that the correlations found between SAD scores and some personality scores can be attributed to genetic origin(s).

Questions

1 Which personality trait correlated most strongly with SAD in monozygotic twins?

2 What do the results suggest to us about SAD and genetics?

research methods

correlation: the genetics of personality disorders

Jang, K.L., Livesley, W.J. and Vernon, P.A. (1998) A twin study of genetic and environmental contributions to gender differences in traits delineating personality disorder. *European Journal of Personality*, 12, 331–44

Aim: To examine relationships between monozygotic pairs of twins and dizygotic pairs of twins (both male and female) on measures of personality disorders to assess the potential role of genetics in personality disorders.

Method: A total of 681 volunteer pairs of twins (128 monozygotic [MZ] male, 208 monozygotic female, 75 dizygotic [DZ] male, 174 dizygotic female, 96 dizygotic opposite-sex) completed a personality disorder questionnaire called the Dimensional Assessment of Personality Pathology. The questionnaire measures 24 dimensions of personality disorders.

Results: The vast majority of correlations were higher for monozygotic twins irrespective of gender compared to the correlations for dizygotic twins. Examples from 4 of the personality disorder dimensions are shown below (all figures are Pearson's *r* – see Chapter 11):

Dimension	MZ male	MZ female	DZ male	DZ female	DZ opposite
Identity problems	+0.54	+0.56	+0.25	+0.44	+0.23
Callousness	+0.67	+0.51	+0.08	+0.39	+0.32
Social avoidance	+0.48	+0.51	+0.25	+0.37	+0.10
Self-harm	+0.20	+0.28	+0.01	+0.30	+0.19

Conclusion: Some elements of personality disorders appear to be genetic because there are many higher correlations of MZ twins compared to DZ twins on the same personality disorder dimensions.

Questions

1 Using the table above, what are the three strongest correlations that Jang *et al.* discovered?

2 Which of the personality traits in females has the weakest genetic influence? Justify your answer.

3 Why did Jang *et al.* decide that some of the personality traits were due to genetics?

4 Note one limitation of this research.

research
methods

correlation: extraversion, introversion – genetic?

Jang, K.L., Livesely, W.J. and Vernon, P.A. (1999) The relationship between Eysenck's P-E-N model of personality and traits delineating personality disorder. *Personality and Individual Differences*, 26, 121–8

Aim: To examine whether there is a relationship between Eysenck's model of personality (Psychoticism, Extraversion and Neuroticism: P-E-N) and personality disorders.

Method: A total of 200 general population participants completed an Eysenck Personality Questionnaire and the Dimensional Assessment of Personality Problems. The latter assesses personality disorders.

Results: There were lots of correlations between the Psychoticism, Extraversion and Neuroticism scores with dimensions on the personality disorder questionnaire. Five of the correlations are noted below:

- correlation between Neuroticism and Identity Problems was +0.59

- correlation between Extraversion and Stimulus Seeking was +0.35

- correlation between Psychoticism and Conduct Problems was +0.40

- correlation between Extraversion and Social Avoidance was –0.41

- correlation between Neuroticism and Insecure Attachment was +0.47

Conclusion: The rather simple P-E-N model of personality proposed by Eysenck has some validity in predicting personality problems in the general population. In particular, the N dimension predicts general psychological distress. The E dimension appears to be part of antisocial disorders, whilst the P dimension appears to be involved in conduct, drug and violent behaviour problems.

Questions

1 Which of the above correlations is negative? What does that indicate?

2 Which of the above correlations is the strongest? What does it indicate?

3 How could Jang *et al.* assess if the P-E-N model of personality is genetic or not?

for and against

correlations

+ Data may already have been collected (e.g. archives of data such as governmental publications).

– There may be other factors that are affecting the correlation, but you are only focusing on *two* variables.

– Sometimes impossible to determine cause and effect (e.g. is the first measure causing the change in the second measure, or vice versa).

– The correlation could be caused by a third factor that you did not measure.

+ Ideal for showing a link between two measures.

where to now?

▶ **Howitt, D. and Cramer, D. (2000)** *First Steps in Research and Statistics*. **London: Routledge** a nice introduction to correlational research including coefficients.

what do you know?

1 Draw on separate graphs a positive correlation and a negative correlation.

2 Describe *one* strength and *one* weakness of using correlations in psychological research.

3 What is meant by the term correlation coefficient?

4 Which correlation is stronger: +0.78 or –0.85?

8

Descriptive Statistics

Measures of Average and Measures of Dispersion

There are three measures of average that we can choose from when we want to analyse data. These are used to summarise data via a comparable single index. Measures of average are sometimes called measures of central tendency, which are supposed to represent a typical score from your data set. Measures of dispersion (sometimes called measures of spread) represent how spread out your data are around the measure of average.

In this chapter the following measures of average will be introduced: mode, median and mean. Also the following measures of dispersion will be introduced: the variation ratio, range, interquartile range and standard deviation.

Measures of average (central tendency)

The mode

This measure of average is the *most common score* in your data set. Therefore, on inspecting your data set you can discover the mode by seeing which score or value is represented the most times. If two scores are equally represented then we call the distribution of scores *bi-modal*. If there are three 'modes' then it is *tri-modal* and so on. The best way of calculating the mode is to draw up a frequency table and see which score has the highest frequency, for example:

Shoe colour choice in males	Frequency
Brown	10
Green	15
Blue	18
Black	27
White	17
Red	4

From the frequency column we can easily conclude that the modal shoe colour for this data set is *Black* with a frequency of 27.

Do cats make their owners happy?

research methods

the mode: do pets make older adults happy?

Ory, M.G. and Goldberg, E.L. (1983) Pet possession and well-being in elderly women. *Research on Aging*, 5(3), 389–409

Aim: To investigate whether there was an association between pet ownership and happiness in elderly women.

Method: Participants were asked a single question about how happy they were. The question 'Taken all together, how would you say things are these days? Would you say you were very happy or not too happy?' (p. 395) had three set responses: **very happy**, **pretty happy** or **not so happy**. A total of 388 pet owners and 685 non-pet owners answered the question.

Results: The data collected were *nominal* (the answer to the question was a category: very happy, pretty happy or not so happy – you can argue that the data are ordinal because you can put the data in order) and the research team were looking for an association between pet ownership status and level of happiness. The following contingency table was produced from the data collected:

Category	Pet owner	Non-pet owner	Total
Very happy	161	296	457
Pretty happy	196	351	547
Not so happy	31	38	69
Total	388	685	1073

Conclusion: From the reported scores above, the modal responses for each group under investigation were the same (pet owners – pretty happy: 196; non-pet owners – pretty happy: 351). Therefore, there appears to be little difference in reported happiness between pet owners and non-pet owners.

The median

This measure of average is the *middlemost score*. That is, when you have placed your data in rank order from the smallest number to the largest number (including every repetition of a score), it is the score that lies in the middle of your data set. To calculate a median, follow these steps:

1 Rank your data from the smallest number to the largest number.

2 Eliminate one score from the lowest end of the ranked data and the highest end of the ranked data (called a pair of scores).

3 Continue eliminating these pairs of scores until either one or two scores are left. If you have an *odd number of scores* in your data set then you should be left with just one number (this is the median). If you have an *even number of scores* in your data set then you should be left with two numbers. In this case, you must complete step four below.

4 Add up the two remaining numbers and divide the total by 2. This is the median.

Let's look at an example. The following are questionnaire scores generated from a Likert-type scale.

11   13   13   13   15   17   17   17   18   19   19

Therefore, the median is *17*. Now, re-calculate with an extra score:

11   13   13   13   13   15   17   17   17   18   19   19

The two remaining numbers are 15 and 17. If we now execute step 4, we get:

$$15 + 17 = 32$$

We then divide this by 2 to get 32/2 = 16. The median score is *16*.

research methods

the median: what do we think of our pets?

Serpell, J.A. (1996) Evidence for an association between pet behaviour and owner attachment levels. *Applied Animal Behaviour Science*, 47, 49–60

Aim: One of the aims of this research was to examine differences in actual behaviour between dogs and cats on a series of dimensions, for example, playfulness, active, clean.

Method: One year after acquiring their pet, participants were asked to rate their pet on 12 dimensions (dog owners, $n = 37$; cat owners, $n = 47$). A *semantic-differential* questionnaire was completed with a 50-mm gap between the bi-polar adjectives (see Chapter 4). The participant had to place a mark between the bi-polar adjectives and this was measured using a ruler. The larger the score, the *less* of that behaviour was seen. For example, for playfulness, a low score indicated playful, while a high score indicated not so playful.

Results: The median scores for four of the dimensions are listed below:

Behaviour measured	Dog owners	Cat owners
Playful	5.7	15.0
Obedient	12.2	12.2
Intelligent	7.5	19.3
Aggressive	4.8	5.0

Conclusion: From the reported median scores above, in this sample dogs were seen as being more playful and more intelligent. There were no median differences between the cats' and dogs' ratings on obedience and aggressiveness.

Serpell (1996) discovered that dogs are seen as more playful than cats!

The mean

This is usually called the 'average' but, as we now know, there are another two types! Therefore, this is more correctly called the *arithmetic mean*. To calculate this we must complete the following procedure:

1   Add up all of the scores we have collected to form our data set.

2   Divide this total by the *number* of scores that we have just added up.

Let's look at an example. We measured the height of 10 people and the results were as follows (in centimetres):

158   163   165   165   165   168   170   170   170   175

So, firstly we add up all of the scores:

158 + 163 + 165 + 165 + 165 + 168 + 170 + 170 + 170 + 175

Next, we divide the total score by the number of scores which is *10*.

$$1669/10 = 166.9$$

Therefore the mean height is *166.9 centimetres*.

research methods

the mean: forget stress balls – hold a hamster!

DeMello, L.R. (1999) The effect of the presence of a companion-animal on physiological changes following the termination of cognitive stressors. *Psychology and Health*, 14, 859–68

Aim: To measure the blood pressure of people before, during and after a cognitive task with or without a companion-animal (pet) present.

Method: Participants were given a variety of cognitive tasks (e.g. mental arithmetic) in a counterbalanced design of pet absent (Condition A) and pet present (Condition B). Blood pressure was monitored and recorded. Participants were not expecting a pet to appear during the pet present task as they were told that the assistant to the experimenter had brought their dog into work and it may have to enter the experimental room with the assistant at some point. They were told not to let that bother them.

Results: Baseline mean measures of blood pressure were approximately the same for both conditions (A = 112.72 mm Hg; B = 112.64 mm Hg). While condition B's mean blood pressure rose more than that for condition A (A = 115.94 mm Hg; B = 121.42 mm Hg), at the rest phase after the cognitive task, condition B's mean blood pressure dropped significantly more than condition A (A = 113.04 mm Hg; B = 110.60 mm Hg).

Conclusion: This research provided evidence that the mere presence of an unknown dog can reduce blood pressure significantly after a person has undertaken cognitive tasks.

interactive
angles

Collect the following data:

● The time it takes people to open and eat a chocolate bar.

● People's favourite type of chocolate: dark, milk, white, none.

● Get people to rate themselves on a scale of 1–10 on their current 'need for chocolate'.

From the scores, calculate an appropriate measure of average. You may wish to split it into male and female averages.

Measures of dispersion (spread)

Measures of dispersion give us an index of how *spread* your data set is around the measure of central tendency. You can use it to see if your participants' scores cluster around your average or are spread widely from your average. It is possible to have roughly equal averages but vastly differing dispersion figures for different groups. There are four main measures of dispersion: the variation ratio, the range, the interquartile range and the standard deviation.

The variation ratio

This measure of dispersion is used in conjunction with the *mode*, it can be used with nominal data (as well as continuous data). Basically, the variation ratio is the percentage of scores that are not the mode. For example:

Eye colour	Frequency
Green	12
Brown	7
Blue	11

The *modal eye colour is green*. So, to calculate the variation ratio, complete the following steps:

1   Calculate the modal score (a category as above).

2   Add up your total number of scores.

3   Calculate how many scores are *not the modal score*.

4   Divide the figure you get from step 3 by the total number of scores (step 2) and multiply by 100.

The equation for the variation ratio is as follows:

$$\frac{\text{No. of scores } not \text{ in the modal category}}{\text{Total no. of scores}} \times 100$$

For this example:

1   The modal score is *green – frequency of 12 people*.

2   The total number of scores is 12 + 7 + 11 = 30.

3   The number of scores that are not the mode is brown + blue, which is 7 + 11 = 18.

4   18/30 = 0.6; to express this as a percentage, 0.6 × 100 = 60%.

Therefore, the *variation ratio of this data set is 60 per cent.* It indicates that 60 per cent of the scores recorded were *not* the mode.

The range

This measure of dispersion is used in conjunction with the *median* but can be used with any continuous data. It is the simplest to calculate as follows:

1   Rank your data from the smallest to the largest number (as for calculating the median).

2   Subtract the smallest number from the highest number then add 1.

The interquartile range

This measure of dispersion is also used in conjunction with the *median*. This is a more stringent measure of dispersion than the range as it is not affected by outliers (extreme scores), which can distort the calculation of the range. The *interquartile range* is essentially the range of the middle 50 per cent of scores in your data set. To calculate the *interquartile range* complete the following steps:

1   Rank data from the smallest number to the largest number (as for calculating the median).

2   **For an odd set of data,** find the median value. Then, divide the rest of the data into set A (those less than the median data point) and set B (those greater than the median data point) – so the actual median data point is *not* in this part of the calculation. Then find the median for both set A and set B (the middle score as if you were finding the median for set A and set B). Or **for an even set of data,** find the median value. As above, divide the rest of the data into set A (those scores less than the median data point) and set B (those greater than the median data point). Then find the median for both set A and set B (the middle score, as if you were finding the median for set A and set B).

3   Subtract set A median (middle score) from set B median (middle score) and then add 1.

It should be noted that the term given to the set A median (middle score) is the *lower quartile* and the term given to the set B median (middle score) is the *upper quartile*.

The standard deviation

This measure of dispersion is used in conjunction with the *mean*. This measure is the spread of data around the mean point. It is the most stringent measure of dispersion as it uses all the data in the calculation. To calculate, you need to use the following table headings:

x	$\bar{x}$	$x - \bar{x}$	$(x - \bar{x})^2$

1   List all of the scores in the x column.

2   Calculate the *mean* and write it in the $\bar{x}$ column as many times as there are data points.

3   Calculate $x - \bar{x}$ for each row of the table.

4   Square each row figure you have in the $x - \bar{x}$ column and write the number in the $(x - \bar{x})^2$ column.

5   Add up the $x - \bar{x}$ column (if it is roughly 0 then you have calculated them all correctly).

6   Add up the scores in the $(x - \bar{x})^2$ column. This is called $\Sigma (x - \bar{x})^2$.

Place the numbers in the following equation:

$$\text{Standard deviation (sd)} = \sqrt{\frac{\Sigma (x - \bar{x})^2}{n - 1}}$$

interactive angles

For the data from previous chocolate-based exercise (on page 119), calculate an appropriate measure of dispersion for each data set.

When do I use each measure of average and each measure of dispersion?

Each particular measure of average and measure of dispersion cannot be used on any data collected. That is, you do not simply calculate the mode, median and mean for the data and report them all on every occasion (this also applies to the measures of dispersion). The following table shows that the type of measure of average and measure of dispersion you use depends on the type (level) of data collected.

Level of measurement	Appropriate measure of average	Appropriate measure of dispersion
Nominal	Mode	Variation ratio
Ordinal	Median	Interquartile range
Interval/ratio	Mean	Standard deviation

Nominal data

As already described, nominal data are categorical in nature. The data are represented in discrete categories, for example the grades given for AS Level Psychology are A, B, C, D, E and U; each is a category. It is easiest to report the *mode* as this is the most common grade. The median or mean cannot be calculated because the data are not numerical. For example, if we attempted to calculate the mean all of the data points have to be added together. How could you add up A + A + A + B + C + C + D + D + E? It cannot be calculated. The *mode* requires the most basic form of data, categorical, for calculation.

research methods

nominal data: chillin' with da right sounds

North, A.C. and Hargreaves, D.J. (2000) Musical preference during and after relaxation and exercise. *American Journal of Psychology*, 113, 43–67

Aim: To test experimentally the observation that we use music in our everyday lives to optimise our mood.

Method: Participants experienced five minutes of either an exercise condition, in which they rode on an exercise bike, or a relaxation condition, in which they lay on a quilt and rested. They were asked to select a piece of music to listen to, either during or after their five-minute session. There were two pieces of electronically generated music, which were identical in every respect except tempo and volume. The *high-arousal* version was played at 140 beats per minute (bpm), 80 dB while the *low-arousal* version was at 80 bpm and 60 dB.

Results: During exercise the participants selected the fast tempo version whereas the relaxing participants selected the slow version. When tested after the sessions, the choices were reversed; those who had exercised selected the slow version whereas those who had been relaxing opted for the faster version.

Conclusion: Music appears to be used to enhance mood during an activity but to moderate it afterwards.

Questions

1 Although North and Hargreaves used many other more sophisticated measures, the participants' choice of music illustrates nominal data. What are the two named categories?

2 If the study were to be repeated with a condition where the participants could opt to listen to no music at all, the data generated would still be nominal. What would you call the third response?

The *variation ratio* is also used with nominal data and is the measure of dispersion that should be reported with the *mode*. This is because you need to have calculated the *mode* before you can calculate the *variation ratio*.

The inferential statistics available for use with nominal data include the chi-squared test and the sign test, described on pages 146 and 151.

In general, ordinal and interval/ratio data can be converted to nominal form, so the mode and variation ratio could be used with any level of measurement, but this is less informative than using the median or mean as noted below.

Ordinal data

This level of measurement is numerical where scores can be ranked in an order specified by the researcher. For example, the scores could be the cumulative score on a *Likert scale* questionnaire where the scores represent how much a participant agrees with an *attitude object*. Although participants may gain the same score, these may not be directly comparable. We know that for any particular individual a higher score has the same meaning, the absolute values of these scores may not be 'equivalent'. For example, imagine the following statement was included on the Likert scale: 'Pets give support and happiness'.

Strongly agree   Agree   No opinion   Disagree   Strongly disagree

Participant A circles 'agree' as their response. For them to 'strongly agree' they have to be very positive about their attitude. On the other hand, participant B circles 'strongly agree' as their response. They do not have to be as sure about their response to 'strongly agree' as participant A. Therefore, participant A and B could be 'feeling' the same response but they have given different responses on the Likert scale. Both scores are not comparable as we are not comparing like with like. Therefore, it is quite meaningless to add their scores together to calculate a *mean* so a *median* should be calculated as this only examines scores in rank order from the highest score to the lowest score.

Think of a horror film you have seen recently. How frightening did you find this film: (1) *mildly disturbing*, (2) *scary*, (3) *terrifying* or (4) *utterly horrific?* Now consider whether it made you shake, sweat, cry or scream. Do you think everyone who answered the same as you would have found it equally scary?

The inferential statistics available for use with ordinal data include the Mann–Whitney *U*-test, Wilcoxon matched pairs signed ranks test and the Spearman rank correlation (described on pages 155, 160 and 165).

The interquartile range is also used with ordinal data and is the measure of dispersion that should be reported with the *median*. This is because you have to know where the median lies to calculate the *interquartile range*.

Interval data and ratio data

These types of data are generated from scales that are either directly comparable (*interval*) or universal (*ratio*). As with the example above, the responses of participant A and participant B were not directly comparable, so could not be added together. In common with ordinal data, *interval data* are generated from a scale with points of increasing magnitude. In this instance, however, the gaps between one point and the next are equivalent, hence 'interval' data. Thus, two sets of interval data are directly comparable, unlike results on an ordinal scale. This is the case because each individual item on the scale is of *equal* value. For example, in a simple maths test a child might be asked to do the following sums: 23 + 35 = _, 14 + 61 = _, 35 + 42 = _, 21 + 58 = _, 42 + 56 = _. All of the sums are of equal difficulty, each has the smaller value first, none expects the child to 'carry over' or to use the 'hundreds' column and they are all written in the same format. We could therefore assume that to get each sum right is 'worth the same amount' in terms of measuring a child's ability in maths. If this is so then their total out of five is an interval score. The distinguishing feature of an interval scale compared to the next category, ratio data, is that an interval scale has no real zero, it is not measured from an absolute baseline. Think back to the child's maths test. Supposing a child scored zero on the test; could we safely assume that they had no mathematical ability? No, we could not: perhaps they just have not learned to use the tens column yet. If such a child were given a simpler test (such as: 2 + 3 = _, 1 + 6 = _, 3 + 4 = _, 2 + 5 = _, 4 + 5 = _) they may exhibit an ability that had been missed by the harder test. We therefore cannot assume that a score of zero on an interval scale really indicates an absence of that characteristic.

research methods

interval data: clever people don't get up in the morning

Roberts, R.D. and Kyllonen, P.C. (1999) Morningness–eveningness and intelligence: early to bed, early to rise will make you anything but wise! *Personality and Individual Differences*, 27, 1123–33

Aim: There has long been a popular belief that people who like to get up early in the morning are in some way advantaged over those individuals who prefer to get up later and continue working later. This belief is captured in the saying 'early to bed, early to rise makes you healthy, wealthy and wise'. This study was not concerned with health or wealth, but it did investigate the association between intelligence and preferences for early or late rising.

Method: A quasi-experimental design was used, in which the IQ of 'morning types' and 'evening types' was compared. Researchers asked 420 United States Air Force recruits, the majority of whom were women, to complete two questionnaires designed to measure their circadian rhythms. Participants were classified on the basis of these questionnaires. 'Morning types' were identified as individuals who woke early and liked to get up and begin the day's activities early, being most active in the morning. 'Evening types', by contrast, rose later and were at their most active in the evening. Participants also completed two different IQ tests, the Cognitive Abilities Measurement (CAM) and the Armed Services Vocational Aptitude Battery (ASVAB), in order to assess their intelligence. The IQ of the two groups (morning types and evening types) was compared.

Results: A significant difference emerged between the intelligence of the 'morning' and 'evening' types. The evening group emerged as significantly higher in IQ than the morning group.

Conclusion: Based on these results, it appears that evening types are brighter than morning types. This is in direct contrast to popular stereotypes. One possible explanation is that the ability to work in the evenings shows adaptability because of the extra difficulties involved, such as working in artificial light.

Questions

1 Scores from IQ tests are usually treated as interval data: why?

2 Suggest a non-directional alternative hypothesis for this study.

However, if a measure is taken from a universal scale (e.g. time, speed) then all participants' data can be compared directly. In common with interval data, *ratio data* are generated by a linear scale that has equal intervals between the points. In addition, a ratio scale has a real zero, that is, the measurements are made against an absolute baseline. In physics, temperature can be measured in °C (Celsius), °F (Fahrenheit) or K (Kelvin). In the first two, the gaps between the points on the scale are equal; the increase in temperature from say 10 °C to 20 °C is the same amount as the increase from 40 °C to 50 °C. However, for degrees Celsius and degrees Fahrenheit the baseline is not a real zero; it is possible to have temperatures lower than 0 °C and 0 °F. This is not the case for Kelvin: 0 K is the lowest possible temperature (at which the random motion of particles due to their kinetic energy ceases). Thus Celsius and Fahrenheit are interval scales, whereas Kelvin is a ratio scale.

Ratio scales are commonly used in psychology to measure physiological variables: body temperature, heart rate and blood pressure. Remember, in a ratio scale it is the measure itself that must have a baseline of zero; it does not mean that your participants have to start from a score of zero.

Other more elaborate tests include the galvanic skin response (a measure of electrical resistance of the skin) which indicates perspiration and therefore fear and the electroencephalograph (EEG) which detects electrical activity in the brain.

In addition, many psychological variables can be measured on ratio scales, such as time. Many tests use speed as a measure of performance, others may use latency (the time to begin to respond).

research methods

ratio data: do your eyes sleep?

Dement, W. and Kleitman, N. (1957) The relation of eye movements during sleep to dream activity: an objective method for the study of dreaming. *Journal of Experimental Psychology*, 53 (5), 339–46

Aim: To investigate the relationship between dream content and the rapid eye movements (REMs) observed during periods of dreaming. There was a secondary aim of the study – to establish whether dreams take place in real-time, or whether they are condensed into a shorter period, as is popularly thought.

Method: Nine volunteers, seven men and two women, took part in the experiment. Each participant turned up at the sleep laboratory shortly before his or her bedtime. They had instructions not to consume any drugs such as alcohol or coffee because these tend to reduce REM sleep. Each participant then went to bed in a dark, quiet room. An EEG and an electro-occulogram (EOG) to detect REMs were run for the entire period of sleep. At a series of times during the night the participants were awakened by means of a bell, both from REM and quiet sleep. When awakened they were instructed to describe the nature of their most recent dream into a tape recorder. They were then allowed to go back to sleep. Participants were given no feedback about what period of sleep they had been awakened from. In order to see how closely the REMs corresponded with dream content the participants were woken following particularly distinctive eye movements. The researchers examined the accounts of dreams and the recordings of brain and eye activity, and looked for associations.

Results: Many more dreams were reported when participants were woken from REM sleep than non-REM sleep. There was a significant correlation between the length of periods of REM and the length of the dreams reported. Participants were fairly accurate in estimating the length of their dreams, indicating that the dreams were experienced in real-time. Of particular interest was a strong association between the distinctive eye movements noted and the content of dreams. For example, one participant had a minute of very little eye movement followed by several large movements to the left. Their dream was of driving down the street and being crashed into by a car coming from the left. Another had been seen to have only vertical movements (as in looking up and down), and their dream was of climbing up and down ladders.

Conclusion: The results show that people dream in real-time and that their REMs are closely related to the content of their dreams. The most fundamental finding was that people dream much more often and more vividly in REM sleep than in non-REM sleep.

Questions

1 The time the participants had spent in REM sleep was a ratio measure. What scale was their own estimate of the time they had spent dreaming?

2 What other information, recorded in the study, could provide information on a ratio scale about the participant?

inter**active**
angles

Read the following examples of possible ways to test psychological variables. Decide which level of measurement is being used in each case and justify your answer.

- A test of whether drinking coffee at night affects our sleep. The participant was monitored using an electroencephalogram (EEG), which records changes in brain activity from sleep to waking. The time spent asleep was measured.

- A measure of vocabulary size was taken to compare men and women by asking participants to select appropriate words from a list to complete a Cloze task (fill-in-the-gaps). The list included words such as album, asymptote, back, beguile, creator, crepuscular, diameter, dorp, embarrass and embrasure.

- A study that compared how good memory is in different senses. Participants were allowed to see, hear or smell stimuli for three seconds and were asked to identify them two hours later. They could answer yes or no to each stimulus.

- An investigation into jetlag in which the adjustment to a new time zone biorhythm is measured as the rise in body temperature after three days, measured in °C during the 'old time' night.

As all scores are directly comparable with interval and ratio data, it is meaningful to add scores to each other and this is of course how you calculate the *mean*. The addition of all scores divided by the number of scores is the *mean*.

The *standard deviation* is also used with interval/ratio data and is the measure of dispersion that should be reported with the *mean*. You have to know the value of the mean to calculate the *standard deviation*.

T-tests (independent and related) and Pearson's product moment correlation are the appropriate inferential tests for interval and ratio data and are discussed on pages 174, 178 and 184.

Exam tip

So, you've designed a great experiment but you don't know what the level of measurement is. Here's a rough guide:

- If there are two or more categories and each participant only gets a *yes* or *no* for each one then it's probably nominal.

- If your scores are rated, such as opinions, attitudes or emotions or if you cannot be sure that every point on your scale is the same, even if you've assigned them numbers, then assume it's ordinal.

- You are relatively unlikely to have interval data. Are you sure that the points are equivalent? Does the scale get harder as you go up?

---

where to now?

▶ **Dyer, C. (1995)** *Beginning Research in Psychology*. **Oxford: Blackwell** – some nice worked examples of each descriptive measure. Good for pointing out the importance of dispersion measures in research.

---

what do you know?

1 How would you calculate the mode, the median and the mean?

2 Under what conditions would you calculate the variation ratio?

3 Distinguish between nominal, ordinal, interval and ratio data.

4 If I were interested in comparing how quickly males and females completed a psychology test, what measure of average and what measure of dispersion would I use and why?

9

Plotting Your Data

what's
ahead?

It is sometimes easier to describe data sets via pictures. Graphical representation of data is a useful way of doing this.

There are four main ways of plotting your data: bar charts, histograms, scattergraphs and frequency polygons. Each will be introduced with examples and a rationale behind each technique. The examples will be from 'real-life' psychological research.

Bar charts

These are usually used for *nominal* data (results in named categories) or for plotting the average scores for the groups of data collected. The *x*-axis (horizontal axis) should always have the categories of data while the *y*-axis (vertical axis) should always have the frequency of occurrences or the average value that is to be represented.

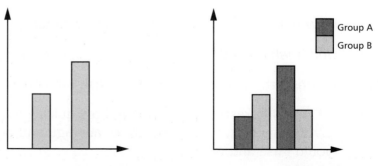

A bar chart   A dual bar chart

Variations on the bar chart

There are two variations that are worth noting: the *bar-and-whisker plot* and the *standard error bar*. Both of these are useful for representing a measure of average and a measure of dispersion on the same graph. The bar-and-whisker plot is used to represent the median and the interquartile range while a standard error bar represents the mean and the standard deviation.

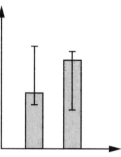
A bar-and-whisker plot

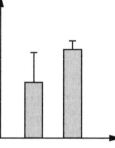
A standard error bar chart

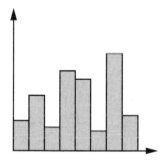
A histogram

Histograms

These are usually used when the data are continuous (on a numerical scale) and are plotted on the *x*-axis (horizontal axis). The *y*-axis (vertical axis) should always be used for the frequency of occurrences.

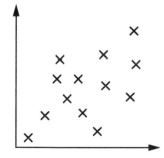
A scattergraph

Scattergraphs

Sometimes scattergraphs are referred to as scatterplots or scattergrams. These are used for plotting *correlations*, the relationship between two numerical measures. From these, it is clear what type of correlation has been found. The *x*-axis (horizontal axis) should represent one of the numerical measures and the *y*-axis (vertical axis) should represent the other.

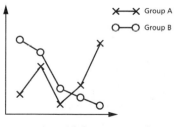
A frequency polygon

Frequency polygons

Frequency polygons are also referred to as line graphs. They are generally used when there are two sets of data that can be directly compared on one graph. An example would be plotting the *distribution* of scores for males and females on a questionnaire measuring attitudes towards safe sex. The *x*-axis (horizontal axis) should always have the scores which have be attained on the task while the *y*-axis (vertical axis) should represent the frequency of occurrences of the participants' scores.

The golden rules of plotting data

The following are guidelines that should be applied every time you are plotting data:

- Tabulate the data either as a frequency tally chart or where each participant's score on one variable for the scattergraph is next to the score on the other variable.

- Choose an appropriate graph for the type of data you have and the information that you are intending to get across to the reader through the graph.

- Label the axes fully and clearly. For example, if you are representing age groups on the *x*-axis, state whether the axis represents years, months or whatever.

- Give the graph an appropriate title. Anyone should be able to read the title and know what the graph is representing.

- Interpret the graph as part of the data analysis. Graphs are not just to fill the space in a report; they should be used as part of your report!

Worked examples of the graphical techniques

For each of the graphical techniques mentioned above, worked examples will be shown below based on *real psychological research*. For many, raw data are not available so the first golden rule of plotting data will not be adhered to in some cases. This is mainly due to research papers in journals rarely reporting the actual data. They usually state measures of average and measures of dispersion alongside inferential statistical test results. For the purposes of this chapter, the *results* sections below in the featured research will focus on the graphical representation of the data collected.

Bar charts

These types of graph are good for representing nominal data or measures of average.

research methods

bar charts: alien attraction

Stone-Carmen, J. (1992) Personality characteristics and self-identified experiences of individuals reporting possible abduction by Unidentified Flying Objects (UFOs). Dissertation as part fulfilment of a Doctorate in Philosophy and Psychology, San Diego, USA, 10–59

Aim: To examine whether people who could consciously remember an alien abduction had a different personality profile from those who could remember the alien abduction only under hypnosis.

Method: The participants were given a Minnesota Multiphasic Personality Inventory (MMPI: a widely used personality profile questionnaire). Two groups were formed: Group H were those who only retrieved their alien abduction via hypnosis; Group C were those who had some clear conscious recollection of their alien abduction.

Results: The following *bar charts* show the average score generated by Group H and Group C on the **Schizophrenia**, **Hypochondriasis** (high score indicates preoccupation with one's health) and **Paranoia** scales of the MMPI.

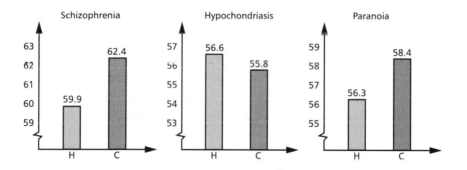

Values: schizophrenia H = 59.9, C = 62.4; hypochondriasis H = 56.6, C = 55.8; paranoia H = 56.3, C = 58.4.

Conclusion: The participants who could remember the alien abduction only under hypnosis (group H) had lower levels of schizophrenia, slightly higher levels of hypochodriasis and lower levels of paranoia than those participants who could consciously remember their account (group C).

interactive
angles

dual bar charts: do pets help Alzheimer's sufferers?

Fritz, C.L., Farver, T.B., Kass, P.H. and Hart, L.A. (1995) Association with companion animals and the expression of noncognitive symptoms in Alzheimer's Disease. *The Journal of Nervous and Mental Disease*, 183 (7), 459–63

Aim: To examine the role a companion animal (pet) had on mood, movement, health and psychiatric symptoms in a group of Alzheimer's disease patients.

Method: A total of 64 patients were observed; 34 were exposed to a pet (pet exposed) while 30 were not (non-pet exposed). Prevalence of various behaviours (e.g. verbal aggression, anxiety, hallucinations, depression) were noted and a percentage of patients showing these behaviours were calculated.

Results: The following results were collected:

Category	Pet	No pet
Verbal aggression	8%	43%
Anxiety	38%	63%
Hallucinations	28%	48%
Depression	41%	34%

Conclusion: Those exposed to a pet showed less verbal aggression, less anxiety, less hallucinations and more depression compared to those not exposed to a pet. Therefore, the results indicate that pets may be beneficial to those suffering from Alzheimer's disease.

Plot the data: Plot a *dual bar chart* to show the difference in *verbal aggression*, *anxiety*, *hallucinations* and *depression* between the pet-exposed group and the non-pet exposed group.

Bar-and-whisker plots

These graphs are ideal for displaying the median and interquartile range.

research
methods

bar-and-whisker plots: dogs, cats and depression

Roberts, C. (2000a) Pet ownership, social support and psychological health in community-dwelling older adults in the United Kingdom. *Hunden på 2000-talet: Om hundens roll i dagens samhälle, dess medicinska och sociala betydelse*, 52–4. Spånga: Svenska Kennelklubben

Aim: One aspect of this paper was to examine whether there were any differences between dog owners, cat owners and non-pet owners on a measure of depression.

Method: A total of 94 participants (dog owners *n* = 27; cat owners *n* = 18; non-pet owners *n* = 49) completed the Hospital Anxiety and Depression Scale (Zigmond and Snaith, 1983). The questionnaire responses generated a total depression score. The higher the score, the more depressed the participant was.

Results: The following *bar-and-whisker plot* shows the median, lower quartile and upper quartile for the dog owners, cat owners and non-pet owners for total depression scores:

dog owners	LQ = 0	median = 1.5	UQ = 5
cat owners	LQ = 1	median = 2	UQ = 3.5
non-pet owners	LQ = 1	median = 2	UQ = 3.5

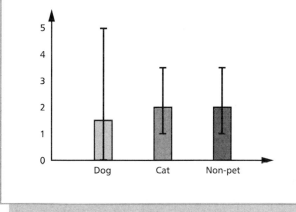

Conclusion: Overall, dog owners appear to be less depressed than cat owners and non-owners. However, there is a greater spread of scores for dog owners. Both the cat owning group and the non-pet owning group generated the same average and spread scores, indicating no difference between the two groups with respect to depression.

interactive angles

bar-and-whisker plot: it's cool for cat owners!

Roberts, C. (2000a) Pet ownership, social support and psychological health in community-dwelling older adults in the United Kingdom. *Hunden på 2000-talet: Om hundens roll i dagens samhälle, dess medicinska och sociala betydelse, 52–4.* Spånga: Svenska Kennelklubben, 52–4

Aim: One aspect of this paper was to examine whether there were any differences between dog owners, cat owners and non-pet owners on a measure of loneliness.

Method: A total of 94 participants (dog owners *n* = 27; cat owners *n* = 18; non-pet owners *n* = 49) completed the Loneliness Scale (de Jong-Gierveld and van Tilburg, 1991). The questionnaire responses generated a total loneliness score. The higher the score, the more lonely the participant was.

Results: The following results were collected:

dog owners	LQ = 0.5	median = 1	UQ = 3
cat owners	LQ = 0	median = 1	UQ = 3
non-pet owners	LQ = 1	median = 2	UQ = 6

Conclusion: Overall, cat owners and dog owners appear to be the least lonely with non-pet owners being the most lonely according to the median scores calculated. There is just a smaller spread of scores for dog owners than for cat owners. However, non-pet owners have a large spread of scores, indicating that many of that group felt lonely.

Plot the data: Plot a *bar-and-whisker plot* to show the median, lower quartile and upper quartile for the dog owners, cat owners and non-pet owners for total loneliness scores

Standard error bars

These are ideal for representing the mean and standard deviation.

research
methods

standard error bars: are alien abductees schizophrenic?

Spanos, N.P., Cross, P.A., Dockson, K. and DuBreuil, S.C. (1993) Close encounters: an examination of UFO experiences. *Journal of Abnormal Psychology*, 102 (4), 624–32

Aim: To discover if there were any psychological/personality differences between people who claim UFO encounters and those who do not.

Method: Four groups of participants were asked to complete a battery of questionnaires that assessed things such as schizophrenia, IQ, self-esteem, aggression and fantasy proneness. The UFO-intense group ($n = 31$) were those people who had reported some contact with a UFO and its occupants, the UFO non-intense ($n = 18$) were those who reported seeing a UFO in its strict definition (Unidentified Flying Object, shapes in sky or lights in sky that were not identified as anything terrestrial), the community comparison group ($n = 53$) consisted of members of the public recruited through a newspaper advertisement, and finally the student group ($n = 74$) were introductory class psychology students.

Results: The following *standard error bar* shows the results for the schizophrenia measure used by the research team.

Scores: UFO-intense, 12.1, sd = 8.0; UFO non-intense, 9.2, sd = 7.2; community, 19.3, sd = 11.6; student = 19.6, sd = 8.6.

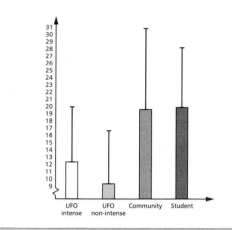

Conclusion: Rather surprisingly, the two UFO groups score much less on the schizophrenia scale, indicating that they were exhibiting much fewer schizophrenic symptoms than the community and student groups! This does not back up the idea that people claiming close encounters with 'alien spaceships' are more schizophrenic than the normal population.

inter**active**
angles

standard error bar: is there something different about UFO-seers?

Parnell, J.O. and Sprinkle, R.L. (1990) Personality characteristics of persons who claim UFO experiences. *Journal of UFO Studies*, 2, 45–58

Aim: To assess the personality of people who claimed UFO encounters and/or contact with extraterrestrial beings.

Method: The participants were given a Minnesota Multiphasic Personality Inventory (MMPI: a widely used personality profile questionnaire). Two groups were compared: those who simply claimed to have seen a UFO (non-communicators) and those who claimed interaction with extraterrestrial beings, usually aboard a spaceship (communicators).

Results: The following results were collected:

Category	Non-communicator mean	Non-communicator standard deviation	Communicator mean	Communicator standard deviation
Depression	51	11	52	10
Psychopathic deviate	61	10	63	11
Paranoia	59	10	63	13
Schizophrenia	59	11	62	13

Conclusion: There is little difference between the two groups. However, those claiming communication with alien beings score higher on the paranoia and schizophrenia measures in this research.

Plot the data: Plot a *dual standard error bars* to show the results for the depression, psychopathic deviate, paranoia and schizophrenia measures used by the research team.

Histogram

Histograms show the distribution of scores that are measured along a continuous (numerical) scale.

research methods

histogram: psychological health in older adults

Roberts, C.A., Horn, S., McBride, E.A., Bradshaw, J.W.S. and Rosenvinge, H. (1998) Pet ownership and psychological health in community-dwelling older adults. *The Changing Role of Animals in Society Abstract Book: 8th International Conference on Human–Animal Interactions*, p. 77. Prague: Ceska Republika

---

Aim: One of the aims of this research was to examine the distribution of psychological well-being in a sample of community-dwelling older adults.

Method: A total of 780 participants completed the Psychological General Well-being Scale (Dupuy, 1985). The responses generated a total score. The higher the score, the more psychologically healthy the participant was.

Results: The following *histogram* shows the distribution of total scores for the sample of 780 participants:

Total psychological well-being score	Number of participants
30–39	3
40–49	4
50–59	6
60–69	27
70–79	57
80–89	108
90–99	134
100–109	200
110–119	180
120–129	61

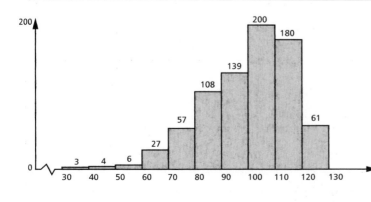

Conclusion: The peak in the histogram was at 100–109. These high scores indicate that the sample, in the main, was psychologically healthy. However, 40 participants scored below 70 total points indicating quite poor psychological health. Overall, it would appear that these community-dwelling older adults are psychologically healthy!

Scattergraph

These are ideal for representing correlations.

research methods

scattergraph: patients are bad for doctors!

Neumayer, L., McNamara, R.M., Dayton, M. and Kim, B. (1998) Does volume of patients seen in an outpatient setting impact test scores? *American Journal of Surgery*, 175 (6), 511–14

Aim: To explore whether the amount of outpatients medical students encounter affects their examination scores.

Method: Students had to log how many outpatients they saw over a period of two years. Test scores were collected from the examination database at the university.

Results: The following table shows the amount of outpatients seen and test scores from 20 medical students:

Medical student number	Number of outpatients seen	Average test scores (%)
1	6925	37
2	4752	65
3	6520	52
4	5301	77
5	4733	65
6	8003	32
7	4119	82
8	3014	81
9	5193	72
10	6448	61
11	7101	48
12	5497	76
13	4410	92
14	4002	97
15	4010	98
16	5931	85
17	4939	72
18	3692	98
19	4508	90
20	5849	81

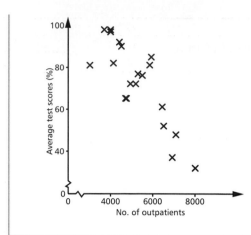

Conclusion: There was a negative correlation between test scores and the amount of outpatients seen by the students.

Frequency polygon

These are ideal for representing the distributions of two groups' data on the same graph.

research methods

frequency polygon: loneliness and pet ownership in older adults

Roberts, C.A., McBride, E.A., Rosenvinge, H.P., Stevenage, S.V. and Bradshaw, J.W.S (1996) The effect of pet ownership and social support on loneliness and depression in a population of elderly people living in their own homes. *Proceedings of Further Issues in Research in Companion Animal Studies* (J. Nicholson and A. Podberscek, eds), p. 64. Callender: SCAS

Aim: One of the aims of this research was to examine if there were any differences in loneliness between pet owners and non-pet owners.

Method: A total of 60 participants (30 pet owners and 30 non-pet owners) completed the Loneliness Scale (de Jong-Gierveld and van Tilburg, 1991). The questionnaire responses generated a total loneliness score. The higher the score, the more lonely the participant was.

Results: The following *frequency polygon* shows the distributions of pet owner's scores and non-pet owners' scores on the Loneliness Scale:

Loneliness score	Non-pet owners	Pet owners
0	5	7
1	7	9
2	3	8
3	4	1
4	3	3
5	2	1
6	0	1
7	1	0

8	1	0
9	3	0
10	1	0

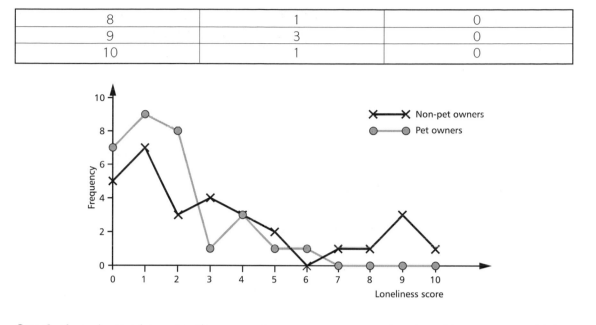

Conclusion: As can be seen, the non-pet owners were more lonely, with many more higher scores (7+ as the total score). Also, more pet owners score at the low end of the scale (0, 1 or 2 as the total score).

where to now?

▶ **Jarvis, M., Russell, J., Flanagan, C. and Dolan, L. (2000)** *Angles on Psychology*. **Cheltenham: Nelson Thornes** – a good, basic introduction to plotting data.

what do you know?

1 Distinguish between a bar chart and a histogram.

2 If you wanted to plot the distribution of scores from two groups of participants on the same graph, which type of graph would you use?

3 When would you use a scattergraph?

4 What does a standard error bar represent?

10

Non-parametric Inferential Statistics

This chapter will deal with non-parametric inferential statistical tests. These statistical tests are predominantly used on data that are nominal or ordinal. Unlike parametric statistical tests (see Chapter 11), non-parametric tests do not make assumptions about the data you have collected. A great deal of psychological data are nominal or ordinal, so these tests are useful to examine differences, associations (links between the independent variable and dependent variable) and correlations in the data you have collected.

Introduction to inferential statistics

Inferential statistics allows us to draw firmer conclusions based on our data. They are tests that attempt to show whether there is a *significant* difference, association or correlation. Descriptive statistics (see Chapter 8) compares the levels of the independent variable with a single numerical value. Inferential statistics in experiments takes the analysis a step further by *testing* whether the two data sets are distinctly different. It allows the researcher to conclude whether the independent variable is having a true effect on the dependent variable. Essentially, inferential statistics allows for a 'battle' between the alternative hypothesis and the null hypothesis where one will win and the other will lose. After executing an inferential statistical test, you will be left with an accepted hypothesis and a rejected hypothesis.

There are a variety of tests that can be used to look for a *significant* difference, association or correlation. There are five non-parametric tests that are commonly used in statistical testing: χ^2 test of association, the Mann–Whitney U-test, the Wilcoxon signed rank matched pairs test, the binomial sign test and the Spearman's rank order correlation coefficient.

Before each test is described, it will be useful to introduce concepts that are part of all tests: the concept of p-values, levels of significance, type I and II errors, observed (calculated) values and critical values.

P-value (probability value)

A p-value represents the probability of something happening by chance. P-values range from 0 to 1, with 0 representing no influence of chance and 1 representing a complete influence of chance. P-values are written as a proportion, that is, $p < 0.05$ represents a less than 5 in 100 probability that you would get these results if they were due to chance. This allows you to have confidence that your results are more likely to be due to the manipulation of your independent variable, or that your two measures are truly correlated. Therefore the closer the p-value is to 0, the less the influence of chance.

Levels of significance

The level of significance refers to the p-value we set that makes us believe the results are due to the independent variable and not due to chance, but what value should we set? We would like to be 100 per cent sure that our results are not due to chance, but in the social sciences there are many *extraneous variables* that can affect a result so this figure is impossibly high for inferential tests. Unlike the physical sciences where *more* variables are controlled, psychological research cannot do this as we are dealing with humans and each one is different! The standard usually set for a level of significance is 5 per cent, or $p \leq 0.05$. There is less than a 5 per cent probability that these results would occur if they were due to chance or other factors such as uncontrolled variables. The less likely that a particular difference has arisen due to chance, the more confident we can be about the difference, association or correlation that we have observed. We can be more stringent with the level of significance we set. For example, we could set a p-value of $p \leq 0.01$ so there is a 1 per cent probability that the results would occur if they were due to chance. On the other hand, we can be less stringent and set a p-value of $p \leq 0.1$ so there is a 10 per cent probability that the results would occur if they were due to chance. However, if we become more stringent or less stringent with the levels of significance we set, a type I or type II error may be committed.

Type I and Type II errors

If we are less stringent with our level of significance (e.g. $p \leq 0.1$ or $p \leq 0.2$) it will be less difficult to find a significant difference, association or correlation. That is, it is easier to *reject the null hypothesis* (which states that the results are due to chance) but because we are being less stringent, this rejection may be incorrect. The null hypothesis may well be correct and this is a *Type I error*. For example, if we set a level of significance of $p \le 0.1$, there is still a 10 per cent probability that the results would occur if they were due to chance, and our results may have fallen into that 10 per cent. A logical way to avoid Type I errors would be to set a more stringent level of significance, say $p \le 0.01$ or $p \le 0.001$. However, as a result of doing this we may be committing a *Type II error* where we *accept the null hypothesis* when in fact we should reject it in favour of the alternative/experimental hypothesis. For example, if we set a level of significance of $p \le 0.01$, there is a 1 per cent probability that the results would occur if they were due to chance. We may well have a significant difference, association or correlation, but because we are being too stringent, the test may not pick up on the difference and we *incorrectly accept the null hypothesis*.

Therefore, to balance the chance of committing either a Type I or a Type II error it is advised that the level of significance is set at $p \le 0.05$.

The higher significance levels are used for replications when we want to be more confident that the result is significant.

Exam tip

You can remember the difference between Type I and Type II errors by noting that Type **O**ne errors are **O**ptimistic (and Type II errors are pessimistic)!

Observed (calculated) values and critical values

Each of the inferential statistical tests essentially reduces your data down to one number called an *observed (calculated) value*. This value has to be compared to a *critical value*, which helps to conclude whether there is a *significant difference, association* or *correlation*. For some tests the observed (calculated) value has to be *greater* than the critical value to show a significant result. On other tests the observed (calculated) value has to be *less* than the critical value to indicate a significant result. For each of the five tests featured in this chapter, it will be explained why the observed (calculated) value has to be greater than or less than the critical value for a significant result.

The critical value that is compared to the observed (calculated) value is read from a critical value table (which can be found in the appendix). There is one of these for each test. The value is revealed by looking at the number of participants (called N; however, this is replaced by degrees of freedom for the χ^2 test and the parametric tests featured in Chapter 11) and whether your experimental hypothesis is directional or non-directional.

The ranking of data

In two of the tests, the Mann–Whitney U test and Spearman's rank order correlation coefficient, you must rank the data collected. That is, each data point is assigned a rank value from 1 to N where N is the total number of data points used in the analysis. The following procedure will help you to rank data:

1   Using all of the data, write down the data in numerical order from the smallest to the largest value(s). For example:

| 12 | 13 | 15 | 15 | 17 | 18 | 18 | 18 | 20 | 21 | 21 | 26 |

2   Starting with the smallest value, assign ranks (beginning with 1) to the data points as follows. This tells you if you have written down all of the data points:

12	13	15	15	17	18	18	18	20	21	21	26
1	2	3	4	5	6	7	8	9	10	11	12

3   However, this is not the end of the procedure. Note that there are some data points represented more than once (e.g. 15 is represented twice, 18 three times and 21 twice). It would not be correct for these data points to have different rank values! This is rectified by calculating the *mean* of the rank values that the data points cover. Then you assign that rank value to all the data points that are numerically the same.

For example, the two 15 data points cover the rank positions of **3** and **4**. The *mean* of these rank values is **3.5** so that is the new rank value given to *both* of the 15 data points.

The three 18 data points cover the rank positions of **6, 7** and **8**. The *mean* of these rank values is **7** so that is the new rank value given to *all* of the 18 data points.

Finally, the two 21 data points cover the rank positions of **10** and **11**. The *mean* of these rank values is **10.5** so that is the new rank value given to *both* of the 21 data points.

4   Re-write the original table with the new, correct rank values as follows:

12	13	15	15	17	18	18	18	20	21	21	26
1	2	3.5	3.5	5	7	7	7	9	10.5	10.5	12

5   Now you can use the data set correctly for the Mann–Whitney U-test and the Spearman's rank order correlation coefficient.

For each of the tests, there are certain criteria that have to be met to allow us to use the test. These criteria will be introduced with a description of each test. Also, each test will be introduced with two worked examples. Even though there are many computer programs that will calculate the observed (calculated) value, executing an inferential statistical test 'by hand using pen and paper' is gratifying. It also allows for a clearer understanding of the mechanisms of the test and why the observed (calculated) value must be greater or less than the critical value for a significant result to be obtained.

The χ^2 test of association

The criteria that have to be met if we are going to use this test are as follows:

- The dependent variable has *nominal* level of measurement.

- The design of the research is *independent groups*.

- Looking for an association between the independent variable and the dependent variable.

The basis for the χ^2 test of association involves comparing the data actually collected with a data set based on the null hypothesis. Therefore, any deviation from this will be noted to reveal a potential significant association. That is, the test will discover if there is a significant deviation from chance.

How to calculate a χ^2 test of association

The following step-by-step guide should help you calculate the observed (calculated) value for a χ^2 test:

1 From the collected data, create a *contingency table* that shows the distribution of scores across the levels of the independent variable. You will need to calculate the totals for each column and each row. For example:

Categorical data/IV	Level 1 of IV	Level 2 of IV	Total
Category A			
Category B			
Total			

2 The next step is to calculate the *expected frequencies* based on the *null hypothesis* for each cell in the contingency table. The following equation allows you to calculate these:

$$\frac{\text{Row total} \times \text{Column total}}{\text{Grand total}}$$

3 Create a table with the following column headings:

Observed (O) value	Expected (E) value	O – E	(O – E)^2	(O – E)^2/E

4 Make sure the correct O and E scores for each cell are next to each other and complete the table.

5 Complete the third column, O – E, for all rows of the table.

6 Calculate the degree of freedom necessary to read the critical value for the χ^2 test. Use the following equation:

(number of rows – 1) × (number of columns – 1)

7 If the answer to step 5 equals 1, then you must use Yate's Correction when mentioned below. If the answer is greater than 1, then there is no need to use Yate's Correction (see step 8).

8 **Using Yate's Correction:** if the degrees of freedom for the test equal 1, then you must use this correction in the fourth column of the table, using the following equation: $(|O – E| – ^1/_2)^2$. The | symbol indicates the modulus, that is, calculate ignoring the sign (making all values positive).

Not using Yate's Correction: simply calculate $(O – E)^2$.

9 Calculate the values in the final column using the equation $((O – E)^2/E)$ for each row of the table.

10 Add up the final column $((O – E)^2/E)$. This is the observed (calculated) value for the χ^2 test.

11 You now need to read off the critical value for the test. To do this you need the following information:

● the degrees of freedom;

● whether your alternative hypothesis is directional or non-directional;

● the level of significance you have set (*p*-value).

12 If the observed (calculated) value you have generated is greater than the critical value, then the result is significant and you *reject the null hypothesis* and *accept the experimental hypothesis*. If the observed (calculated) value you have generated is less than the critical value, then the result is significant and you *reject the experimental hypothesis* and *accept the null hypothesis*.

An example should clarify this from an actual research project.

research methods

χ^2: children and UFOs – what on Earth are they drawing?

Roberts, C.A., Russell, J. and Chandler, E. (in press) What do children produce when asked to draw how an alien would travel to Earth? Submitted to the *European Journal of UFO and Abduction Studies*

Aim: Children were asked to draw how they thought an alien would travel to Earth. Each drawing was classified on many criteria and it was hoped that some gender differences would be unveiled.

Method

Data collected: One particular area that was assessed looked into whether boys or girls drew more aggressive pictures. Each of the 321 pictures were rated either *friendly* (aliens smiling, greeting humans), *neutral* (simply a spacecraft, or alien not showing emotion), *moderate aggression* (some sign of armour, guns, but nothing being used against humans!) or *severe aggression* (including death of humans, guns firing, attacking humans). A total of 164 boys and 157 girls drew a picture for analysis.

Hypotheses: Experimental – there will be a significant association between sex and the aggressiveness level of UFO pictures drawn. Null – any association between sex and the aggressiveness level of UFO pictures drawn will be due to chance.

Data analysis: The data collected were *nominal* (pictures placed into one of the four categories above), the research design was *independent groups* (male or female) and the research team were looking for an association between gender and level of aggression in the pictures. The following contingency table was produced from the data collected:

Category	Male	Female	Total
Friendly	10	29	39
Neutral	98	120	218
Moderate	42	6	48
Severe	14	2	16
Total	164	157	321

A severely aggressive spaceship picture drawn in the research of Roberts *et al.* (in press)

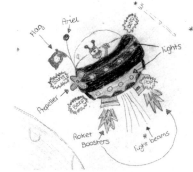

A friendly spaceship picture drawn in the research of Roberts *et al.* (in press)

Calculating the observed (calculated) value for Roberts *et al.* (in press)

1   Create a contingency table:

Category	Male	Female	Total
Friendly	10	29	39
Neutral	98	120	218
Moderate	42	6	48
Severe	14	2	16
Total	164	157	321

2   Calculate the expected frequencies:
For example, the expected frequency for the cell relating to Male–Friendly will be:

$$(39 \times 164)/321 = 19.9$$

Repeat this procedure for each cell and write it in the bottom right-hand corner of the cell it is the expected frequency for:

Category	Male		Female		Total
Friendly	10	19.9	29	19.1	39
Neutral	98	111.4	120	106.6	218
Moderate	42	24.5	6	23.5	48
Severe	14	8.2	2	7.8	16
Total	164		157		321

3   Create a table as below:

Observed (O)	Expected (E)	O – E	$(O-E)^2$	$(O-E)^2/E$
10	19.9			
98	111.4			
42	24.5			
14	8.2			
29	19.1			
120	106.6			
6	23.5			
2	7.8			

4   The observed and expected columns are completed – ensure they are in the correct rows.

5   Calculate the degrees of freedom:

$$(4-1) \times (2-1) = (3) \times (1) = 3$$

6   As the degrees of freedom is greater than 1 we do not need to use Yate's Correction.

7 The third column of the table, O – E, can now be completed.

Observed (O)	Expected (E)	O – E	$(O - E)^2$	$(O - E)^2/E$
10	19.9	−9.9		
98	111.4	−13.4		
42	24.5	17.5		
14	8.2	5.8		
29	19.1	9.9		
120	106.6	13.4		
6	23.5	−17.5		
2	7.8	−5.8		

8 The fourth column of the table can now be completed.

Observed (O)	Expected (E)	O – E	$(O - E)^2$	$(O - E)^2/E$
10	19.9	−9.9	98.01	
98	111.4	−13.4	179.56	
42	24.5	17.5	306.25	
14	8.2	5.8	33.64	
29	19.1	9.9	98.01	
120	106.6	13.4	179.56	
6	23.5	−17.5	306.25	
2	7.8	−5.8	33.64	
			Total =	

9 The final column of the table can now be calculated.

Observed (O)	Expected (E)	O – E	$(O - E)^2$	$(O - E)^2/E$
10	19.9	−9.9	98.01	4.93
98	111.4	−13.4	179.56	1.61
42	24.5	17.5	306.25	12.50
14	8.2	5.8	33.64	4.10
29	19.1	9.9	98.01	5.13
120	106.6	13.4	179.56	1.68
6	23.5	−17.5	306.25	13.03
2	7.8	−5.8	33.64	4.31
			Total =	47.29

10 Add up the numbers in the final column. In this example it equals 47.29. This is the observed (calculated) value.

11 We now need to read off the critical value using the following criteria:

- the degrees of freedom = **3**

- whether the experimental hypothesis is directional or non-directional = **non-directional**

- the level of significance set (p-value) = **0.05**

	0.2	0.1	0.05	0.02	0.01	two-tailed
d f	**0.1**	**0.05**	**0.025**	**0.01**	**0.005**	**one-tailed**
2	4.605	5.991	7.378	9.210	10.597	
3	6.251	7.815	9.348	11.345	12.838	
4	7.779	9.488	11.143	13.277	14.860	
5	9.236	11.070	12.833	15.086	16.750	

A section of the critical value table for the x^2 test of association

As can be seen, the critical value for the criteria above is **7.815**. Our observed (calculated) value is **47.29**. Therefore, the observed (calculated) value is *greater than* the critical value so we can *reject the null hypothesis* and *accept the experimental hypothesis*.

Other factors to note with the χ^2 test

If any of the *expected frequencies* are 5 or less the χ^2 test becomes invalid. To overcome this you must merge the *observed* and *expected* values for the cells that are closest in similarity. For instance, with the Roberts *et al.* example, if the expected frequency for the female–severe was less than 5 it would be most logical to merge it with female–moderate as this is the closest category. The equivalent 'male' cells must also be merged and the degrees of freedom recalculated.

If the data collected consist of only *one* row of data, for example comparing the amount of aggressive acts in four different TV programmes (and all you have recorded are the number of aggressive acts), a χ^2 *goodness of fit test* can be performed. This involves calculating expected values based on the null hypothesis again. So, for instance if 100 acts of aggressiveness were recorded, we would expect 25 in each of the four TV programmes by chance. The same procedure applies as with the χ^2, but the degrees of freedom are calculated by subtracting 1 from the number of categories present. So, in the TV example, the degrees of freedom would be $4 - 1 = 3$. Read off critical values as you would with the χ^2 test of association.

The binomial sign test

The criteria that have to be met if we are going to use this test are as follows:

- The dependent variable has *nominal* level of measurement.

- The design of the research is *repeated measures*.

- Must be looking for a difference between the effect each level of the independent variable has on the dependent variable.

The basis for the sign test is rather straightforward. It examines the number of differences that occur in one direction compared with the other direction. Therefore, if students were asked to rate two teaching methods using the descriptors: Excellent (rated 1), Very Good (rated 2), Good (rated 3), Average (rated 4) or Poor (rated 5), the test would examine whether one of the teaching methods had 'better' ratings than the other. If both teaching methods were rated about the same, then the test would pick out no significant difference. However, if in a sample of 20 students, the first teaching method was rated better on 17 occasions, then it is very unlikely that we will retain the null hypothesis. Instead of examining the magnitude of difference between the two teaching methods, the sign test merely looks at how many times one particular method is rated better than the other method.

How to calculate a sign test

The following step-by-step guide should help you calculate the observed (calculated) value for a sign test:

1   Create a table with the following column headings:

Participant no.	Score for condition A	Score for condition B	Direction of difference

2   Enter the data into the first three columns.

3   Examine the difference between *each pair* of scores. If the score for condition A is greater than that for condition B, write a plus sign (+) in the final column. If the score for condition A is less than that for condition B, write a minus sign (–) in the final column. If the scores for condition A and condition B are the same, write 'tied' in the final column (this participant's score is dropped from the analysis).

4   Count the number of + signs and the amount of – signs that occur in the final column. The one that is smaller is now called *s*. This represents the observed (calculated) value for the sign test.

5   You now need to read off the critical value for the test. To do this you need the following information:

   - the number of pairs of scores (N) – remember to only include those that have a + or – sign in the final column (therefore, the value of N may not be the same as the amount of participants in the study);

   - whether your experimental hypothesis is directional or non-directional;

   - the level of significance you have set (p-value).

6   If the observed (calculated) value you have generated is greater than the critical value, then the result is not significant and you *accept the null hypothesis* and *reject the experimental hypothesis*. If the observed (calculated) value you have generated is less than the critical value, then the result is significant and you *accept the experimental hypothesis* and *reject the null hypothesis*.

A research example should help clarify the calculation of the observed (calculated) value.

research methods

binomial sign test: bias in investigating UFOs

Roberts, C.A. (2000b) UK UFO Organisations: what do they have knowledge of and what do they investigate? *European Journal of UFO and Abduction Studies*, 1 (1), 26–32

Aim: To investigate which theory is preferred as an explanation for UFO activity in the United Kingdom by UFO groups.

Method

Data collected: UFO groups were asked to rate the knowledge they had for each of the listed theories using the following responses: **excellent knowledge (1)**, **good knowledge (2)**, **some knowledge (3)**, **poor knowledge (4)**, **heard of it but no knowledge (5)**, **never heard of it (6)**. A total of 12 groups responded.

Hypotheses: Experimental – there will be a significant difference between the ratings of knowledge given to Extraterrestrial Approach and Earthlights Approach by UFO organisations. Null – any difference between the ratings of knowledge given to Extraterrestrial Approach and Earthlights Approach by UFO organisations will be due to chance.

Data analysis: The data collected were *nominal* (each UFO group rated the theory using the categories above – it should be noted that the data could also be seen as ordinal as the categories are in rank order), the research design was *repeated measures* (the independent variable was Spacecraft or Earthlights [geological phenomenon] and each group rated both levels of the independent variable) and the research team were looking for a difference in knowledge of Spacecraft and Earthlights between the UFO groups. The following data was collected:

Group number	Extraterrestrial rating	Earthlights rating
1	3	2
2	1	3
3	1	2
4	1	2
5	6	6
6	1	1
7	1	3
8	1	2
9	1	3
10	1	1
11	1	2
12	3	2

Calculating the observed (calculated) value for Roberts (2000b)

1 Create a table as follows:

Group no.	Extraterrestrial rating	Earthlights rating	Direction of difference
1			
2			
3			
4			
5			
6			
7			
8			
9			
10			
11			
12			

2 Enter the data collected into the second and third columns.

Group no.	Extraterrestrial rating	Earthlights rating	Direction of difference
1	3	2	
2	1	3	
3	1	2	
4	1	2	
5	6	6	
6	1	1	
7	1	3	
8	1	2	
9	1	3	
10	1	1	
11	1	2	
12	3	2	

3 Complete the final column, placing a + where the first score is greater than the second score, a − where the first score is less than the second score or the word 'omit' if the first score and second score are the same.

Group no.	Extraterrestrial rating	Earthlights rating	Direction of difference
1	3	2	+
2	1	3	−
3	1	2	−
4	1	2	−
5	6	6	omit
6	1	1	omit
7	1	3	−
8	1	2	−
9	1	3	−
10	1	1	omit
11	1	2	−
12	3	2	+

4   Count the number of + and − signs represented in the final column. In this instance, + = 2; − = 7, the smaller number represents the observed (calculated) value *s*. So here it is 2.

5   We now need to read off the critical value using the following criteria:

- the number of pairs of scores used in the analysis = **9 (3 omitted)**;

- whether the experimental hypothesis is directional or non-directional = **non-directional**;

- the level of significance set (*p*-value) = **0.05**

N	Level of significance for one-tailed test				
	0.05	0.025	0.01	0.005	0.0005
	Level of significance for two-tailed test				
	0.10	0.05	0.02	0.01	0.001
8	1	0	0	0	−
9	1	1	0	0	−
10	1	1	0	0	−
11	2	1	1	0	0

A section of the critical value table for the binomial sign test

As can be seen, the critical value for the criteria above is **1**. Our observed (calculated) value is **2**. Therefore, the observed (calculated) value is *greater than* the critical value so we can *accept the null hypothesis* and *reject the experimental hypothesis*.

The Mann–Whitney *U*-test

The criteria that have to be met if we are going to use this test are as follows:

- The dependent variable has *ordinal* level of measurement.

- The design of the research is *independent groups*.

- Must be looking for a difference between the effect each level of the independent variable has on the dependent variable.

The basis for the Mann–Whitney U-test involves ranking the entire data set (irrespective of the level of independent variable) then examining how the ranks lie per level of the independent variable. To retain the null hypothesis, which would state that a difference would be due to chance, we would expect the ranks to be randomly distributed across the two levels of independent variable. However, one level may contain more of the lower ranks for instance, and the Mann–Whitney test will examine whether the distribution of ranks is random or not.

How to calculate a Mann–Whitney test

The following step-by-step guide should help you calculate the observed (calculated) value for a Mann–Whitney test:

1 Create a table with the following column headings:

Scores for condition A	Ranks for condition A	Scores for condition B	Ranks for condition B

2 Enter the data in the first and third columns.

3 Let N_1 be the number of scores in the smallest group of scores and N_2 be the number of scores in the largest group of scores.

4 Rank *all* of the scores, *irrespective of condition*, so that each score has a rank value. Begin with the smallest score obtaining a rank value of 1, the next smallest 2 and so on until all scores have a rank value.

5 Write the rank values in the appropriate place in both columns labelled 'Ranks for condition…' so that each score has its own rank value written beside it.

6 Calculate the sum of the rank values for the smaller group (N_1), calling this value R_1.

7 Place the values for N_1, N_2 and R_1 in the following equation, calling this value U:

$$U = N_1 N_2 + \frac{N_1(N_1 + 1)}{2} - R_1$$

8 Place the values of N_1, N_2 and U in the following equation, calling this value U':

$$U' = N_1 N_2 - U$$

9 Examine the value you have calculated for U and U'. Whichever is the smaller value represents the observed (calculated) value.

10 You now need to read off the critical value for the test. To do this you need the following information:

- the values for N_1 and N_2;

- whether your experimental hypothesis is directional or non-directional;

- the level of significance you have set (p-value).

11 If the observed (calculated) value you have generated is greater than the critical value, then the result is not significant and you *accept the null hypothesis* and *reject the experimental hypothesis*. If the observed (calculated) value you have generated is less than the critical value, then the result is significant and you *accept the experimental hypothesis* and *reject the null hypothesis*.

research methods

Mann–Whitney *U*-test: loneliness, older adults and the pet owner

Roberts, C.A., McBride, E.A., Rosenvinge, H.P., Stevenage, S.V. and Bradshaw, J.W.S. (1996) The pleasure of a pet: the effect of pet ownership and social support on loneliness and depression in a population of elderly people living in their own homes. *Proceedings for the Society for Companion Animal Studies workshop September 1996, University of Cambridge*, Nicholson, J. and Podberscek, A. (eds). Callender: SCAS, p.64

Aim: To examine whether older adults with pets and older adults without pets show differences in the amount of loneliness they feel.

Method
Data collected: Participants completed the Loneliness Scale (de Jong-Gierveld and van Tilburg, 1991) which is a questionnaire of 11 items. The higher the score, the more lonely the person feels. A total of 30 pet owners and 30 non-pet owners completed the scale.

Hypotheses: Experimental – there will be a significant difference between pet owners and non-owners on their subjective feelings of loneliness. Null – any difference between pet owners and non-owners on their subjective feelings of loneliness will be due to chance.

Data analysis: The data collected were *ordinal* (the data could be ranked from most lonely to least lonely but for instance, a participant scoring 8 points is *not* twice as lonely as a participant scoring 4 points), the research design was *independent groups* (pet owner or non-pet owner) and the research team were looking for a difference between the levels of loneliness reported by pet owners and non-pet owners. The following results are a portion of those collected (10 pet owners and 10 non-pet owners):

Pet owners	Non-pet owners
0	0
0	1
0	1
0	2
1	3
2	5
2	7
3	9
4	9
5	10

Calculating the observed (calculated) value for Roberts *et al.* (1996)

1 Create a table with the following headings:

Scores for pet owners	Ranks for pet owners	Scores for non-pet owners	Ranks for non-pet owners

2 Enter the data into the first and third columns (it does not matter in what order the numbers are written down):

Scores for pet owners	Ranks for pet owners	Scores for non-pet owners	Ranks for non-pet owners
0		0	
0		1	
0		1	
0		2	
1		3	
2		5	
2		7	
3		9	
4		9	
5		10	

3 Write down the number of scores in each group. So, $N_1 = 10$ and $N_2 = 10$.

4 Rank *all* of the scores. Make sure you use all of the data:

S	0	0	0	0	0	1	1	1	2	2	2	3	3	4	5	5	7	9	9	10
R	3	3	3	3	3	8	8	8	10	10	10	12.5	12.5	14	15.5	15.5	17	18.5	18.5	20

S = score; R = rank value

5 Write these rank values next to the appropriate score in the table:

Scores for pet owners	Ranks for pet owners	Scores for non-pet owners	Ranks for non-pet owners
0	3	0	3
0	3	1	8
0	3	1	8
0	3	2	10
1	8	3	12.5
2	10	5	15.5
2	10	7	17
3	12.5	9	18.5
4	14	9	18.5
5	15.5	10	20

6 As both groups are of the same size, we can choose either group to add up the ranks to become the value R_1. In this example, we will use the pet owners group. Therefore $R_1 = 82$.

7 Place the values for N_1, N_2 and R_1 into the equation below. $N_1 = 10$; $N_2 = 10$; $R_1 = 82$.

$$U = N_1 N_2 + \frac{N_1(N_1 + 1)}{2} - R_1$$

This gives a value of 73.

8 Place the values for N_1, N_2 and U into the equation below. $N_1 = 10$; $N_2 = 10$; $U = 73$.

$$U' = N_1 N_2 - U$$

This gives a value of 27.

9 Note which value (U or U') is smaller: this is the observed (calculated) value. In this example it is U' with a value of 27.

10 We now need to read off the critical value using the following criteria:

- the values for N_1 and N_2 = **$N_1 = 10$; $N_2 = 10$**
- whether the experimental hypothesis is directional or non-directional = **non-directional**
- the level of significance set (p-value) = **0.05**

	n_1											
n_2	1	2	3	4	5	6	7	8	9	10	11	12
9	–	0	2	4	7	10	12	15	17	20	23	26
10	–	0	3	5	8	11	14	17	20	23	26	29
11	–	0	3	6	9	13	16	19	23	26	30	33
12	–	1	4	7	11	14	18	22	26	29	33	37

A section of the critical value table for the Mann–Whitney U-test for two-tailed test; $p = 0.05$

As can be seen, the critical value for the criteria above is **23**. Our observed (calculated) value is **27**. Therefore, the observed (calculated) value is *greater* than the critical value so we can *accept the null hypothesis* and *reject the experimental hypothesis*.

The Wilcoxon signed ranks matched pairs test

The criteria that have to be met if we are going to use this test are as follows:

- The dependent variable has *ordinal* level of measurement.

- The design of the research is *repeated measures* or *matched pairs*.

- Must be looking for a difference between the effect each level of the independent variable has on the dependent variable.

The basis for the Wilcoxon signed rank test is rather simple. It examines the magnitude of differences between two 'scores' generated by the same participant. The test looks at how much difference there is between the scores (remember that with the sign test, differences were looked at but not the magnitude). Therefore, as with the sign test, if there is a large difference between the sets of scores for each participant in one direction (e.g. participants in condition A consistently score higher than condition B), the Wilcoxon test will detect a significant difference between the two conditions. The test investigates the differences between the two conditions by ranking the magnitude of difference between the two sets of scores and then sums the rank values for the difference that has the least frequency (either + or – depending on the results generated).

How to calculate a Wilcoxon test

The following step-by-step guide should help you calculate the observed (calculated) value for a Wilcoxon test:

1 Create a table with the following column headings:

Participant no.	Score for condition A	Score for condition B	Difference $(A - B) = d$	Rank of differences

2 Enter the data into the first three columns.

3 Calculate the difference between the score for condition A and condition B and enter it into the fourth column labelled *d*.

4 Ignoring whether the difference is + or – rank the numbers in the fourth column (*d*), with the smallest difference given the rank value of 1 and so on. If the difference is 0, then this participant's data is ignored for this test (as with the sign test).

5. Enter the ranks into the appropriate row in the table (in the final column).

6. Add together the ranked differences values for the participants with the least frequent sign (+ or –). This value is the observed (calculated) value for the Wilcoxon test and is given the letter T.

7. You now need to read off the critical value for the test. To do this you need the following information:

   - the number of pairs of scores used in the analysis (remember to ignore those scores where the difference, d, was 0);

   - whether your experimental hypothesis is directional or non-directional;

   - the level of significance you have set (p-value).

8. If the observed (calculated) value you have generated is greater than the critical value, then the result is not significant and you *accept the null hypothesis* and *reject the experimental hypothesis*. If the observed (calculated) value you have generated is less than the critical value, then the result is significant and you *accept the experimental hypothesis* and *reject the null hypothesis*.

research methods

Wilcoxon test: does alcohol consumption make you want more and more?

Kirk, J.M. and de Wit, H. (2000) Individual differences in the priming effect of ethanol in social drinkers. *Journal for the Study of Alcohol*, 61 (1), 64–71

Aim: It is known that alcohol-dependent people report an increased desire for alcohol after a single drink. However, in non-problem social drinkers (those not classified as alcoholic), this trend is not consistently found.

Method
Data collected: Participants were asked to rate how much they wanted more alcohol after two drinks: one contained 0.2 g of alcohol per kilogram weight of the participant (low-alcohol drink), the other contained 0.8 g of alcohol per kilogram weight of the participant (high-alcohol drink).

Hypotheses: Experimental – there will be a difference in the rating for how much people will like another drink after consuming a low-alcohol drink compared with a high-alcohol drink. Null – any difference in the rating for how much people will like another drink after consuming a low-alcohol drink compared to a high-alcohol drink will be due to chance.

Data analysis: The data collected were *ordinal* (participants had to rate themselves out of 20 as to how much they desired another drink – the higher the score, the more the desire), the design was *repeated measures* (participants took part on both conditions: the low-alcohol and high-alcohol conditions) and the researchers were looking for a difference in the desire for more alcohol after drinking low- and high-alcohol drinks.

The following table presents fictitious results for this piece of research:

Participant no.	Low-alcohol desire score	High-alcohol desire score
1	3	15
2	12	11
3	2	8
4	7	7
5	3	18
6	12	20
7	14	10
8	0	4
9	5	15
10	2	7
11	12	8
12	3	6

Do you feel like more alcohol after you have drunk one alcoholic drink?

Calculating the observed (calculated) values for Kirk and de Wit (2000)

1. Create a table with the following column headings:

Participant no.	Low-alcohol desire score (A)	High-alcohol desire score (B)	Difference $(A - B) = d$	Ranked difference

2. Enter the collected data into the second and third columns:

Participant no.	Low-alcohol desire score (A)	High-alcohol desire score (B)	Difference (A – B) = d	Ranked difference
1	3	15		
2	12	11		
3	2	8		
4	7	7		
5	3	18		
6	12	20		
7	14	10		
8	0	4		
9	5	15		
10	2	7		
11	12	8		
12	3	6		

3 Calculate the difference between the score for condition A (low alcohol) and condition B (high alcohol) and enter the figure into the fourth column labelled d.

Participant no.	Low-alcohol desire score (A)	High-alcohol desire score (B)	Difference (A – B) = d	Ranked difference
1	3	15	−12	
2	12	11	1	
3	2	8	−6	
4	7	7	0	
5	3	18	−15	
6	12	20	−8	
7	14	10	4	
8	0	4	−4	
9	5	15	−10	
10	2	7	−5	
11	12	8	4	
12	3	6	−3	

4 Ignoring whether the difference is + or − rank the numbers in the fourth column (d) with the smallest difference given the rank value of 1 and so on. If the difference is 0, ignore this score and it is omitted from further analysis.

d	0	1	3	4	4	4	5	6	8	10	12	15
rank	X	1	2	4	4	4	6	7	8	9	10	11

5 Enter the ranks into the appropriate row in the table (the final column):

Participant no.	Low-alcohol desire score (A)	High-alcohol desire score (B)	Difference (A – B) = d	Ranked difference
1	3	15	−12	10
2	12	11	1	1
3	2	8	−6	7
4	7	7	0	omitted
5	3	18	−15	11
6	12	20	−8	8
7	14	10	4	4
8	0	4	−4	4
9	5	15	−10	9
10	2	7	−5	6
11	12	8	4	4
12	3	6	−3	2

6   Add together the rank differences values (d) for the participants with the least frequent sign (+ or −). This value is the observed (calculated) value for the Wilcoxon test and is given the letter T. Least frequent sign is +.

Sum of ranks for the $+d$ values: $1 + 4 + 4 = 9$ (this is the T value)

7   We now need to read off the critical value using the following criteria:

- the number of pairs of scores used in the analysis = **11 (1 omitted)**
- whether the experimental hypothesis is directional or non-directional = **non-directional**
- the level of significance set (p-value) = **0.05**

	Level of significance for one-tailed test			
	0.05	0.025	0.01	0.005
	Level of significance for two-tailed test			
N	0.10	0.05	0.02	0.01
10	11	8	5	3
11	14	11	7	5
12	17	14	10	7
13	21	17	13	10

A section of the critical value table for the Wilcoxon signed rank matched pairs test

As can be seen, the critical value for the criteria above is **11**. Our observed (calculated) value is **9**. Therefore, the observed (calculated) value is *less than* the critical value so we can *reject the null hypothesis* and *accept the experimental hypothesis*.

Spearman's rank order correlation coefficient

The criteria that have to be met if we are going to use this test are as follows:

- The measured variables have *ordinal* level of measurement.

- The design of the research is *a correlation*.

- Looking for a relationship between the two measured variables.

The basis for the Spearman rank order correlation coefficient is initially to rank order each variable separately. Then, the ranks for both of the variables are compared to see if there are any distinct similarities or differences. If the rank orders are very similar then a positive correlation is expected. If the rank orders appear to be randomly distributed and there are large differences in rank per participant's scores, then no correlation is expected. Finally, if the rank orders appear to be a mirror image of one another, then a negative correlation is expected. This expectation can be backed up by plotting a scattergraph (see page 107).

How to calculate a Spearman rank order correlation coefficient

The following step-by-step guide should help you calculate the observed (calculated) value for a Spearman rank order correlation coefficient:

1 Create a table with the following column headings:

Participant no.	First measure	Second measure	Rank of first measure (A)	Rank of second measure (B)	(A – B) = d	d^2

2 Enter the data into the first three columns.

3 Plot a scattergraph to see if there appears to be a correlation.

4 Rank the scores for the first measure *only*. Enter these rank values into the fourth column of the table.

5 Rank the scores for the second measure *only*. Enter these rank values into the fifth column of the table.

6 Calculate the difference between the first measure rank value and the second measure rank value. Enter this into the sixth column of the table with the column heading d.

7 Square each of the values on the d column and enter them in the appropriate row of the final column.

8 Add up all of the d^2 values in the final column. The total is then called Σd^2.

9 Substitute the values into the following equation (remember, unlike the sign or Wilcoxon test, tied values are included so N = the number of participants). This is the observed (calculated) value for the Spearman's rank order correlation coefficient and is given the term *rho*, r_s.

$$r_s = 1 - \frac{6 \Sigma\, d^2}{N(N^2 - 1)}$$

10 You now need to read off the critical value for the test. To do this you need the following information:

- the number of participants (N);
- whether your experimental hypothesis is directional or non-directional;
- the level of significance you have set (p-value).

11 If the observed (calculated) value you have generated is greater than the critical value, then the result is significant and you *reject the null hypothesis* and *accept the experimental hypothesis*. If the observed (calculated) value you have generated is less than the critical value, then the result is significant and you *reject the experimental hypothesis* and *accept the null hypothesis*.

research
methods

Spearman's rank order correlation coefficient: a link between amount of social support and depression?

Roberts, C.A., McBride, E.A., Rosenvinge, H.P., Stevenage, S.V. and Bradshaw, J.W.S. (1996) The pleasure of a pet: the effect of pet ownership and social support on loneliness and depression in a population of elderly people living in their own homes. *Proceedings for the Society for Companion Animal Studies workshop September 1996, University of Cambridge*, J.Nicholson and A.Podberscek (eds). Callender: SCAS, p. 64

Aim: To examine if there was a correlation between the level of social support in older adults and levels of depression. Previous research and theory had suggested that the more social support a person has, the less depressed they are. That is, there should be a *negative correlation* between social support and depression.

Method
Data collected: Participants completed a social support scale designed by the authors and the Geriatric Depression Scale. The social support generated a score that indicated how extensive the participant's social support was. A high score indicated a good network and a low score indicated a poor network. The Geriatric Depression Scale is a 30-item scale. The total score was calculated by examining the proportion of 'yes' answers (showing depression) to the total number of questions answered (many participants did not answer all 30 items). A low score indicated

little depression and a high score indicated more depression. Therefore, given the aim we would expect that if a person scores *low* on the social support score they will also score *high* on the depression scale. This would point towards a *negative correlation* as a poor network (low score) should be correlated with more depression (high score).

Hypotheses: Experimental – there will be a negative correlation between the amount of social support a person has and how depressed they feel. Null – any correlation between the amount of social support a person has and how depressed they feel will be due to chance.

Data analysis: The data collected were *ordinal* (the data could be ranked for each measure) and the research team was looking for a correlation. The following data are a portion of what was collected (12 pet owners and 12 non-pet owners):

Social support score	Depression score
45	0.00
15	0.03
24	0.10
6	0.40
41	0.23
24	0.15
17	0.27
15	0.03
17	0.30
12	0.30
11	0.23
9	0.74

Calculating the observed (calculated) value for Roberts *et al.* (1996)

1.   Create a table as follows:

Participant no.	First measure	Second measure	Rank of first measure (A)	Rank of second measure (B)	(A – B) = d	d^2
1						
2						
3						
4						
5						
6						
7						
8						
9						
10						
11						
12						

2 Enter the collected data into the second and third columns of the table, ensuring that each participant's scores are placed in the correct row.

Participant no.	First measure	Second measure	Rank of first measure (A)	Rank of second measure (B)	(A – B) = d	d^2
1	45	0.00				
2	15	0.03				
3	24	0.10				
4	6	0.40				
5	41	0.23				
6	24	0.15				
7	17	0.27				
8	15	0.03				
9	17	0.30				
10	12	0.30				
11	11	0.23				
12	9	0.74				

3 Plot a scattergraph of the data to give an idea of the type of correlation expected.

4 Rank the scores for the first measure (second column of the table) and then insert them into the fourth column of the table ensuring the correct rank is placed in the correct row.

Score	6	9	11	12	15	15	17	17	24	24	41	45
Rank	1	2	3	4	5.5	5.5	7.5	7.5	9.5	9.5	11	12

Participant no.	First measure	Second measure	Rank of first measure (A)	Rank of second measure (B)	(A – B) = d	d^2
1	45	0.00	12			
2	15	0.03	5.5			
3	24	0.10	9.5			
4	6	0.40	1			
5	41	0.23	11			
6	24	0.15	9.5			
7	17	0.27	7.5			
8	15	0.03	5.5			
9	17	0.30	7.5			
10	12	0.30	4			
11	11	0.23	3			
12	9	0.74	2			

5 Rank the scores for the second measure (third column of the table) and then insert them into the fifth column of the table ensuring the correct rank is placed in the correct row.

Score	0.00	0.03	0.03	0.10	0.15	0.23	0.23	0.27	0.30	0.30	0.40	0.74
Rank	1	2.5	2.5	4	5	6.5	6.5	8	9.5	9.5	11	12

Participant no.	First measure	Second measure	Rank of first measure (A)	Rank of second measure (B)	(A – B) = d	d^2
1	45	0.00	12	1		
2	15	0.03	5.5	2.5		
3	24	0.10	9.5	4		
4	6	0.40	1	11		
5	41	0.23	11	6.5		
6	24	0.15	9.5	5		
7	17	0.27	7.5	8		
8	15	0.03	5.5	2.5		
9	17	0.30	7.5	9.5		
10	12	0.30	4	9.5		
11	11	0.23	3	6.5		
12	9	0.74	2	12		

6 Calculate the difference between the A and B rank (remember to be consistent with the subtraction).

Participant no.	First measure	Second measure	Rank of first measure (A)	Rank of second measure (B)	(A – B) = d	d^2
1	45	0.00	12	1	11	
2	15	0.03	5.5	2.5	3	
3	24	0.10	9.5	4	5.5	
4	6	0.40	1	11	–10	
5	41	0.23	11	6.5	4.5	
6	24	0.15	9.5	5	4.5	
7	17	0.27	7.5	8	–0.5	
8	15	0.03	5.5	2.5	3	
9	17	0.30	7.5	9.5	–0.2	
10	12	0.30	4	9.5	–5.5	
11	11	0.23	3	6.5	–3.5	
12	9	0.74	2	12	–10	

7 Square each of the values on the d column and write the values into the final column of the table.

Participant no.	First measure	Second measure	Rank of first measure (A)	Rank of second measure (B)	(A − B) = d	d^2
1	45	0.00	12	1	11	121
2	15	0.03	5.5	2.5	3	9
3	24	0.10	9.5	4	5.5	30.25
4	6	0.40	1	11	−10	100
5	41	0.23	11	6.5	4.5	20.25
6	24	0.15	9.5	5	4.5	20.25
7	17	0.27	7.5	8	−0.5	0.25
8	15	0.03	5.5	2.5	3	9
9	17	0.30	7.5	9.5	−2	4
10	12	0.30	4	9.5	−5.5	30.25
11	11	0.23	3	6.5	−3.5	12.25
12	9	0.74	2	12	−10	100

8   Add up all of the numbers in the final column to give a value for Σd^2. In this example, $\Sigma d^2 = 456.5$

9   Substitute the values for Σd^2, N and N^2 into the following equation. The values on this example are $\Sigma d^2 = 456.5$, $N = 12$; $N^2 = 144$. This gives the observed (calculated) value.

$$r_s = 1 - \frac{6\,\Sigma\,d^2}{N(N^2 - 1)}$$

This gives a r_s value of −0.60.

10   You now need to read off the critical value for the test. To do this you need the following information:

● the number of participants (N) **= 12**

● whether your experimental hypothesis is directional or non-directional   **= directional**

● the level of significance you have set (*p*-value) **= 0.05**

N	Level of significance for one-tailed test				
	0.1	0.05	0.025	0.01	0.005
	Level of significance for two-tailed test				
	0.2	0.1	0.05	0.02	0.01
11	0.4182	0.5273	0.6091	0.7000	0.7545
12	0.3986	0.5035	0.5874	0.6713	0.7273
13	0.3791	0.4780	0.5604	0.6484	0.6978
14	0.3670	0.4593	0.5385	0.6220	0.6747

A section of the critical value table for the Spearman's rank order correlation coefficient test

As can be seen, the critical value for the criteria above is **0.5035**. Our observed (calculated) value is **–0.60**. Therefore, the observed (calculated) value is *greater than* the critical value so we can *reject the null hypothesis* and *accept the experimental hypothesis*.

It should be noted that the Spearman's rank order correlation coefficient does not look for the strength of a *linear relationship* but looks for patterns in data. Below are three different types of correlation that would achieve an $r = +1.0$.

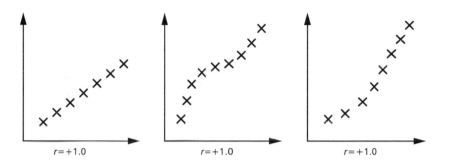

Revision aid for choice of inferential statistics test

The following table should help you to learn when to use each of the tests described in this chapter and under what criteria significant results are achieved.

Research design	Level of data		
	Independent groups	Repeated measures/ matched pairs	Correlation
Nominal	χ^2 test for association	Binomial sign test	X
Ordinal/interval	Mann–Whitney U-test	Wilcoxon test	Spearman's rank order correlation coefficient

To see if the result of the test is significant, for the tests above in a white cell the observed (calculated) value has to be greater than or equal to the critical value. For the tests in the grey cells above, a significant result is attained if the observed (calculated) value is less than the critical value (note how the grey cells make a backward 'L' shape for **L**ess than).

where to now?

▶ **Miller, S. (1984)** *Experimental Design and Statistics.* **London: Routledge** – still one of *the* best statistics books on the market. Clear coverage of all the tests mentioned in the text with worked examples. Plus, it is an easy read for students and teachers!

▶ **Dyer, C. (1995)** *Beginning Research in Psychology.* **Oxford: Blackwell** – good use of worked examples to show how each test works. Student-friendly too

▶ **Greene, J. and D'Oliveira, M. (1999)** *Learning to Use Statistical Tests in Psychology.* **Buckingham: Open University Press** – again, good worked examples, and for the student who wishes to be pushed further there are some great exercises to complete.

what do you know?

1 Describe what is meant by the term *p*-value.

2 Under what conditions would you use a Mann–Whitney *U* test on your data?

3 How would you know if a χ^2 test of association had produced a significant result?

4 What is meant by the terms observed (calculated) values and critical values?

11

Parametric Inferential Statistics

what's
ahead ?

This chapter examines parametric statistical tests. These tests hold certain assumptions about the data under analysis. There are three parametric tests that you need to know about: the *independent t-test*, the *related t-test* and *Pearson's product moment correlation coefficient*.

Introduction to parametric tests

Parametric tests differ from non-parametric tests in the following ways:

- The data are assumed to be *normally distributed* for the population(s) used in the research from which you have drawn your sample.

- The data for both levels of the independent variable have equal variance (the variance is the standard deviation squared – see Chapter 8), or both measured variables have equal variance.

- The data are either interval or ratio (see Chapter 8).

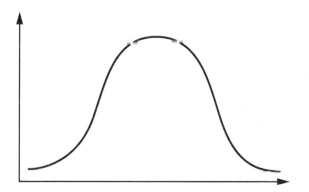

A normal distribution curve

The independent *t*-test

The criteria that have to be met if we are going to use this test are as follows:

- The dependent variable has *interval* or *ratio* level of measurement.

- The design of the research is *independent groups*.

- Must be looking for a difference between the effect each level of the independent variable has on the dependent variable.

- The data are from normally distributed populations.

- The populations for each level of the independent variable have equal variances.

The basis for the *t*-test is as follows. The formula converts the mean and variance of each level of the independent variable into a measure of deviation. Essentially, the test examines the mean and variance of each level of the independent variable to see if there is a large enough difference between them to reach significance. In this respect, the *t*-test is seen as being more robust as it examines the mean *and* the variation in scores to find the observed (calculated) value.

How to calculate an independent *t*-test

The following step-by-step guide should help you to work out the observed (calculated) value for an independent *t*-test:

1 Create a table using the following headings:

Scores for condition 1 (A)	A^2	Scores for condition 2 (B)	B^2

2 Complete the first and third columns of the table by writing in all of the scores for each condition.

3 Complete the second and fourth columns of the table by squaring each of the numbers in turn that you have written in step 2.

4 Write down the number of scores for each condition and call these N_A and N_B.

5 Calculate the mean score for each condition using the following formula:

$$\bar{x}_A = \frac{\Sigma A}{N} \; ; \; \bar{x}_B = \frac{\Sigma B}{N}$$

6 Calculate the variance for each condition using the following formula:

$$S_A^2 = \frac{\Sigma A^2}{N} - \bar{x}_A^2 \; ; \; S_B^2 = \frac{\Sigma B^2}{N} - \bar{x}_B^2$$

7 Write down the values for each of the following:

$$\bar{x}_A = \qquad N_A = \qquad S_A^2 =$$
$$\bar{x}_B = \qquad N_B = \qquad S_B^2 =$$

8 Insert the values written in step 7 into the following equation for the t-test (if N_A and N_B are the same number, use the easier looking equation). This is the observed (calculated) value.

$$t = \frac{(\bar{x}_A - \bar{x}_B)\sqrt{(N_A + N_B - 2)N_A N_B}}{(N_A S_A^2 + N_B S_B^2)(N_A + N_B)} \quad ; \quad t = \frac{(\bar{x}_A - x_B)}{\sqrt{\dfrac{S_A^2 + S_B^2}{N}}}$$

9 You now need to read off the critical value for the test. To do this you need the following information:

- the degrees of freedom (using the equation $N_A + N_B - 2$);
- whether your experimental hypothesis is directional or non-directional;
- the level of significance you have set (p-value).

10 If the observed (calculated) value you have generated is greater than or equal to the critical value, then the result is significant and you *reject the null hypothesis* and *accept the experimental hypothesis*. If the observed (calculated) value you have generated is less than the critical value, then the result is significant and you *reject the experimental hypothesis* and *accept the null hypothesis*.

research methods

independent *t*-test: does a cardiac arrest reduce memory?

Grubb, N.R., Fox, K.A., Smith, K., Blane, A., Ebmeier, K.P., Glabus, M.F. and O'Carroll, R.E. (2000) Memory impairment in out-of-hospital cardiac arrest survivors is associated with global reduction in brain volume, not focal hippocampal injury.
Stroke, 31 (7), 1509–14

Aim: To examine whether people who have experienced a cardiac arrest have memory impairment. A region of the brain called the hippocampus (which is linked to memory) could by affected during a cardiac arrest.

Method
Data collected: Twelve people who had experienced a cardiac arrest and 12 control participants with no heart condition had their amygdala-hippocampal volume in the brain measured.

Hypotheses: Experimental – there will be a significant difference in amygdala-hippocampal volume in cardiac arrest victims compared to those with no heart condition. Null – any difference between the amygdala-hippocampal volume in cardiac arrest victims compared to those with no heart condition will be due to chance.

Data analysis: The data collected were *ratio* (measures of the amygdala-hippocampal volume in centimetre cubed), the research was *independent groups* (cardiac arrest victim or not) and the research team were looking for a difference between the amygdala-hippocampal volume of cardiac arrest victims and those with no heart condition.

The following table of results shows the amygdala-hippocampal volume (in cm²) for 10 participants in each group:

Cardiac arrest group	No heart problem group
3.65	4.65
4.02	4.78
3.93	3.88
3.99	4.52
4.25	4.66
4.99	4.78
4.25	4.21
4.32	4.02
3.95	4.66
4.00	4.82

Calculating the observed (calculated) value for Grubb *et al.* (2000)

1   Create a table with the following headings:

Cardiac arrest group (A)	A^2	No heart problem group (B)	B^2

2   Complete the first and third columns by writing in the scores for each condition.

Cardiac arrest group (A)	A^2	No heart problem group (B)	B^2
3.65		4.65	
4.02		4.78	
3.93		3.88	
3.99		4.52	
4.25		4.66	
4.99		4.78	
4.25		4.21	
4.32		4.02	
3.95		4.66	
4.00		4.82	

3   Complete the second and fourth columns of the table by squaring each of the numbers in turn (to 2 decimal places as the data that have been collected are to 2 decimal places).

Cardiac arrest group (A)	A^2	No heart problem group (B)	B^2
3.65	13.32	4.65	21.62
4.02	16.16	4.78	22.84
3.93	15.44	3.88	15.05
3.99	15.92	4.52	20.43
4.25	18.06	4.66	21.72
4.99	24.90	4.78	22.84
4.25	18.06	4.21	17.72
4.32	18.66	4.02	16.16
3.95	15.60	4.66	21.72
4.00	16.00	4.82	23.23

4   Write down the number of scores for each condition and call these N_A and N_B.

$$N_A = 10$$
$$N_B = 10$$

5   Calculate the mean score for each condition using the formula below:

$$\bar{x}_A = \frac{\Sigma A}{N} \; ; \; \bar{x}_B = \frac{\Sigma B}{N}$$

Mean for condition A = 4.14 cm^2 (this is $\bar{x}_A$)
Mean for condition B = 4.50 cm^2 (this is $\bar{x}_B$)

6   Calculate the variance for each condition using the formula below:

$$S_A^2 = \frac{\Sigma A^2}{N} - \bar{x}_A^2 \; ; \; S_B^2 = \frac{\Sigma B^2}{N} - \bar{x}_B^2$$

Variance for condition A = 0.07 cm^2 (this is S_A^2)

Variance for condition B = 0.08 cm^2 (this is S_B^2)

7   Write down the values for each of the following:

$$N_A = 10$$
$$N_B = 10$$
$$\bar{x}_A = 4.14$$
$$\bar{x}_B = 4.50$$
$$S_A^2 = 0.07$$
$$S_B^2 = 0.08$$

8 Insert the values written in step 7 into the following equation (as the values of N_A and N_B, we use the simpler version of the *t*-test equations in this example). This is the observed (calculated) value.

$$t = \frac{(\bar{x}_A - \bar{x}_B)}{\sqrt{\dfrac{S_A^2 + S_B^2}{N}}} \qquad t \text{ value} = -2.94$$

9 We now need to read off the critical value using the following criteria:

- the degrees of freedom (using the equation $N_A + N_B - 2$) = **18**

- whether the experimental hypothesis is directional or non-directional = **non-directional**

- the level of significance set (*p*-value) = **0.05**

| df | Level of significance for one-tailed test | | | | |
	0.1	0.05	0.025	0.01	0.005
	Level of significance for two-tailed test				
	0.2	0.1	0.05	0.02	0.01
17	1.333	1.740	2.110	2.567	2.898
18	1.330	1.734	2.101	2.552	2.878
19	1.328	1.729	2.093	2.539	2.861
20	1.325	1.725	2.086	2.528	2.845

A section of the critical value table for the independent *t*-test

As can be seen, the critical value for the criteria above is **2.101**. Our observed (calculated) value is **−2.94** (the minus sign indicates that condition B, the no heart problem group, scored higher on the amygdala-hippocampal volume). Therefore, the observed (calculated) value is *greater than* the critical value so we can *reject the null hypothesis* and *accept the experimental hypothesis*.

The related *t*-test

The criteria that have to be met if we are going to use this test are as follows:

- The dependent variable has *interval* or *ratio* level of measurement.

- The design of the research is *repeated measures*.

- Must be looking for a difference between the effect each level of the independent variable has on the dependent variable.

- The data are from normally distributed populations.

- The populations for each level of the independent variable have equal variances.

The basis for the related *t*-test involves the examination of the *magnitude* of differences between the two sets of scores (remember that the sign test and Wilcoxon test do not look at the amount of difference between the scores, only the *direction* of difference). The related *t*-test examines the *mean* difference in scores and also examines the deviation all scores have from this.

How to calculate a related *t*-test

The following step-by-step guide should help you work out the observed (calculated) value for a related *t*-test:

1 Create a table with the following headings:

Participant no.	Score for condition A	Score for condition B	Differences $(A - B = d^2)$	d^2

2 Complete the first three columns of the table, making sure that each participant has the correct scores for condition A and condition B.

3 Complete the fourth column by using the formula A − B where A is the score for condition A and B is the score for condition B. Remember to write down whether the score is positive or negative.

4 Complete the final column of the table by squaring each of the numbers in the fourth column, making sure you write it in the correct row.

5 Calculate the mean for the fourth column. This is calculated by adding all the scores in the fourth column and dividing the total by the number of scores (the equation is below). Make sure you take account of the minus signs (you can have a minus figure for this mean).

6 Add up all of the scores in the final column. Call this number Σd^2.

7 Calculate the standard deviation for the differences between the scores by using the following formula (call this value sd):

$$sd = \sqrt{\frac{\Sigma d^2}{N} - \bar{d}^2}$$

8 Write down the numbers that correspond with the following (mean of *d*; standard deviation (sd) of *d*; N):

$$\bar{d} =$$
$$sd =$$
$$N =$$

9 Substitute the values you have written down in step 8 in the following equation. This is the observed (calculated) value.

$$t = \frac{\bar{d}}{sd/\sqrt{N-1}}$$

10 You now need to read off the critical value for the test. To do this you need the following information:

- the degrees of freedom (using the equation $N - 1$);

- whether your experimental hypothesis is directional or non-directional;

- the level of significance you have set (*p*-value).

11 If the observed (calculated) value you have generated is greater than or equal to the critical value, then the result is significant and you *reject the null hypothesis* and *accept the experimental hypothesis*. If the observed (calculated) value you have generated is less than the critical value, then the result is significant and you *reject the experimental hypothesis* and *accept the null hypothesis*.

research methods

related *t*-test: depression in Alzheimer sufferers – does a drug alleviate the depression?

Magai, C., Kennedy, G., Cohen, C.I. and Gomberg, D. (2000) A controlled clinical trial of sertraline in the treatment of depression in nursing home patients with late-stage Alzheimer's disease. *American Journal of Geriatric Psychiatry*, 8 (1), 66–74

Aim: To assess whether an antidepressant drug (sertraline) alleviated depression in late-stage Alzheimer's disease sufferers.

Method
Data collected: Facial expressions of happiness were coded by the research team (e.g. smiling, laughing, grinning) to increase reliability. This formed the score each patient received. A total of 12 patients took part in the drug trial. All patients were rated after taking the drug and also when a placebo was taken.

Hypotheses: Experimental – there will be a significant difference in the facial expressions of happiness in Alzheimer's sufferers who take the drug sertraline compared with those who take a placebo. Null – any difference in the facial expressions of happiness in Alzheimer's sufferers who take the drug sertraline compared with those who take a placebo will be due to chance.

Data analysis: The data collected were *interval* (the number of facial expressions recorded), the research design was *repeated measures* (each patient was rated after taking the drug and the placebo) and the research team was looking for a difference in the number of facial expressions of happiness between when the patient had taken the drug and when they had taken a placebo.

The following table of results shows the facial expressions of happiness recorded for drug and no-drug observations.

Participant no.	Drug condition (A)	Placebo condition (B)
1	8	6
2	4	2
3	5	5
4	3	5
5	7	2
6	8	6
7	3	5
8	4	8
9	5	3
10	6	7
11	2	1
12	0	3

Calculating the observed (calculated) value for Magai *et al.* (2000)

1 Create a table as follows:

Participant no.	Drug condition (A)	Placebo condition (B)	Differences $(A - B - d)$	d^2
1				
2				
3				
4				
5				
6				
7				
8				
9				
10				
11				
12				

2 Complete the second and third columns of the table making sure the drug condition and placebo condition have the correct scores in them:

Participant no.	Drug condition (A)	Placebo condition (B)	Differences (A − B = d)	d^2
1	8	6		
2	4	2		
3	5	5		
4	3	5		
5	7	2		
6	8	6		
7	3	5		
8	4	8		
9	5	3		
10	6	7		
11	2	1		
12	0	3		

3 Complete the fourth column by using the formula A − B where A is the score for the drug condition (A) and B is the score for the placebo condition (B). Remember to write down if the score is positive or negative.

Participant no.	Drug condition	Placebo condition	Differences (A − B = d)	d^2
1	8	6	2	
2	4	2	2	
3	5	5	0	
4	3	5	−2	
5	7	2	5	
6	8	6	2	
7	3	5	−2	
8	4	8	−4	
9	5	3	2	
10	6	7	−1	
11	2	1	1	
12	0	3	−3	

4 Complete the final column of the table by squaring each of the values you calculated in step 3.

Participant no.	Drug condition	Placebo condition	Differences (A − B = d)	d^2
1	8	6	2	4
2	4	2	2	4
3	5	5	0	0
4	3	5	−2	4
5	7	2	5	25
6	8	6	2	4
7	3	5	−2	4

8	4	8	−4	16
9	5	3	2	4
10	6	7	−1	1
11	2	1	1	1
12	0	3	−3	9

5 Calculate the mean for the fourth column. Add up all of the scores and then divide by the number of scores in the column.

$$\text{The mean of } d = 0.2$$

6 Add up all of the scores in the final column (Σd^2):

$$\Sigma d^2 = 76$$

7 Calculate the standard deviation of the scores in the fourth column using the equation below. Call this value sd.

$$sd = \sqrt{\frac{\Sigma d^2}{N} - \bar{d}^2}$$

$$sd = 2.75$$

8 Write down the values for the following:

$$\text{Mean of } d \ (\bar{d}) = 0.2$$
$$sd = 2.75$$
$$N = 12$$

9 Substitute the values you have written down in step 8 into the following equation. This is the observed (calculated) value.

$$t = \frac{\bar{d}}{sd/\sqrt{N-1}}$$

$$t \text{ value} = 0.24$$

10. We now need to read off the critical value using the following criteria:

- the degrees of freedom (using the equation $N - 1$) = **11**

- whether the experimental hypothesis is directional or non-directional = **non-directional**

- the level of significance set (p-value) = **0.05**

df	Level of significance for one-tailed test				
	0.1	0.05	0.025	0.01	0.005
	Level of significance for two-tailed test				
	0.2	0.1	0.05	0.02	0.01
10	1.372	1.812	2.228	2.764	3.169
11	1.363	1.796	2.201	2.718	3.106
12	1.356	1.782	2.179	2.681	3.055
13	1.350	1.771	2.160	2.650	3.012

A section of the critical value table for the related t-test

As can be seen, the critical value for the criteria above is **2.201**. Our observed (calculated) value is **0.24**. Therefore, the observed (calculated) value is *less than* the critical value so we can *reject the experimental hypothesis* and *accept the null hypothesis*.

Pearson's product moment correlation coefficient

The criteria that have to be met if we are going to use this test are as follows:

- The dependent variable has *interval* or *ratio* level of measurement.

- The design of the research is *correlational.*

- Must be looking for a *linear relationship* between each of the variables that have been measured.

- The data are from normally distributed populations.

- The populations for each measured variable have equal variances.

The basis for the Pearson's product moment correlation coefficient is straightforward. The scores generated are compared to an imaginary line that 'exists' in the centre of all the scores (a line of best fit). Therefore, the test measures the amount of spread around the line and reports the deviation. If no deviation occurs then we are left with an r value of 1 (r values are interpreted in the same way as the Spearman's rho value – see page 166). A small deviation could result in an r value of $+0.8$ or -0.8 while a large deviation could result in an r value of $+0.2$ or -0.2. As with the Spearman test, the higher the value, the stronger the correlation. The Pearson's test examines whether there is a *linear relationship* between the two measured variables.

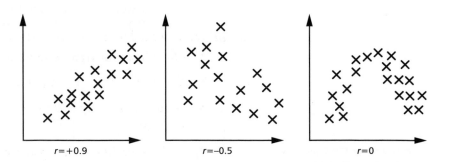

$r = +0.9$ $r = -0.5$ $r = 0$

How to calculate a Pearson's product moment correlation coefficient

The following step-by-step guide should help you calculate the observed (calculated) value for a Pearson's product moment correlation coefficient:

1 Create a table with the following headings:

Participant no.	Score for first measure (X)	Score for second measure (Y)	XY	X^2	Y^2

2 Complete the first three columns of the table making sure that each participant has the correct scores for score X and score Y.

3 Add up the scores for each of the measures. Call these ΣX and ΣY.

4 Plot a scattergraph to examine the correlation.

5 Complete the fourth column of the table (XY) by multiplying the X and Y score for each participant and writing it into the correct row.

6 Add up all of the scores you now have in the XY column of the table. Call this number ΣXY.

7 Complete the fifth column of the table (X^2) by squaring the X score for each participant and writing it into the correct row.

8 Add up all of the scores you now have in the X^2 column of the table. Call this number ΣX^2.

9 Complete the final column of the table (Y^2) by squaring the Y score for each participant and writing it into the correct row.

10 Add up all of the scores you now have in the Y^2 column of the table. Call this number ΣY^2.

11 Substitute the values you have calculated above into the following equation. This is the observed (calculated) value.

$$r = \frac{\Sigma XY - \dfrac{(\Sigma X)(\Sigma Y)}{N}}{\sqrt{\left(\Sigma X^2 - \dfrac{(\Sigma X)^2}{N}\right)\left(\Sigma Y^2 - \dfrac{(\Sigma Y)^2}{N}\right)}}$$

12 You now need to read off the critical value for the test. To do this you need the following information:

- df, the number of participants minus 2 ($N - 2$);

- whether your experimental hypothesis is directional or non-directional;

- the level of significance you have set (p-value).

13 If the observed (calculated) value you have generated is greater than or equal to the critical value, then the result is significant and you *reject the null hypothesis* and *accept the experimental hypothesis*. If the observed (calculated) value you have generated is less than the critical value, then the result is significant and you *reject the experimental hypothesis* and *accept the null hypothesis*.

research methods

Pearson's product moment coefficient: clever cabbies

Maguire, E.A., Gadian, D.G., Johnsrude, I.S., Good, C.D., Ashburner, J., Frackowiak, R.S. and Frith, C.D. (2000) Navigation-related structural changes in the hippocampi of taxi drivers. *Proceedings of the National Academy of Sciences USA*, 97 (8), 4398–403

Aim: One of the aims of the study was to examine whether taxi drivers have an increased hippocampal volume (linked to navigational skills) the longer they have been in the occupation. It has long been a belief that certain regions of the hippocampus deal with spatial representations and will increase in capacity if the area is consistently used.

Method
Data collected: Each taxi driver had their hippocampal volume recorded via a brain scan and they were asked how long they had been a taxi driver.

Hypotheses: Experimental – there will be a positive correlation between the hippocampal volume in taxi drivers and the number of years they have been a taxi driver. Null – any correlation between the hippocampal volume in taxi drivers and the number of years they have been a taxi driver will be due to chance.

Data analysis: The data collected was *ratio* (the hippocampal volume was measured in cubic centimetres and the second measure was the number of years the participant had been a taxi driver), the research design was *correlational* and the research team were looking to see if there was a positive correlation between hippocampal volume and the number of years the participant had been a taxi driver.

The following table shows the results for 12 of the participants:

Participant no.	Hippocampal volume (X)	Years as a taxi driver (Y)
1	2.45	12
2	2.65	15
3	1.86	5
4	2.33	12
5	2.00	9
6	2.56	15
7	2.59	18
8	1.93	6
9	2.11	8
10	2.05	7
11	2.66	22
2	2.91	25

Calculating the observed (calculated) value for Maguire *et al.* (2000)

1   Create a table as follows:

Participant no.	Hippocampal volume (X)	Years as a taxi driver (Y)	XY	X^2	Y^2
1					
2					
3					
4					
5					
6					
7					
8					
9					
10					
11					
12					

2 Complete the second and third columns of the table by inserting the data collected.

Participant no.	Hippocampal volume (X)	Years as a taxi driver (Y)	XY	X^2	Y^2
1	2.45	12			
2	2.65	15			
3	1.86	5			
4	2.33	12			
5	2.00	9			
6	2.56	15			

7	2.59	18			
8	1.93	6			
9	2.11	8			
10	2.05	7			
11	2.66	22			
12	2.91	25			

3 Plot a scattergraph to examine the correlation:

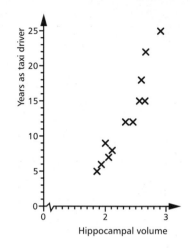

4 Add up the scores for each of the measures. Call these ΣX and ΣY.

$$\Sigma X = 28.1$$
$$\Sigma Y = 154$$

5 Complete the fourth column of the table (XY) by multiplying the hippocampal volume score (X) and years as a taxi driver score (Y) for each participant.

Participant no.	Hippocampal volume (X)	Years as a taxi driver (Y)	XY	X^2	Y^2
1	2.45	12	29.40		
2	2.65	15	39.75		
3	1.86	5	9.30		
4	2.33	12	27.96		
5	2.00	9	18.00		
6	2.56	15	38.40		
7	2.59	18	46.62		
8	1.93	6	11.58		
9	2.11	8	16.88		
10	2.05	7	14.35		
11	2.66	22	58.52		
12	2.91	25	72.75		

6 Add up all of the values in the XY column of the table. Call this number ΣXY.

$$\Sigma XY = 383.51$$

7 Complete the fifth column of the table (X^2) by squaring the X score for each participant.

Participant no.	Hippocampal volume (X)	Years as a taxi driver (Y)	XY	X^2	Y^2
1	2.45	12	29.40	6.00	
2	2.65	15	39.75	7.02	
3	1.86	5	9.30	3.46	
4	2.33	12	27.96	5.43	
5	2.00	9	18.00	4.00	
6	2.56	15	38.40	6.55	
7	2.59	18	46.62	6.71	
8	1.93	6	11.58	3.72	
9	2.11	8	16.88	4.45	
10	2.05	7	14.35	4.20	
11	2.66	22	58.52	7.08	
12	2.91	25	72.75	8.47	

8 Add up all of the values in the fifth column (X^2). Call this value ΣX^2.

$$\Sigma X^2 = 67.09$$

9 Complete the final column of the table (Y^2) by squaring the Y score for each participant.

Participant no.	Hippocampal volume (X)	Years as a taxi driver (Y)	XY	X^2	Y^2
1	2.45	12	29.40	6.00	144
2	2.65	15	39.75	7.02	225
3	1.86	5	9.30	3.46	25
4	2.33	12	27.96	5.43	144
5	2.00	9	18.00	4.00	81
6	2.56	15	38.40	6.55	225
7	2.59	18	46.62	6.71	324
8	1.93	6	11.58	3.72	36
9	2.11	8	16.88	4.45	64
10	2.05	7	14.35	4.20	49
11	2.66	22	58.52	7.08	484
12	2.91	25	72.75	8.47	625

10 Add up all of the values in the fifth column (Y^2). Call this value ΣY^2.

$$\Sigma Y^2 = 2426$$

11 Substitute the values below into the following equation. This is the observed (calculated) value.

$\Sigma X = 28.1$
$\Sigma Y = 154$
$\Sigma XY = 383.51$
$\Sigma X^2 = 67.09$
$\Sigma Y^2 = 2426$

$$r = \frac{\Sigma XY - \dfrac{(\Sigma X)(\Sigma Y)}{N}}{\sqrt{\left(\Sigma X^2 - \dfrac{(\Sigma X)^2}{N}\right)\left(\Sigma Y^2 - \dfrac{(\Sigma Y)^2}{N}\right)}} \qquad r = +0.95$$

12 We now need to read off the critical value using the following criteria:

- df, the number of participants minus 2 $(N - 2) = 10$

- whether the experimental hypothesis is directional or non-directional = **directional**

- the level of significance set (p-value) = **0.05**

n	Level of significance for one-tailed test				
	0.1	0.05	0.025	0.01	0.005
	Level of significance for two-tailed test				
	0.2	0.1	0.05	0.02	0.01
11	0.4187	0.5214	0.6021	0.6851	0.7348
12	0.3981	0.4973	0.5760	0.6581	0.7079
13	0.3802	0.4762	0.5529	0.6339	0.6835
14	0.3646	0.4575	0.5324	0.6120	0.6614

A section of the critical value table for Pearson's product moment correlation coefficient test

As can be seen, the critical value for the criteria above is **0.4973**. Our observed (calculated) value is **0.95**. Therefore, the observed (calculated) value is *greater than* the critical value so we can *reject the null hypothesis* and *accept the experimental hypothesis*.

where to now?

▶ **Miller, S. (1984)** *Experimental Design and Statistics*. **London: Routledge** – easy to follow examples of parametric tests showing step-by-step guides to calculate values by hand. Very good on describing the rationale behind each test

▶ **Greene, J. and D'Oliveira, M. (1999)** *Learning to Use Statistical Tests in Psychology*. **Buckingham: Open University Press** – again, good worked examples, and for the student who wishes to be pushed further there are some great exercises to complete.

what do you know?

1 What criteria are required to execute a parametric test?

2 Under what conditions would you use a related *t*-test?

3 How would you know if a Pearson's product moment correlation coefficient test had produced a significant result?

4 Draw a normal distribution curve.

12

Controlling Variables

what's ahead?

This chapter introduces the concepts of validity, reliability and generalisability. We describe the problems of situation and participant variables, order effects, participant reactivity, researcher bias, investigator effects, demand characteristics and issues of location. We also discuss ways to reduce the effects of confounding variables.

Generalisability

As we learned in Chapter 2, we can only test a sample from the population that we are investigating and we must take steps to ensure that this sample is representative. This is because we will generalise from our results, that is, extrapolate the implications of the findings from the sample back to the whole population. We can justify generalisations such as this only if the findings really do apply to the whole population. Sampling is only one factor that affects the value of the results of a study, the reliability and validity of the findings are also important.

media watch

> ### STOP PRESS: IF YOU HAVE AT LEAST SIX CLOSE FRIENDS YOU'RE LESS LIKELY TO GET A COLD
>
> *Company* magazine, April 2000

1   Would you believe the results of this report?

2   What would you want to know before you were prepared to place any faith in the findings?

Validity

Validity refers to whether a technique can achieve the purpose for which it was designed. A valid test should therefore measure what it claims to measure. For example, a test designed to gauge sexual promiscuity should successfully measure the number of partners an individual has over a fixed period of time. Metzler *et al.* (2000), see page 83, measured this variable by asking their participants to answer questions about:

- number of partners in the last three months;
- sex with non-monogamous partners;
- sex with partners not well known.

Do you think they are likely to have obtained truthful responses? If not, the test may have been measuring the participants' responsiveness to social desirability rather than their risky sexual behaviour.

Validity can be described in a number of different ways, as discussed below.

Face validity

This is the least sophisticated measure. *Face validity* is simply whether the measure *appears* (at *face value*) to test what it claims to. Face validity is more worthwhile if an opinion is obtained from an expert.

Concurrent validity

In an estimate of *concurrent validity* the new test in question is compared with other tests of the same phenomenon to see if they produce similar results. If the tests agree, they have concurrent validity. For example if a consumer organisation wishes to use a new measure of cats' preferences for different brands of tinned food it might validate this by asking cat owners which brands their cat consumes most quickly.

How would you measure the concurrent and predictive validity of a test that demonstrated that most cats preferred to eat Whiskas?

media watch

Does this quiz *look* as if it tests sensation seeking?
If so it has *face validity*

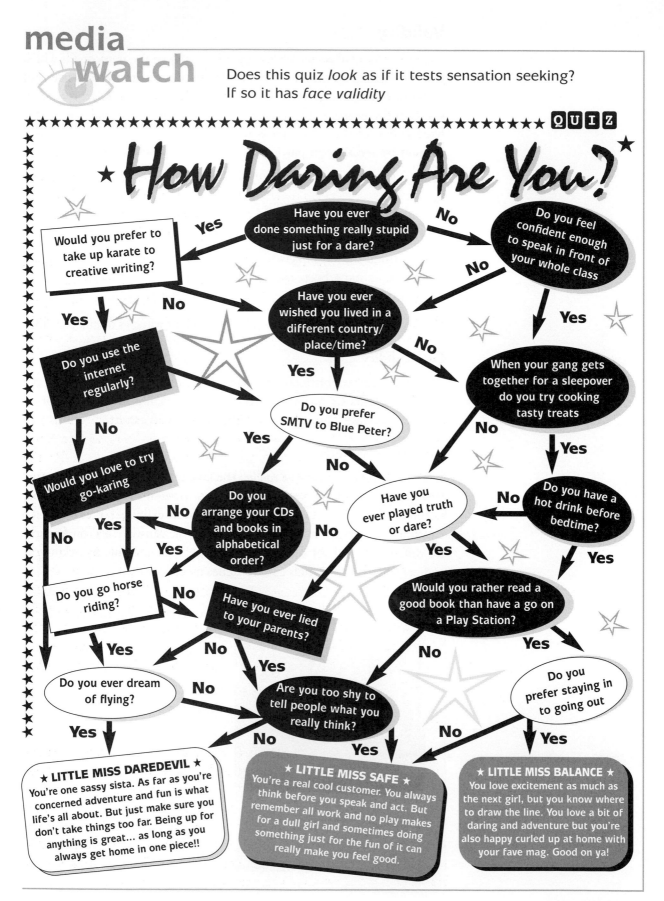

Construct validity

To test for *construct validity* it must be demonstrated that the phenomenon being measured actually *exists*. So, the construct validity of a test for intelligence, for example, is dependent on a model or theory for intelligence.

Predictive validity

Predictive validity indicates that the measure is valid because it can accurately *predict* performance on the measure under scrutiny. If an intelligence test has predictive validity it should be able to forecast participants' success on intellectually demanding tasks such as examinations.

In relation to the three measures listed above, Metzler *et al.* (2000) found that the sexual behaviour of the participants in the intervention group was much less risky than that of the usual care group so we would expect that the experimental participants would experience fewer STDs. This, however, was not the case, suggesting that the measures of behaviour change were not valid.

Ecological validity

The approaches to validity that we have discussed so far relate only to *internal validity*, that is, the validity of the test items *themselves* in relation to the objective, for instance, does the task assess the issue raised by the research question? We also need to consider *external* or *ecological validity*, the extent to which a test measures a real-world phenomenon, that is, whether the results would generalise to the rest of the population, other populations or other contexts. The three studies reported by MacDonald *et al.* (2000) on the effects of alcohol on social judgements differ in their ecological validity. The first administered a fixed quantity of alcohol in the laboratory whereas the second and third studies used participants who were spending their evening at a bar, some of whom were drinking alcohol. The first study therefore had lower ecological validity than subsequent tests. This is not simply because it was conducted in the field but because findings from this context are more likely to apply to other situations.

Reliability

Reliability is a measure of whether replications would produce similar results: if they do then the test or technique is reliable. Think about yourself: do you always turn up at the same time in the same place? If so, you're *reliable*. There are several ways to assess the reliability of a psychological test, all of which are based on the assumption that if one source of scores from the test correlates with another source then the test is reliable (see Chapter 7 for an explanation of correlations). The measures of reliability differ in the way they select test material to compare.

Test–retest method

In a *test–retest* assessment of reliability a group of participants completes the test twice, at different times. Their first and second scores are then correlated and if the correlation coefficient is highly positive then the test is reliable. This works well if the test is not highly memorable, otherwise the effect of practice may be a problem.

Equivalent forms

To overcome the effect of practice on any test it may be produced in *equivalent forms*, that is, different but comparable versions of the same test. This would be like IQ test books where each test claims to be of equal difficulty and is composed of identical style questions. The principle here is the same as with test–retest: a group of participants is tested twice, once with each form of the test and their results should correlate strongly if the tests are reliable.

Split-half method

This is a measure of the *internal reliability* of the test, that is, the extent to which the items on the test are all measuring the same phenomenon. All participants take the test only once. Their scores on one half of the test (e.g. the even-numbered questions) are then correlated with their scores on the other half of the test (e.g. the odd-numbered questions). A high correlation indicates that the test items are 'equivalent', i.e. that the test has internal reliability.

Inter-observer reliability

In Chapter 3 (page 37) we discussed the need for observers to generate the same records when they are watching the same behaviours. The extent to which they do so is their *inter-observer* or *inter-rater reliability*. Leaper (2000) (page 41) illustrates how inter-observer reliability is measured and improved.

inter**active**
angles

Are each of the measures described below valid, reliable, neither or both? Explain why.

- A student is testing whether dyslexic readers are better when the text they are reading is covered with a transparent coloured film. She times their reading speed with and without the coloured sheet in place and asks them whether they found the passages easier to read in one or the other condition. The general consensus was that the coloured sheets made reading easier but there was no difference in reading speed.

- In a study of first and third year students a psychologist measured anxiety levels using a device that recorded how tightly a participant clenched their jaw. You happen to score highly because you've just experienced an episode of road rage on the way to the laboratory. The following week you decide to walk quietly through the park instead. How will this affect your score? Another participant grinds their teeth at night. Their score is also very high.

- A group of students decides to observe affection and affiliation between couples using a field experiment. They take photos of couples in parks, restaurants, bars and the student lounge and estimate the distance between the two people.

Controls

The control of extraneous variables is particularly important in the experimental setting but should also be considered in other situations. For example, in Chapter 3 we looked at the observational technique and ways to limit the effects of the observer on those individuals being observed. The steps taken are a means to limit factors that could distort the collection of valid and reliable data; they are *controls*. Similarly in Chapter 4, we considered ways to dissuade participants from answering questions in a patterned way, an attempt to reduce responder bias. This, again, involves the implementation of controls. But it was in Chapter 6, on experimentation, where we considered most about the control of variables.

Confounding variables

A variable is any factor that is free to vary or can be changed, altered or examined to gauge an effect. In experiments we have two key categories of variable, the IV and the DV. In addition we must pay attention to those variables that could disrupt the effect of the IV, *confounding variables*. In some cases such effects act on only one level of the IV: these are called *constant errors*. They may act in the same direction as the predicted effect, enhancing the apparent impact of the IV and hence potentially increasing the risk of a type I error (see page 143). On the other hand, an uncontrolled variable might act counter to predictions, obscuring the effect of the IV and causing a type II error. Finally, uncontrolled variables may act in unsystematic ways, resulting in *random errors*.

media watch

Snack attack

Want to slim for summer but have the willpower of Homer Simpson? Then put your hands together for those lovely scientists at University College London. They've discovered a way to trick your body into hating snacks. The secret? Simply scoff some choc straight after a meal. Chocolate junkies who ate half a bar after lunch and dinner lost their cravings in just two weeks while choc-haters (?!) who indulged on an empty stomach started craving the stuff. Better pass the After Eights then…

Company magazine, April 2000

Questions

1 What is the IV in the study described in this article?

2 Psychologists have identified many variables that affect appetite, such as smell, time of day, time since last meal and social factors. How can you control for these and other factors that you suspect might affect the perception of hunger?

3 What other controls would you impose if you conducted this study?

How would you test whether the motivation to eat chocolate differed from that to eat fruit? What factors would you try to control in such a study?

One way in which experimentation allows for control of variables is in the selection of materials as we discussed in Chapter 6. In textual material it may be important to control for meaning, complexity, word or letter frequency, similarity to other words, font and size. For example, in the study by Duncan and Seymour (2000) described on page 12 non-words such as *tal*, *nal* and *zuf* were used. What characteristics are being controlled for in these examples? Chawarski and Sternberg (1993) (see page 93) used eight stories, which were matched for length. Each was approximately 220 words and all were extracted from the same source (the *Reader's Digest*) to control for ease of reading and understandability.

In studies using pictorial stimuli it may be important to control for image content, colour, complexity, clarity and size. For example, MacDonald *et al.* (2000), described in Chapter 6, used hand-stamps as an immediate visual cue to convey different messages to participants. Each stamp was the same size, colour and overall shape, they differed only in the image or words within the circular border (see page 101).

Experiments using auditory stimuli may need to control pitch, volume, familiarity, tempo and style. It may be possible to control many of these variables using computer-generated music as described by North and Hargreaves (2000) in Chapter 8.

interactive
angles

The following words might, for the reasons suggested, be unsuitable for inclusion in an experiment. Try to construct two word lists, each containing ten words. Consider how you will control for meaning(s), sounds, plurals, frequency, etc.

bat – has two meanings
bee – is not consonant/vowel/consonant
calf – is a juvenile animal rather than a species
duck – has two meanings
ewe – is a female animal rather than a species
fish – both noun and verb
gnat – has a silent g
lamb – has a silent b
        – is a juvenile animal rather than a species
lice – is plural rather than singular
mice – is plural rather than singular
owl – is not consonant/vowel/consonant
ram – has two meanings
yak – is uncommon

research
methods

pouring a perfect pint

Cabe, P.A. and Pittenger, J.B. (2000) Human sensitivity to acoustic information from vessel filling. *Journal of Experimental Psychology: Human Perception and Performance,* 26, 313–24

Aims: To ascertain the extent to which people are able to use acoustic information to detect changes in the acoustic properties of a vessel as it fills with water.

Method: Participants were observed in situations where they detected the status of a vessel containing water. The design involved five independent variables: vision status (blind or sighted), vessel size, flow rate, sex and number of trials. The participants were tested on their ability to detect water level rising, falling or not changing and when filling a vessel to the brim or to drinking level either blindfold or sighted. Aspects of the situations that were controlled included the following:

- Participants were naïve to the purpose of the study.

- No participants had hearing problems, sighted participants had normal or corrected-to-normal vision.

These controlled for participant variables.

- All participants heard the same tape of filling, emptying, and constant level events in a vessel.

- The speed of flow into the vessel was controlled to a maximum rate.

- Tube diameter and position were the same.

- The height of the water was kept at a constant level.

These controlled for water pressure and flow rate.

- Participants listened from approximately 1 metre from the loudspeaker.

- All participants sat in the same position in relation to the apparatus.

These controlled for situational variables.

- Participants responded during 10-second intervals.

- Participants responded to multiple-choice answers.

● No feedback was given to a participant until the end of all their trials.

● Different vessels were used for demonstrations to participants than for the experiment itself.

These controlled for other aspects of the procedure.

In general it was not possible to counterbalance the order of events. When filling below the brim, participants were asked to fill to their 'preferred drinking level'.

Results: Participants reliably identified water level rising, falling or not changing and were readily able to use auditory information alone to control filling (whether blind, sighted or blindfold) although where available the use of both sources of information improved accuracy. Filling to the brim was more accurate than to drinking level.

Conclusion: Changing acoustic information appears to afford good prospective control of vessel filling.

Questions

1 Select three controlled variables and explain why they are important.

2 Why was it important to compare blind *and* blindfold participants?

interactive angles

Look at the following studies described elsewhere in the text. What variables are being controlled? What other, uncontrolled variables might still have existed?

● McNicholas and Collis (2000), page 44.

● Seyfarth and Cheney (1986), page 29.

● Roberts *et al.* (in press), page 148.

Situational variables

One source of uncontrolled variables is the research setting. Variables arising from this are called *situational variables*. They are confounding effects arising from the influence of the environment on the behaviour of participants, such as lighting, noise levels and temperature. Within reason the absolute conditions are less important than consistency across conditions. You cannot expect to get reliable data if you test one group of participants in a quiet place such as the canteen early in the morning and another at lunchtime when it is busy and crowded.

It is clear, therefore, that *location* can be an issue both in the sense that all participants should share a similar experience and that the environment *per se* can have an effect on the outcome of the research. This is clearly demonstrated by experiments in which the location is the IV itself. Studies of context-dependent memory such as Abernethy (1940) showed that environment affects recall using students tested in the same room as they had learned, or in a different location.

research methods

issues of location: is scary sexy?

Dutton, D.C. and Aron, A.P. (1974) Some evidence for heightened sexual attraction under conditions of high anxiety. *Journal of Personality and Social Psychology*, 30, 510–17

Aims: To demonstrate that a high arousal state induced by fear could be misinterpreted internally as sexual arousal.

Method: An interviewer (either an attractive female or a male) asked male passers-by to fill out a questionnaire in which they devised a short story using an ambiguous picture of a woman as a prompt (this was from a Thematic Apperception Test, TAT). Eighty-five males aged 18–35 years and unaccompanied by a female companion were interviewed as they crossed the Capilano River. Experimental participants were interviewed on a suspension bridge only 1.75 metres wide and 160 metres long, built of wooden boards held up by wire cables spanning from one side of the canyon to the other. Hanging 70 metres above the rocky riverbed the bridge sways, tilts and wobbles precariously. Control participants were interviewed in the same way but on a solid bridge, further upstream that had higher handrails, was wider, was only 3.5 metres above a small rivulet and did not sway. Scorers working blind to the condition the participant was from later rated the story for sexual content. The inter-rater reliability was +0.87.

Results: When interviewed by a woman, the men in the high arousal condition on the suspension bridge invented stories with greater sexual imagery than those interviewed in the less arousing location. No difference was found between the conditions with a male interviewer.

Conclusion: Dutton and Aron concluded that fear increased the participants' attraction to the female interviewer. Arousal level in this study was the IV (rather than a situational variable). However, it does show that the situation in which people are placed during a study can affect the results obtained.

Questions

1 Which of the following terms would you use to describe this study: field experiment, natural experiment, quasi-experiment, observation, interview, survey?

2 What is the DV in this study? How was it measured?

3 What variables should have been controlled to ensure that the only difference between the two situations was the level of arousal?

4 What does an inter-rater reliability of +0.87 mean?

Participant variables

In addition to the setting, the participants themselves can be a source of uncontrolled variables. *Participant variables* are confounding effects that arise from the characteristics of the people performing in a study, such as their age, sex, state of hunger or level of arousal. A participant who attends an experiment asking about sources of frustration when they have just spent 40 minutes in a car getting to the laboratory is likely to answer differently from one who has arrived in 10 minutes by foot.

interactive angles

What are the potential confounding variables in each of these situations?

- Testing participants for auditory reaction time in the canteen.

- Asking participants outside a video store after a fight has broken out over the loan of *Texas Chainsaw Massacre* whether they believe that violent TV affects behaviour.

- Interviewing people about their sleeping habits in an airport lounge.

Demand characteristics

A well-planned experiment represents a pay-off between ethics – how much participants should know about the study in order to make informed choices – and scientific rigour – how little participants should know in order to ensure that this knowledge does not affect their behaviour. As a consequence we must attempt to minimise the cues in an experimental setting which might enable participants to guess, correctly or incorrectly, about the purpose of the investigation. The features of an experiment that inform participants about the aim and influence their behaviour independently of the experimental objectives thereby confounding the results are called *demand characteristics*.

research methods

demand characteristics: participants prove to be pathetic

Orne, M.T. (1962) On the social psychology of the psychological experiment: with particular reference to demand characteristics and their implications. *American Psychologist*, 17, 776–83

Aim: To devise a task so psychologically noxious, meaningless and boring that it would counter the power of social influence, which results in participants continuing to perform in order to fulfil an experimenter's expectations even when their requests demand toleration of discomfort, boredom or pain.

Method: Participants were asked to complete 224 additions of random numbers presented to them on a sheet, to tear this into a minimum of 32 pieces, and start on the next sheet (from a stack of 2000). When the experimenter left the room saying 'Continue to work, I will return eventually' he expected the participants to give up working.

Results: After five and a half hours, it was the experimenter who gave up!

Conclusion: Orne reports that 'Thus far, we have been singularly unsuccessful in finding an experimental task which would be discontinued, or, indeed, refused by subjects in an experimental setting'. Such is the power of compliance.

Questions

1 What research method is used in this study?

2 What pressures in this situation were acting as demand characteristics?

Participant reactivity

Responder bias or *participant reactivity* is the tendency of a participant to produce responses that are socially desirable, that are what the experimenter wants or that are biased. This problem can be overcome with a *blind* procedure in which allocation to levels of the IV is achieved by the researcher in such a way that the participants themselves are unaware of the condition in which they are performing. For example, in the laboratory experiment by MacDonald *et al.* (2000) reported on page 100, participants did not know whether they were in the *alcohol* or *control* (no alcohol) group. To ensure that the participants were blind, the rims of the glasses from which the control group were drinking had been dipped in alcohol.

Researcher bias

Researcher bias is a tendency of experimenters or observers to record the response they expect from the participants in different conditions. Unless effective control measures are taken, the results can simply become the consequence of a self-fulfilling prophecy; you just find what you expected to find. Being aware of which participants are in the experimental group may cause researchers to act differently towards them, or attribute different explanations to their behaviour.

One way to overcome researcher bias is to use *standardised instructions*, which ensure that participants in all conditions are treated in an identical manner in every respect other than the independent variable. For example, in an investigation into the effects of viewing different televised material on mood, an experimenter could say to participants going to view news reports that they will 'fill in a questionnaire, watch some TV then have to fill in another questionnaire', implying the processes will be dull. Participants destined for the comedy programmes might receive the same instructions but without the '*then have to*', since the experimenter believes it will not seem like such a chore after having had fun. Although nothing has been said about the content of their differing experiences, participants in the 'news' condition may have been unintentionally affected by the additional wording, thus any differences between the groups that arise may be due to the procedure rather than the IV. This would be an example of an *investigator effect*: a prejudgement by the researcher has affected the way in which the participants behave. It is sometimes called the *experimenter expectancy effect* because it is the effect of the experimenter's expectations that is affecting the behaviour of the participants.

research
methods

researcher bias: puzzled primate picks the poles

Kohler, W. (1925) The *Mentality of Apes.* New York: Harcourt, Brace

Aim: To observe insight learning in chimpanzees (*Pan troglodytes*) by requiring chimpanzees to use information available in the situation and to reapply this knowledge to solve a problem.

Method: In one demonstration, a chimpanzee named Sultan was given two bamboo rods with which to retrieve some fruit from outside his cage. Each individual stick was too short to reach the fruit.

Results: Kohler observed that Sultan attempted to reach the fruit with only one stick and having failed, abandoned his efforts and simply played with the sticks. During this play, Sultan held the sticks together so that one fitted inside the other. He immediately joined the sticks and ran to the edge of the cage to retrieve the fruit. Although the sticks fell apart while Sultan was raking the fruit in, he immediately reconnected them. However, Kohler also reports Sultan's 'bad errors'; the chimpanzee engaged in behaviours irrelevant to the situation. Before solving the double stick problem, Sultan had dragged a box up to the bars then abandoned it and had lost one of the sticks. He pushed one stick so far out of the cage with the other that he could not retrieve it himself, and it had to be returned to him for the experiment to continue. Furthermore, when Sultan failed to recognise that one stick could be joined to the other, the observer assisted him by putting a finger into the end of the wider stick, right under his nose.

Conclusion: Kohler believed that Sultan recognised that fitting the sticks together was essential to solving the problem of retrieval, his success was the product of time spent with the elements of the problem in mind, the solution arising as a result of insight rather than manipulation.

Questions

1 Do the additional events reported, which are often omitted from descriptions, reduce the credibility of the insightful solutions assumed in such situations?

2 Kohler's descriptions often suggest that the chimpanzees' behaviour was far from instant or insightful. In fact, they are often described as 'angry' or 'fatigued', and they frequently made efforts with a range of inappropriate tools (including their keepers and Kohler himself) to access their goal. Does this suggest that Kohler was unbiased in his interpretation of the chimpanzees' behaviour?

Researcher bias may also affect the way data are recorded. For example, a study might observe the effects on attention of drinking fruit juice containing tartrazine, a food additive implicated in hyperactivity. An observer who sees a control participant looking out of the window might assume they have heard a noise outside whereas the same behaviour from an experimental participant might be classified as inattention. This can be overcome by an individual other than the researcher who will conduct the study, allocating the members of the sample to the different levels of the IV. This assistant ensures that the participants themselves are unaware of the condition in which they are performing and that the researcher who will continue to conduct the study cannot differentiate between them. This is called a *double blind* procedure. For example, Scholey *et al.* (2000) studied the effects of actual caffeine consumption on cognitive performance. In their experiment, participants were allocated to groups which were informed either that they would be given caffeinated coffee or decaffeinated coffee. In each group, half the participants were given the coffee they had been told they would receive, and the other half were not (although the participants were unaware of this). In addition, when the cognitive tests were administered it would not have been apparent to the experimenters which participants had received caffeinated or decaffeinated coffee.

Order effects

In Chapter 6, we discussed the role of variables in experiments, a situation that presents additional needs for controls. In an experiment with a repeated measures design the participants are exposed to the experimental situation on more than one occasion and this *repetition* may affect their performance. Consider how several consecutive attempts at running a 100-m race would affect your chances of success. Similarly, how repeated attempts to flick a pile of beer mats would affect ability to catch the stack effectively.

inter**active**
angles

Try these tasks and see if your performance changes. If it does, this would have implications for experimental design. If these tests were used to provide a measure of the DV, steps would need to be taken to avoid the effects of practice and fatigue.

● Link your fingers as illustrated then draw your linked hands up towards your face under your arms. Ask a partner to point at (but not touch) individual fingers on each of your hands. Can you raise them as indicated?

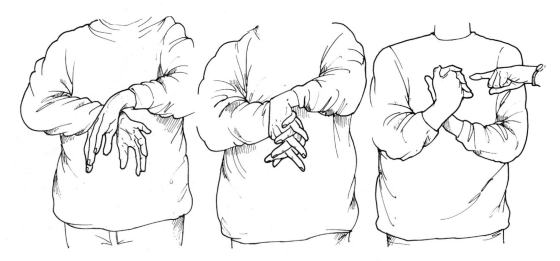

● Time yourself on this task. Place a pack of playing cards in front of you. Lift the top one off the pile with one hand, tap the middle of the next card with the index finger of the other hand, lift that card off, tap the next card and continue to the end of the pack. Then repeat the task. What happens to your speed and accuracy?

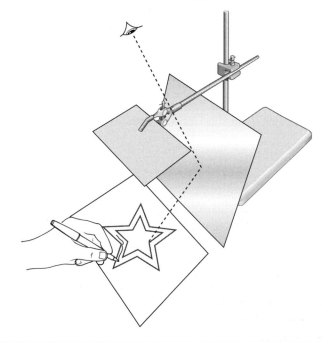

● Set up a mirror and a piece of card, using a retort stand and clamp. With your non-dominant hand, trace around a shape drawn on a piece of paper, keeping your hand out of view. Can you keep between the lines using only the view in the mirror to guide you?

The experimental effects that arise as a result of the order in which two levels of the IV are presented to participants are called *order effects*. These may be of two kinds. *Fatigue effects* arise when the participants become tired or bored as they repeat the task so their performance worsens in later conditions. This might occur if tests are highly repetitive or very demanding, for example insoluble mathematical problems or vigilance tasks (such as looking for a dot on a screen). *Practice effects* arise when the participants become more skilled in familiar tasks so their performance improves in later conditions. This might occur if a researcher uses an unfamiliar task, which, although difficult at first because of its novelty, rapidly becomes easier with practice. Mirror drawing (as described on page 208) would be an example of such a task. By counteracting the effects of practice and fatigue the IV rather than the order of conditions must be responsible for differences between conditions.

One way in which order effects can be controlled, although not eliminated, is by the use of *counterbalancing*. This is the systematic variation of the order of presentation of the levels of the IV in a repeated measures design. For example, in Chapter 2 (page 25) we described Graham *et al.* (2000), an experiment in which women were tested prior to ovulation and menstruation. Half of the sample was tested after menstruation and then in their post-ovulatory stage later the same month. For the other half the post-ovulation testing was conducted first and the post-menstrual tests were conducted the subsequent month. In this instance the experimenters could not control the occurrence of the levels of the IV; this is not, however, always the case. In Leaper (2000), the experimenter ensured that equal numbers of parent–child interactions were observed in the order mother–father as father–mother (see page 41).

interactive
angles

Counterbalancing has been used in the following studies described elsewhere in the text. Find them and describe how the conditions were counterbalanced. In each case suggest why this was necessary. Were practice or fatigue effects more likely to occur? What factors would be responsible for these order effects?

- Williamson *et al.* (2000).
- Chawarski and Sternberg (1993).
- Neer *et al.* (1987).

As an alternative to counterbalancing, the order of conditions can be randomised as in Baenninger *et al.* (2000), see page 55. *Randomisation* attempts to overcome the effects of practice and fatigue by allocating participants to randomised orders for participation in each condition. In a truly randomised order it may be possible for several subsequent participants to experience the same order of conditions by chance. To avoid this, *blocked randomisation* can be used. Here, pairs of participants are allocated to each randomly generated order, one participant performing the conditions as indicated, the other performing them in reverse.

Randomisation

BA BA BA BA BA AB AB BA AB AB AB BA AB BA BA AB AB AB AB AB AB BA BA BA

Using this list of random pairs in a truly randomised allocation of participants to different orders of conditions in an experiment, the first five participants would all perform condition B followed by condition A. Using blocked randomisation, the first five pairs of participants would perform alternately in the order BA and AB.

Conclusions

Validity and reliability affect the extent to which the results of a study can be generalised back to the parent population. Confounding variables, such as order effects, participant reactivity, researcher bias, investigator effects, demand characteristics and situation, and participant variables can each be controlled in different ways. Experimental controls may be exerted through the use of blind and double-blind procedures, standardised instructions, counterbalancing and randomisation.

where to now?

▶ **Barber, T.X. (1976)** *Pitfalls in Human Research: Ten Pivotal Points*. **Oxford: Pergamon Press** – this book draws a clear distinction between researcher bias and investigator effects

▶ **Howitt, D. and Cramer, D. (2000)** *First Steps in Research and Statistics, A practical Workbook for Psychology Students*. **London: Routledge** – this book provides good explanations of counterbalancing and randomisation.

what do you know?

1 Define *order effects* and illustrate how they may arise in an experiment.

2 What is *counterbalancing* and when is it used?

3 Describe the possible consequences of *researcher bias* and indicate how these may be counteracted.

4 Define reliability and describe one way in which it may be measured.

13

Ethics in Research

what's ahead?

In this chapter we discuss the issues raised by psychological research. The guidelines set out by the British Psychological Society for work with human participants are described in detail, covering such issues as consent, conduct, competence, confidentiality, debriefing and the right to withdraw. We will look at the use of non-human animals in psychology and the legal and ethical constraints that apply to the use of animals in research.

Research with human participants

Some of your friends do psychology. They ask you to volunteer for an experiment. When you ask what it is they say 'it's for our coursework'. You ask 'what's it about?' The reply is an unintelligible 'it's a test of so-and-so's theory'. You go along and are given a piece of paper that says all you have to do is listen to the time the guy says, count the seconds in your head then put your hand up when you've estimated that length of time. Easy. But, somehow, everyone else seems to put their hand up earlier than you. At first you stand your ground, then you begin to feel awkward and start to believe you must be overestimating, so you put your hand up earlier and earlier along with everyone else. At the end you're allowed to ask questions; you feel a bit stupid and say 'What was going on?' The explanation, that it was a test of conformity, doesn't help. It turns out that all the other would-be participants had different instructions saying 'The experimenter will say "session number X" and you have to time the length indicated on your sheet even if this contradicts the time he then reads out'. This simply makes you feel worse: it was bad enough feeling different, now you appear to be a fool in front of all these people. And as if that wasn't enough, they all know and are asking *you* why you did it…*they're* the psychologists….

Do psychologists really do this sort of thing?

212

research issues

ethics: as long as a piece of string

Asch, S.E. (1955) Opinions and social pressure. *Scientific American*, 193, 31–5

Aim: To investigate the effect of conformity. Would participants give answers that were obviously untrue to avoid contradicting the responses or other participants?

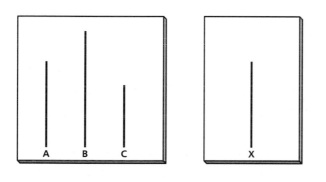

Method: Each participant was part of a group of seven individuals each of whom was also apparently a participant but was actually a confederate of the experimenter. As a group, they were shown one large card followed by a smaller one. They were asked to match the length of the line on the second card with one of those on the first. They were arranged around a table so that the real participant always answered second to last.

In the experimental trials, the confederates sometimes all gave the same wrong answer. The participants were interviewed individually afterwards.

Results: In 32 per cent of the experimental trials where the confederates gave the wrong answers, the real participants conformed and also answered incorrectly. Some 75 per cent of all participants conformed and gave the wrong answer at least once. When interviewed, the participants said that they knew they were giving the wrong answers but were doing so to avoid being disruptive but felt very anxious.

Conclusion: The desire to avoid feeling different is sufficient to induce conformity in individuals.

Questions

1 In what ways did this experiment deceive the participants?

2 How might the participants have felt about themselves following the experiment?

Ethical guidelines

The British Psychological Society (BPS) has, since 1985, published a Code of Conduct for psychologists. This, together with the Ethical Principles, first published in 1978, is central to British provision against the misconduct of psychologists in research and professional practice.

These two documents have been revised most recently as the BPS *Code of Conduct, Ethical Principles and Guidelines* (1998). These are described in detail below and summarised in the box.

BPS *Code of Conduct, Ethical Principles and Guidelines* (1998)

- *Competence* – work within your limit and strive to maintain and develop your skills.

- *Consent* – ensure that you have provided sufficient information for your participants or clients to make an informed choice about their commitment:

  (a) *deception* – do not mislead participants unless it is unavoidable, justifiable and accepted by appropriate authorities;

  (b) *debriefing* – after completion of your study, participants must be fully informed of the purpose and expected outcomes;

  (c) *right to withdraw* – participants must be reminded that they are free to leave a study at anytime or to remove their results at the end, regardless of any payment they have received.

- *Confidentiality* – ensure that you have disguised participants' identities and stored their data securely.

- *Conduct* – be responsible. Treat participants or clients safely and without discrimination or exploitation.

BPS Code of Conduct

The aim of this document was to guide practising psychologists in their conduct, for instance to ensure that they value integrity, impartiality and respect for individuals. This establishes the highest possible ethical standards and to ensure that work is being carried out with the greatest possible scientific integrity. The four key elements in the Code of Conduct, competence, consent, confidentiality and conduct are discussed below.

Competence

Psychologists should endeavour:

- to maintain and develop their professional competence;

- to work within their own limitations;

- to identify and attempt to overcome restrictions to their competence.

In order to do this, psychologists should not claim competencies they do not have. For instance, a student studying children's writing should not claim to be able to identify dyslexic individuals. Nor should they misrepresent their qualifications or capabilities; the same student should not, for example, imply that they are more advanced in their studies than they are. In addition, they should be prepared to advise an individual to seek out a more appropriate service when requested for assistance outside their own abilities. Our student might suggest that a suitable professional such as the classroom teacher should look at a particular piece of work by a child they are concerned about.

interactive
angles

What should a psychologist do in each of these situations?

- A researcher conducting a study on the effects of viewing text through transparent coloured acetate finds that a participant who says they are dyslexic can read more easily in this condition than with a colourless overlay. The participant asks if they should always read with a coloured sheet.

- During a consultation, a psychologist in clinical practice realises that his client would benefit more from therapy of a kind he is, as yet, unqualified to provide.

- A university student finds that in her experiment participants who are overweight are less stressed than those who are underweight. She is asked whether it is therefore better to be overweight since it protects you from the negative effects of stress.

Consent

Psychologists carrying out investigations or interventions should always obtain the valid consent of the participants, ensuring that they can make an informed decision about the nature of their contribution and its potential consequences. Specifically psychologists should:

- withhold information only when necessary to the objectivity of the investigation or future professional practice and only after consultation with experienced colleagues (such as a teacher);

- give full information in advance to those participating in an investigation or intervention (via the brief in a study) and to provide full information afterwards regarding the aims, rationale and outcome as appropriate to the welfare of participants (via the debrief in a study);

- refrain from making exaggerated, sensational or unjustified claims about the effectiveness of their work, for instance to avoid unrealistic expectations about the consequences of participation;

- obtain consent from those persons who participate and take steps to ensure that this is valid, except where intervention is compulsory;

- recognise and uphold the rights of those who may be unable to give valid consent such as the young, individuals with learning difficulties, the elderly and those in the care of an institution or detained by law;

- seek permission from the person(s) with legal authority to give consent for those who cannot give valid consent for themselves.

For students this means providing prospective participants with a full *brief* of the experiment, a description of what will be expected of them during the experiment and its general purpose such that they can give their informed consent to participate.

interactive
angles

In a continuation of Dutton and Aron (1974) described on page 202, participants were left in a laboratory with an array of electrical equipment and some copies of 'previous experiments in the area' to read, which discussed the effects of electric shocks on learning and pain in general. The experimenter went to find another participant and returned with a woman who was, in fact, a confederate. She had been told that the study involved sexual attraction but did not know the experimental hypothesis. Her actions had been rehearsed to avoid differences among conditions and she had been instructed to call either heads or tails when she flipped a coin. Eighty male students volunteered for whom the experimental protocol was as follows. The confederate took off her coat and hung it up. They were (mis)informed about the experiment and shocks and were then asked if they wanted to leave, but no one did. They were told that there were two levels of shock, quite painful or a mere tingle and a coin was tossed for allocation to conditions. (Both participants tossed the coin: in half the confederate called the same as the participant, in half the opposite.) The experimenter then said 'Today heads receives the high shock level' and explained how the shock series would take place, about the electrodes, etc. While the experimenter 'set up the equipment', the participants were taken to private cubicles to fill in a questionnaire about their feelings towards the experimental situation, including their co-participant. The questions included 'How much would you like to ask her out on a date' and 'How much would you like to kiss her' (an alternative set of questions was provided for participants who ostensibly had a male co-partner) and TAT pictures as used previously. The results showed that participants in the high anxiety (painful shock) condition demonstrated attraction to the confederate on all measures but for the TAT only when she too was in the 'painful shock' condition.

Questions

1 Were the participants able to give informed consent?

2 Justify your answer to (1) as if you were Dutton and Aron.

3 Why was a confederate used?

4 What aspect of the BPS Ethical Guidelines would the use of the confederate have contravened?

5 Did any participants ever receive electric shocks?

Confidentiality

Although psychologists must maintain adequate records, both of clinical practice and scientific research, it is essential in either case that the privacy of individuals and organisations and confidentiality of any information acquired from them is upheld. The identity of participants should not be revealed except with their expressed permission. Specifically psychologists should:

- communicate information without identifying individuals or organisations;

- convey personally identifiable information to others only with expressed permission except where this would either be contrary to the best interests of the individual, in contravention of the law or when information is shared within a team when this has been made clear to the participants;

- in exceptional circumstances when the safety or interests of the recipients are at risk, or when others may be at risk, inform appropriate third parties without prior consent, having first consulted an experienced and disinterested colleague unless the delay in so doing would result in a significant risk to life or health;

- maintain records which can be personally identifiable only as long as necessary, rendering them anonymous once this is no longer essential;

- make audio, video or photographic recordings of clients or participants (except recordings of public behaviour) only with expressed agreement to the recording and subsequent access to it;

- safeguard the security of records, including those on computer;

- take steps to ensure that other persons with whom they work also respect the need for confidentiality.

In practice, these require us to ensure that raw data from our research is kept securely, to use participant numbers rather than names and to ensure that other identifying characteristics, such as handwriting, are disguised.

interactive
angles

- Why are some participants, such as HM (Corkin, 1984), identified by only their initials?

- Explain two situations under which it would be appropriate to photograph participants.

- In an observation where independent raters watch video of recorded behaviour of participants, what obligations do those assistants have?

Conduct

The personal conduct of psychologists should not damage the recipients of their services or participants in their research. Nor should their conduct undermine public confidence in their own ability or in that of other psychologists or members of related professions. Specifically they should:

- refrain from improper conduct in their work that would be detrimental to the recipients of their services or participants in their research;

- not request or accept significant payment other than has been agreed;

- not exploit any relationship of influence or trust;

- not allow their professional standards to be diminished by consideration of religion, sex, race, age, nationality, party politics, social standing, class, self-interest or other extraneous factors;

- refrain from practice if their personal judgement is seriously impaired such as by alcohol, drugs or personal stress;

- value all relevant information when expressing a professional opinion;

- value and respect scientific evidence and the limits of such evidence when making public statements that provide psychological information;

- not claim credit for the work of others;

- ensure that safe procedures and equipment are used in professional practice and research;

- act responsibly in cases of the alleged misconduct of others.

For students of psychology, some key issues above are: striving for equal opportunities for individuals to participate in their experiments, ensuring that when work is reported as their own, their contribution is accurately represented and that they treat participants in a safe and responsible way.

interactive
angles

Which aspects of the Code of Conduct would be contravened in each of these scenarios and why would this be important?

- A psychologist in clinical practice is finding their personal life stressful and often arrives at work very hung-over.

- A group of students conducting a project on the effects of music on concentration know that they should have the cassette player they are using tested by their college Health and Safety Officer but have not done so.

- The colleague of a research psychologist has been challenged with an unfair allegation of misconduct and has asked for assistance. The colleague, however, is after promotion and hopes he will lose the case.

media watch

How plain Janes trick those poor men with a bit of chemical warfare

Men have know it for centuries. They are completely powerless against feminine wiles.

Now scientists have revealed that women have even resorted to chemical warfare to snare a mate. Female pheromones trick men into thinking women are more attractive than they are.

While a woman may look plain from a distance, once she gets close enough to a man for him to smell her, the odourless chemical which affects behaviour takes control giving her instant sex appeal.

Strangely, pheromones, which contain up to 240 different substances, make good-looking women seem less attractive, according to a study by Professr Karl Grammer and Astrid Juette.

Women taking the Pill lose their attractiveness because it stops them producing pheromones.

Prof Grammer found the Pill also wipes out a woman's sensitivity to male pheromones, causing her to lose her natural ability to pick the right partner through his smell.

Speaking at a conference of the British Psychological Society in London, he said: 'Females exploit male brains for their own advantage. The most astonishing thing is that the attractive ones lose, and what they lose the others gain.'

In the study, 66 men were either exposed to a synthetic vaginal pheromone called copulin or water, which was used as a control. They were then asked to rate the attractiveness of women and their voices.

The professor found that usually faces and voices were rated more positive under the influence of copulin. The more negative a woman was rated in attractiveness without smell, the more she gained through smell.

Testosterone levels also increased among the copulin sniffers but remained the same among those given water.

Scientists already know that pheromones play a vital role in animals finding a mate, but are only just beginning to study their role in human sexual relations.

Prof Grammer said oral contraceptives caused 'all types of problems' by upsetting the scent signals between men and women. He believed it was no accident that 40 per cent of women with unexplained fertility problems were on the Pill.

Scientists suspect that one purpose of pheromones is to help women find biologically compatible mates. 'A woman taking the contraceptive pill loses all sensitivity to pheromones,' said Prof Grammer. 'She picks out the genetically wrong mates.'

The Express, 17 December 1998

As a public statement that provides psychological information, to what extent do you think that this report values all of the relevant information and respects scientific evidence and its limitations?

BPS *Ethical Principles for Conducting Research with Human Participants*

The current *Ethical Principles* (1998), revised from the 1978 version, aims to recognise the debt owed by psychologists to those who give their time to take part in their studies. This is reflected in the change from the term *subjects* to *participants*. For psychologists exposed to the term 'subjects' as part of their professional jargon it is not derogatory but it could be interpreted as impersonal by someone without that experience. In many ethical dilemmas, the appropriate course of action is to discuss the issue with uninvolved but experienced colleagues or an Ethics Committee. This is described below as 'consultation'.

Consent

- The investigator should, where possible, inform all participants of the objectives of the investigation, including aspects that might influence their willingness to participate. Where fully informed consent is not obtained, additional safeguards relating to deception must protect the participants' welfare and dignity.

- Efforts should be made to obtain the real consent of children and adults with impairments of understanding or communication and if they are unable to give it, special safeguarding procedures must be employed. For participants less than 16 years of age permission must additionally be obtained from parents or those *in loco parentis*. Where the nature of the research precludes such permission the investigator must seek appropriate consultation.

- Where real consent cannot be obtained from adults with impairments, permission must be sought from a person well placed to judge for the participant and from disinterested advisors.

- In research with detained persons special care must be taken to ensure that their circumstances do not affect their ability to give free informed consent.

- The investigator's position of responsibility should not be used to pressurise participants to take part in or remain in the investigation.

- Payment of participants must not be used to encourage them to take risks beyond that which they would experience in their normal lifestyle.

- If harm or unusual discomfort or other negative consequences for the individual might occur in the future, additional steps must be taken to obtain approval from other researchers and real consent from the participants.

- In longitudinal research, consent may be required on more than one occasion.

Deception

- Withholding information or otherwise misleading the participants is unacceptable if they are likely to object or show unease once debriefed. In such cases additional consultation is required with experienced psychologists or with individuals sharing the same social and cultural background as the participants.

- Intentional deception of participants over the purpose and general nature of the investigation should be considered only where there is extremely strong scientific or medical justification. Even then strict controls and the approval of independent advisors is necessary.

- Deception may be unavoidable in the study of some psychological processes. In these cases the investigator must (a) be sure that other procedures are not available, (b) provide participants with sufficient information as early as possible and (c) consult appropriately about the way that such deception will be received.

Debriefing

- Following studies in which participants are aware that they have taken part the investigator should debrief them by providing sufficient information to complete their understanding of the research. They should then discuss the participants' experience and monitor any unforeseen negative effects or misconceptions.

- Debriefing is not a justification for unethical procedures.

- Where the effects of an experiment cannot be negated by a verbal description of the research, investigators should employ active intervention before the participants leave the research setting.

Withdrawal from the investigation

- Participants should be made aware from the outset that they have the right to withdraw from the investigation at any time, irrespective of payment. Children may indicate their desire to withdraw by avoidance of the situation and this should be acknowledged.

- Following participation or debriefing a participant may withdraw their consent retrospectively and require that their data be destroyed.

Confidentiality

- Information obtained during an investigation must remain confidential unless otherwise agreed with the participant in advance and published data must not be individually identifiable. If confidentiality and/or anonymity cannot be guaranteed, participants must be warned in advance of the investigation.

Protection of participants

- Investigators must protect participants from risk of physical or mental harm during the investigation. Participants must be asked about any factor in the planned procedure that might create a risk such as pre-existing medical conditions and advised appropriately.

- Participants should be informed of procedures for contacting the investigator should unforeseen stress, potential harm or related issues arise following participation.

- In the case of research that involves behaviour or experiences that the participant may regard as personal and private, participants must be appropriately protected from stress and assured that answers to all questions need not be given. There should be no deception when seeking information that might encroach on privacy.

- Caution should be exercised in discussing the results of research on children with their parents, teachers or those *in loco parentis*.

Observational research

- Unless those being observed give their consent, observational research should be carried out only in situations where those being observed would expect to be seen by strangers. Account should be taken of local cultural values and of the possibility of intruding upon the privacy of individuals who, while in a public space, may believe they are unobserved.

Giving advice

- If an investigator discovers evidence of physical or psychological problems of which the participant is apparently unaware they should inform the participant if they believe that failure to do so may endanger the participant's future well-being.

- If participants solicit advice from the investigator concerning educational, personality, behavioural or health issues, caution should be exercised and professional advice recommended if the investigator is not qualified to offer assistance.

- Advice may be offered if this is intrinsic to the research and has been agreed in advance.

Colleagues

- Responsibility for the ethical treatment of participants is shared among the investigator and their collaborators, assistants, students and employees. Psychologists also have a responsibility to encourage other investigators to conduct research in accordance with the ethical principles.

interactive
angles

- Which aspects of the Ethical Principles would be contravened by the following procedures?

(a) A psychologist employing relaxation techniques allows participants to leave the experimental setting very sleepy to get into their cars to return home.

(b) A team of researchers studying workplace bullying describes the setting as a large manufacturing company in the south-west of England. It becomes apparent from extracts of dialogue that the company manufactures widgets. There is, however, only one widget-maker in the south-west.

(c) A psychologist using hypnosis debriefs the participants but does not tell them that they may later recall some disturbing aspects of the research.

(d) A psychology student working on stress is measuring the blood pressure of participants before and after they have attempted an insoluble logic problem as an indicator of anxiety. One participant has a very high blood pressure at the start of the experiment and the student suggests that they should cut down the amount of fat they eat and get more exercise.

● How might each of the situations (a)–(d) have been adapted so that the procedures fell within the BPS guidelines?

● A student is conducting a replication of Piaget's conservation experiments at a primary school. Two children look into the room where he is working and run away. When asked to come back they say no and hide in the playhouse. What should the student do?

● A researcher is investigating road rage by photographing drivers in a long queue of traffic to see how many of them are drumming their fingers on the steering wheel or biting their nails. She finds that in many of the photographs the drivers are engaging in behaviours we would not normally see, such as picking their nose. Is her observational study ethical?

interactive
angles

Return to the description at the beginning of the chapter. In what ways does the study reported (which was conducted as part of an introduction to psychology for medical students at a British university in the 1980s) contravene the ethical guidelines?

research
issues

ethics: is just being part of a group sufficient to lead to prejudice?

Tajfel, H. (1970) Experiments in intergroup discrimination. *Scientific American*, 223, 96–102

Aim: Tajfel was interested in whether being categorised as belonging to one of two groups was sufficient to induce prejudice against another clearly identifiable group even when they were not competition.

Method: In one experiment the participants, 64 British schoolboys aged 14–15 years, were told that the researchers were investigating vision. They were shown clusters of dots on a screen and asked to estimate the number of dots. The boys were then randomly allocated into two groups but were told that they were being divided into groups (either *underestimators* and *overestimators* in one condition or *accurate* and *inaccurate* in the other) on the basis of their number-estimates. The next task was to allocate points to each other, choosing which one of a pair of boys should receive points for their estimates of the numbers of dots. They were told that points could later be converted into money. The participants did not know which individuals they were allotting the money to but they did know which group each boy was in. In different conditions, the choices were between two boys in the in-group, two boys in the out-group or between one boy from the in-group and one from the out-group.

Results: The boys overwhelmingly chose to allocate points to others who had been identified as being in the same group as themselves regardless of the accuracy of the boys' estimates.

Conclusion: Although there was no competition between groups, the participants consistently displayed a prejudice towards those who were identified as being in the same group as themselves and against those identified as in a different group.

Questions

1 Identify as many potential ethical dilemmas as you can in this report.

2 Suggest how one of these might have been overcome.

research
issues

ethics: cool Britannia

Poppe, E. and Linssen, H. (1999) In-group favouritism and the reflection of realistic dimensions of difference between national states in Central and Eastern European nationality stereotypes. *British Journal of Social Psychology*, 38, 85–102

Aim: To investigate the stereotypes European adolescents hold regarding the morality and competence of their own and other European nationalities. Social identity theory would predict that the young people questioned would favour their own country. However, differences in the economic status and recent history of different European countries would suggest that people in some states should rate other countries as more competent and/or moral than their own.

Method: 1143 students aged 15–18 from Russia, Bulgaria, Hungary, Poland, Belarus and the Czech Republic answered a questionnaire that examined beliefs about the characteristics of people from European countries including all those from which participants were taken, plus Italy, Germany and England. The questionnaires required participants to rate each nationality according to their competence and their morality. The questionnaires given to different partici-pants listed the various nationalities in different orders to ensure that they were not influenced by the order of presentation. The responses were analysed to see whether people tended to favour their own nationality over others or whether general national stereotypes (such as German efficiency) proved a more important factor in judgements.

Results: The Eastern Europeans tended to favour their own nationality over those of other Eastern Europeans but not over Western Europeans. Overall, national stereotypes were upheld and participants consistently rated Germans as the most competent (though least moral) and the English as the most moral people.

Conclusion: Social identity appeared to be one factor affecting people's judgements about other nationalities, correctly predicting that the Eastern European countries would show in-group favouritism in relation to other East European countries. However, people did not blindly favour their own nationality and economic and historical factors proved important in creating national stereotypes.

Questions

1 The findings of this study could be used to reinforce rather than reduce stereotypes. To what extent do psychologists have a responsibility to challenge rather than exacerbate social issues such as prejudice?

2 What should a psychologist do to act within the BPS guidelines in conducting and reporting upon a study such as this?

research
issues

ethics: obedience kills

Milgram, S. (1963) Behavioural study of obedience. *Journal of Abnormal and Social Psychology*, 67, 371–8

Aim: To investigate how obedient people would be in a situation where following orders would mean breaking participants' moral code and harming another person.

Method: Milgram advertised for male volunteers to take part in a memory experiment for a fee of $4. When they arrived at the university, the participants were told they would be either a teacher or a learner. They were then introduced to 'Mr Wallace', a mild-mannered and pleasant middle-aged man who was in fact a confederate. In a contrived but apparently random procedure, Milgram ensured that the participant was always the teacher and 'Mr Wallace' was always the learner. Mr Wallace was then strapped into a chair and given a memory task involving remembering pairs of words. The genuine participant was given a 45-volt shock to illustrate that the apparatus was real. Every time Wallace made a mistake the participant was ordered to give him an electric shock. Apart from the one demonstrated to the teacher there were no real shocks but the participants themselves did not know this. Following each mistake the level of the 'shock' appeared to increase. The shock levels on the machine were labelled from 0 to 450 volts and also had signs saying 'danger – severe shock' and, at 450 volts 'XXX'. Milgram ordered participants to continue giving increased shocks while the learner shouted and screamed in pain then appeared to collapse. When participants protested they were told 'the experiment requires that you continue'. After the experiment the participants were fully debriefed about the true purpose of the experiment, assured that no shocks had been delivered to Mr Wallace and saw he was alive and well. Obedient participants were assured that their response in such as situation was entirely normal and that they were not alone in their feelings of tension and conflict. The decision of disobedient participants was also supported. They were followed up a year later when all except one was glad to have participated.

Results: To Milgram's surprise, all the participants gave Mr Wallace some electric shocks and 65 per cent gave the full 450 volts to an apparently dead Mr Wallace! Most participants protested and some wept and begged in their distress, obviously believing that they had killed Mr Wallace. However, most people did not feel that they could stop when ordered to continue by Milgram.

Conclusion: This study demonstrates the power of authority over our behaviour. What is particularly remarkable about the results is that participants were clearly very upset by what they had to do, but saw no alternative except to obey.

Questions

1 List the ethically sound and unsound aspects of this experiment. Relate each of these to a point made in the Ethical Guidelines.

2 Which, if any, of the unsound aspects could have been avoided without introducing demand characteristics that would have obscured the experimental effect?

3 In his criticism of Milgram, Baumrind (1964) argued that the rights and feelings of the participants had been violated and that Milgram's efforts to protect them from stress and emotional conflict were inadequate. Did Milgram *expect* the participants to suffer the stress that they did?

4 Shortly after publication of this paper, Milgram's membership of the American Psychological Association (APA) was suspended while the APA Ethical Committee investigated the research. It was eventually deemed to be ethically sound and, in 1965, Milgram was awarded the prize for outstanding contribution to social psychological research by the American Association for the Advancement of Science. If Milgram's research is considered in terms of the *benefit to society* rather than the *cost to the individual* it becomes easier to understand how the ends justify the means. In the historical context of Milgram's study, what insight did the findings provide?

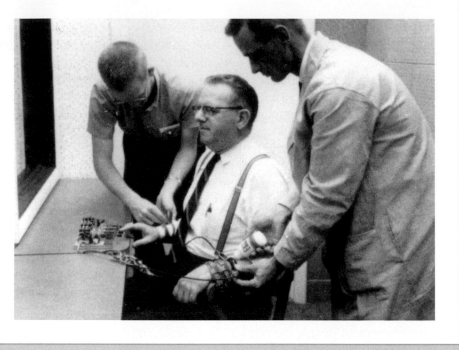

An experimenter shows the 'teacher' how to administer an electric shock to the 'learner'

Compare Milgram's obedience study above with the field experiment described below and consider the differences between them in terms of the ethical issues they present.

research
issues

ethics: do nurses obey doctors' orders?

Hofling, K.C., Brotzman, E., Dalrymple, S., Graves, N. and Pierce, C.M. (1966) An experimental study in the nurse–physician relationship. *Journal of Nervous and Mental Disorders,* 143, 171–80

Aim: To discover whether nurses would obey a doctor if, by doing so, they would breach hospital regulations and endanger the lives of patients. On a practical level, this would have implications for nurse training and hospital policy and on a theoretical level it is interesting to see whether the high levels of obedience reported in Milgram's laboratory studies would be replicated in a real-life setting.

Method: Boxes of capsules labelled 'Astrofen' were placed with other medicines in 22 hospital wards of American hospitals. The capsules contained glucose, harmless to the most patients, but the label said that the maximum safe daily dose was only 10 mg. A researcher calling himself 'Dr Smith from the psychiatric department' telephoned nurses on duty on each ward and instructed them to give a patient, Mr Jones, 20 mg of Astrofen. Although written authorisation was normally required before nurses were allowed give drugs Dr Smith said that he was running late and would get there and sign the necessary authorisation shortly. Meanwhile, 22 other nurses not involved in the field experiment were interviewed and asked whether they would administer more than a safe dose if a doctor telephoned when they were on duty and instructed them to do so.

Results: There was a significant difference between what the nurses interviewed said they would do and the behaviour of the nurses actually put in the situation. Of the nurses interviewed, 21 out of 22 said that they would not obey the doctor's instructions, yet 21 of the 22 nurses told by telephone to give a large dose of Astrofen did so! When questioned later, 11 of these nurses said that they had not noticed the discrepancy between the maximum dose and the dose they were told to give. The other 10 did notice but judged that it must be safe if the doctor ordered them to give it.

Conclusion: Although the nurses believed that they would not obey a doctor unquestioningly if they were ordered to do something that breached regulations and endangered patients, it appeared that in fact they did just that.

Questions

1 Describe the implications this study has for the safety of patients.

2 How do you think the nurses in the experimental condition (who received a telephone call) would have felt? How does this relate to the Ethical Guidelines?

interactive
angles

This exercise is best organised in small groups. Imagine that you were on an Ethical Committee that received a proposal for a study similar to that of Hofling *et al*. What considerations would be important if the study were to go ahead? Would you want to implement any changes or additions? How could you insist that the findings were used for the benefit of patients and not to reprimand nurses? Remember, you would not at the planning stage know the outcome of the study but you would be able to base assumptions on previous, similar studies such as that by Milgram.

Socially sensitive research

Arguably, psychologists have a role in the public domain. The BPS *Ethical Principles* (1978) refers to psychologists as being 'committed to increasing the understanding that people have of their own and others' behaviour in the belief that this understanding ameliorates the human condition'. The 1998 *Ethical Principles* observes that participants in psychological research should have confidence in the investigators. Psychologists cannot hope to 'give psychology away' successfully unless the recipients of the benefits of their findings have both trust in the researchers and belief that the information has the potential to be beneficial. Working within the ethical guidelines helps to ensure that:

- members of the public who come in contact with research or clinical practice encounter mutual respect between themselves and professional psychologists; and

- the community in general can appreciate the outcomes of that research or intervention.

The potential risks and benefits arising from psychology in the public domain are perhaps greatest in the areas of socially sensitive research. Whenever the participating individuals or implicated groups may be adversely affected by their own interpretations of research findings or the interpretations of others, whether accurate or misplaced, the research is described as *socially sensitive*. For example, research into the effects of day-care on children has found wildly differing results. Some have found that children who have spent time in day-care score higher on measures of academic achievement and social skills indicating that day-care can have very positive effects (e.g. Andersson, 1992). Other studies have shown that day-care is associated with insecure attachment, demonstrating that if mothers started work in their first year the children were more likely to have behavioural difficulties or poor intellectual development (e.g. Baydar and Brooks-Gunn, 1991). Yet other studies have found no link between day-care and development (e.g. Clarke-Stewart *et al.*, 1994).

research issues

ethics: does mummy matter?

Melhuish, E.C., Mooney, A., Martin, S. and Lloyd, E. (1990a) Type of childcare at 18 months I. Differences in interactional experience. *Journal of Child Psychology and Psychiatry*, 31, 849–59

Melhuish, E.C., Lloyd, E., Martin, S. and Mooney, A. (1990b) Type of childcare at 18 months II. Relations with cognitive and language development. *Journal of Child Psychology and Psychiatry*, 31, 861–70

Aim: To measure the relative social-emotional and intellectual progress made by children who remained in full-time maternal care and those who experienced day-care and to investigate the factors that differed between different forms of day-care which may have contributed to any differences in the development of the children.

Method: 255 first-born children from two-parent families were followed from birth to three years. All the mothers were in full-time work before they had a child and 75 per cent returned to work before the baby was 9 months old. Of the children in day-care, 30 per cent were cared for by a relative, 50 per cent by a childminder and 20 per cent at a nursery. At 18 months and 3 years the children were all assessed on their social-emotional, intellectual and language development, using observation and interviews with the carers. The day-care environments were also assessed for factors that might contribute to a child's level of development.

Results: Some variables did not vary across the different environments. The amount of crying, playing and physical contact with adults was the same for children cared for by their mother, another relative, a childminder or a nursery. However, there were some differences in the children's behaviour. The amount of vocalisation in 18-month-olds was greatest with the mothers, then with a relative, less with a childminder and least of all in nurseries. On measures of aggression children in nurseries came out highest and those with their mothers lowest. This was reversed for affection, this being greatest with mothers and least in nurseries. No differences emerged in the proportion of children showing secure attachments to their mothers between the four groups. At three years the children with their mothers showed the most affection but those in nurseries the best social skills.

Considerable variations in the quality of care were noted. The nurseries were characterised by low levels of responsiveness to children's communications and a low adult : child ratio (average 4.6 : 1). The nursery staff members were younger than the carers in the other conditions and less likely to have children of their own. The nurseries also had a high turnover of staff, so that the children did not have consistent adults with whom they could form an attachment.

Conclusions: On most, though not all, measures the children in nurseries did less well than the others. However, the real message of this study is not that there is anything wrong with nurseries, but that good care of young children is associated with good responsiveness to the child, a high staff : child ratio, experienced staff and a low staff turnover, whatever the type of child-care.

Questions

1 What differences were exhibited between children receiving different sorts of care?

2 Who are the participant groups affected by the experiment?

3 Who could, potentially, be affected by the social consequences or implications of such findings if these were generalised to groups of individuals?

4 Why might such research be identified as socially sensitive?

inter**active**
angles

Other areas of socially sensitive research include investigations into sexual orientation, race-related research (such as into differences in IQ), investigations into methods of controlling behaviour such as through brain surgery or drugs and research about AIDS.

Attempt to find studies that report sensitive research in some of these areas. Describe in detail *why* the research might be ethically sensitive. This may be in terms of the manner in which it was conducted or the ways in which the findings could be interpreted.

Research with non-human animals

Why use animals?

Driscoll and Bateson (1988) discussed the reasons for using animals in research. They observed that, especially for investigations motivated by an intrinsic interest, it could be difficult to justify the value of the research to the public. There are two problems here. Firstly, it can be difficult to explain how an increasing knowledge of natural systems can ultimately reap immense benefits. For example, it cannot have been apparent to contemporaries of Thorndike that the general laws of learning he was beginning to elucidate through his research with cats in puzzle boxes would eventually have such diverse applications. Secondly, practical benefits of research are not necessarily easy to predict or identify immediately. Driscoll and Bateson identified the following reasons for using animals in research:

- to understand natural principles because an animal can provide a convenient model for a process (such as using pigeons or rats to study the general features of learning);

- when a procedure cannot ethically be carried out on humans (e.g. developmental studies involving isolation);

- when they are especially good examples of a particular phenomenon (such as communication: bird song or bee dances);

- because they are fascinating as animals (e.g. bat sonar or whale song).

Why might you use animals in each of the following investigations?

1   A study of overcrowding where groups are kept in closer confines than they would normally live for several months.

2   An investigation into the role of light on the early development of the retina which requires raising neonates in darkness.

3   An experiment which is investigating the way in which sexual arousal affects the release of hormones.

Why protect animals?

As we observed above, one of the reasons for using non-human animals in psychology is because of *continuity*. The evolutionary link between other species (most apparent in those closest to us) and ourselves enables us to justify the use of animals as reliable models of human action. If this continuity is extended, it seems unlikely that the non-human animals most often selected for studies (those bearing similarities to ourselves) would differ from us so greatly in their capacity to feel pain and suffer. Because animals cannot defend themselves they are protected both by guidelines and by law.

How many animals are used in psychological studies?

Still (1982) reviewed the numbers of animals used in experiments reported in the journal *Animal Behaviour* in 1979. There were 117 articles, which fell into the following categories:

- 49 were experimental studies of vertebrates;
- 38 of these were field studies (they were of wild or domestic animals and inflicted no painful procedures except, in some cases, tagging);
- 19 were experimental studies of invertebrates;
- 10 were theoretical papers.

Of the experimental studies on vertebrates, 18 involved mild suffering (including food deprivation, hormone injections) while in 6 the treatment was more severe (electric shocks, 48-hour food deprivation in cats, pigs and rats and 24-hour water deprivation in rats). He concluded that the numbers of animals used could sometimes be reduced without loss of scientific rigour. It was observed that fewer animals were used in studies relying upon expensive, exotic species such as mink and seals. It is reasonable to assume that if numbers can be reduced on economic grounds similar reductions could be made on ethical grounds. Suggestions for change include using more powerful statistical tests, higher significance levels, better experimental designs, sequential tests and single subject designs.

McConway (1991), in a replication of Still (1982), found the following numbers of articles in the first 1990 edition of *Animal Behaviour*:

- 53 were experimental studies of vertebrates;
- 33 of these were field studies (they were of wild or domestic animals and inflicted no painful procedures except, in some cases, tagging);
- 27 were experimental studies of invertebrates;
- 8 were theoretical papers.

These 122 papers show only slight differences in terms of the proportion of studies in each category compared with Still (1982). However, in comparing the suffering of vertebrate animals (using the same criteria as Still) McConway found fewer studies involved the procedures classified by Still as causing 'mild suffering' (or ones similarly categorised by McConway including electrode implantation and minor surgical procedures but not counting handling). McConway (1991) identified none involving the 'more severe' treatments listed by Still (1982). Nevertheless, McConway concludes that it is still valid to ask whether the numbers of animals used can be reduced. In a comparison of the numbers of subjects used, McConway found that more rather than fewer animals were being used. In some cases this was because very large groups, such as colony-living birds, were being observed, but in general McConway concludes that there is little evidence that the advice of Still (1982) on ways to reduce subject numbers in experiments is being followed by researchers.

research issues

ethics: monkeys' mums matter!

Harlow, H.F. (1965) Love in infant monkeys. *Scientific American*, 200, 68–74

Aim: To determine the role of food and comfort on attachment by rearing baby monkeys in isolation.

Method: Rhesus monkeys (*Macaca mulatta*) were reared alone, without their mothers, in cages containing a pair of 'surrogate mothers'. One of these models provided nourishment; it was made of wire and supplied milk though a teat. The other model provided comfort; it was covered with soft terry towelling.

Results: The infant monkeys clung to the soft surrogates, ran to them if they were afraid and used them as a safe base from which to explore. If the soft surrogate was absent, the infants either froze or became highly active, apparently displaying intense fear. As adults these monkeys displayed social abnormalities; they were easily dominated, often failed to mate and were poor mothers.

Conclusion: The contact with the soft model seemed to be important in the formation of a strong bond between the infant monkey and the soft surrogate. No such bonding was demonstrated towards the wire surrogate. The formation of this bond seemed to be important to subsequent social interactions.

Questions

1 Identify the ethical issues raised by this study.

2 Why might rhesus monkeys have been chosen as the experimental species?

3 Subsequent studies have suggested that the behavioural abnormalities may have be due to the social isolation rather than absence of mothering since some of the effects could be reversed by social housing. Does this finding affect the justification for conducting this study, and if so how?

Assessing pain in non-human animals

Bateson (1991) suggests that until we can reliably identify the experience of stress or pain, it is difficult to implement guidelines that aim to protect animals from suffering. He proposes that from an understanding of comparable mechanisms and behaviour in humans and non-human animals, we could generalise some criteria that are used to identify pain in humans, to animals. For some species such criteria seem to be appropriate; we might feel confident about assessing the stress or pain experienced by a mammal or even a bird, but we might feel less certain in our judgement of the experiences felt by a locust or octopus. What criteria may be used?

- *Continuities between humans and non-human animals* – humans after the age of about 2 years become self aware, that is, they are not only aware that an experience may hurt but be conscious of their own self as distinct from others. While it is difficult to ascertain the extent of self-awareness in non-human animals, Dawkins (1980) has observed that animals may possess some or all of the attributes of self-awareness to differing extents, so we cannot decide categorically that an animal *is* or *is not* conscious. If her assumptions are right we are not forced to choose but to acknowledge a degree of self-awareness in non-human animals. The sensations of pain and self-awareness are not equivalent but any evidence for such awareness in an animal could only strengthen the case for supposing that it could suffer. Conversely, the absence of such evidence would not negate the possibility of an animal experiencing pain.

- *Cognitive abilities* – brain size and structure combined with evidence of reflective consciousness, such as from deception by non-human animals suggests a level of consciousness capable of experiencing pain.

- *Non-verbal signs of pain* such as howling, although a distressed animal may alternatively remain quiet.

- *Behavioural signs of pain* – such as escape, although a distressed animal may alternatively remain immobile, fail to groom, lose its appetite or show avoidance or suppression of social behaviours.

Objective measures of pain?

A normal rat will drink a sugar solution in preference to one containing analgesic. A rat with chronically inflamed joints will choose to drink a solution containing analgesic (Colpaert *et al.*, 1980). What does this tell us about the experience of the rat with inflamed joints?

Assessing the experience of pain in non-human animals more distant from ourselves than mammals is even more challenging. Fish, which are long-lived complex vertebrates, demonstrate flight behaviour in response to substances released from the damaged skin of fish similar to themselves (Hara, 1986). To judge the animals' responses to situations that might be subjectively unpleasant, Dawkins (1983) tested the effort an animal would expend to escape a potentially painful experience. She measured the cost chickens would endure (by forcing themselves through narrow gaps, a behaviour they generally avoid) in order to overcome a potentially aversive situation. Arey (1992) used a similar technique with pregnant sows and found that during their gestation they would 'work' (by pressing a door with their nose) harder for food than for nesting material (straw). Immediately prior to parturition, however, the sows would work almost as hard for straw as food, pressing the door 300 times for access to bedding (on average 17 times per day). This suggests that deprivation of straw is as serious as food deprivation for a sow at the end of her gestation period.

- *Physiological signs of pain* – pilo-erection (raised hair), increased heart and breathing rate.

- *Learning capacities* – some animals can be conditioned in as little as a single trial to avoid a noxious stimulus. On the one hand this may be taken to indicate the severity of the suffering avoided by the learned response. On the other hand, it may be interpreted as a simple association and not necessarily indicative of a brain sufficiently complex to experience suffering.

- *Features of the nervous system* – while there are parallels between the pain perception in humans and non-human animals such as pain receptors and pathways, this does not guarantee the experience of pain or its absence. Evolution has resulted in both analogous systems (such as wings in birds and insects) and homologous ones (such as the use of the pentadactyl limb to fly in bats, to dig in moles and to gallop in horses). This is of particular importance in the assessment of pain in invertebrates, which lack the pain fibres found in mammals. A locust may continue to feed while it is being eaten by a mantis (although a herbivore will also graze normally after severe injury). An octopus in contrast will rapidly learn to avoid visual or tactile stimuli associated with an electric shock (Wells, 1978).

media watch

Strong arm of the law embraces British octopuses

Protection for the octopus

Octopuses are to be protected from painful scientific experiments, the Home Office has ruled. For the first time, an animal lacking a backbone will be included under the regulations that already cover experiments on vertebrates – fish, amphibians, reptiles, birds and mammals. Now, any scientist wanting to experiment on octopuses will have to apply for a licence, and use anaesthetics during surgery.

The Home Office has acted on recommendations from its Animal Procedures Committee, which was set up to advise government on animal experiments. A clear majority of the APC agreed that there was sufficient evidence of sentience to give one species of invertebrate, the common octopus *Octopus vulgaris*, the benefit of the doubt, the APC's chairman, Lord Nathan, wrote in a letter to the Home Secretary.

A minority of the committee voted against extending protection to any of the cephalopods, which include squids and nautiluses as well as octopuses, on the grounds that there is no 'definite, scientific evidence' that these animals experience pain or suffering.

'It is an excellent idea,' says Roger Ewbank, director of the Universities Federation for Animal Welfare and a member of the APC. Octopuses have complex nervous systems and learning abilities that rival those of fish and amphibians, he says. 'But it is a pity that it was not extended to all cephalopods. That would have been scientifically much more tidy.'

Only a handful of British biologists will be affected by the decision, as most research on these animals takes place abroad. Nonetheless, some scientists on the committee fear that it will be 'the thin end of the wedge', says Ewbank, and sets a precedent for further extensions into the invertebrate kingdom, perhaps to include advanced insects as well.

More immediate problems may face Home Office inspectors responsible for policing the act. According to Peter Boyle, at the University of Aberdeen, the use of anaesthetics in these animals is 'at a relatively primitive stage'.

New Scientist, 2 October 1993

Why have octopuses been protected by law?

1876 Cruelty to Animals Act

The first act of parliament to protect animals in scientific experiments was the 1876 Cruelty to Animals Act. This defined an experiment as being 'calculated to cause pain on a living, vertebrate animal, and to be of unknown origin'. Such experiments were regulated by the issue of Home Office licences and exemption certificates, the procedure for which has now changed.

1986 Animals (Scientific Procedures) Act

The 1986 Animals (Scientific Procedures) Act did not abolish the 1876 Act, but replaced it in the context of animal experimentation. The new legislation again depends on the issue of licences by the Home Office but these are issued to specific individuals for particular projects so that research on animals can be more closely monitored. A 'Project Licence' covers three aspects of research:

- *The procedures*: the Home Secretary is required to weigh the likely adverse effects to the animals used (*animal suffering*) against the gains likely to accrue from the work (*certainty of medical benefit*).

- *The animals*: their breeding and supply, daily and veterinary care.

- *The premises*: which are checked by Her Majesty's Inspectorate (HMIs).

How are decisions about animal experiments made?

Bateson (1986) argued that when there is a conflict of interest between experimenters and their critics, this might be resolved by weighing up the degree of suffering for the animal subjects against the value of the research. This balance can be represented by the diagram opposite.

When a research proposal falls into the opaque region of the decision cube, the experiment should not be conducted, those falling in the clear space should proceed.

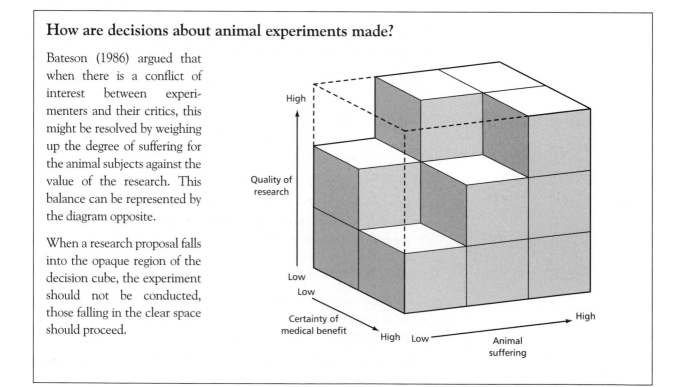

British Psychological Society *Guidelines for the Use of Animals in Research* (1985)

These guidelines were published to assist members of the BPS in the planning of experiments with live animals and to remind them of their general obligation to avoid, or at least to minimise, discomfort to living animals.

- *The law* – Investigators must work within the laws protecting animals.

- *Ethical considerations* – If the animals are confined, restrained, harmed or stressed in any way the investigator must consider whether the knowledge gained justifies the procedure. Options other than animal experiments should be considered.

- *Species* – When research is likely to cause pain or discomfort it should be borne in mind that some species may suffer less than others. An appropriate choice of species usually requires a consideration of its natural history as well as its special needs.

- *Number of animals* – Laboratory studies should use the smallest number of animals necessary, through the prudent choice of experimental design and statistical tests.

- *Endangered species* – Wild animals from endangered species should not be collected or manipulated except as part of a serious attempt at conservation.

- *Animal suppliers* – Investigators should obtain animals only from reputable suppliers and must ensure that they are provided with adequate food, water, ventilation and space during transit, and are not unduly stressed. Where animals are trapped in the wild this must be done in as painless and humane way as possible.

- *Caging and social environment* – This should take account of the social behaviour of the species as this will affect the acceptable density of animals to avoid overcrowding and response to social isolation.

- *Fieldwork* – Animals in the field should be disturbed as little as possible; even observations may affect the breeding and survival of wild animals. Investigators should consider the effects and potential stress of identification marks, radio transmitters and the capture and recapture of animals.

- *Aggression and predation including infanticide* – That animals experience pain and injury in the wild should not be used to defend the occurrence of suffering in the laboratory. Where possible, natural encounters should be observed in preference to staged ones. If this is not possible, models or glass screens should be used to reduce risk and the number of subjects and length of the experiments should be minimised.

- *Motivation* – The normal eating and drinking habits and metabolic requirements of the species and individual should be considered when arranging schedules of deprivation.

- *Aversive stimulation and stressful procedures* – Procedures causing pain or distress to animals are illegal in the UK unless the experimenter holds an appropriate Home Office licence. Options other than aversive stimuli should be considered and where no alternative can be found the investigator must ensure that the suffering is minimised and is justified by the expected outcome.

- *Surgical and pharmacological procedures* – It is illegal to perform any such procedure without an appropriate Home Office licence. Where these are performed, staff must be experienced in the procedures, anaesthesia and toxicity. Steps must be taken to prevent post-operative infection where appropriate and be aware of the implications of using different strains of animal and new environments on behaviour.

- *Anaesthesia, analgesia and euthanasia* – Animals must receive adequate post-operative care, and if post-operative suffering occurs it should be minimised by suitable nursing and local anaesthetic. Recovery should be frequently monitored and if at any time an animal is suffering severe and enduring pain it must be killed in a suitable manner for the species.

- *Independent advice* – Doubts about the condition of an animal should be raised with someone not directly involved in the experiment, preferably a veterinarian.

research
issues

ethics: sleeplessness kills

Rechtschaffen, A., Gilliland, M.A., Bergmann, B.M. and Winter, J.B. (1983)
Physiological correlates of prolonged sleep deprivation in rats. *Science*, 221, 182–4

Aim: To investigate the effect of prolonged sleep deprivation.

Method: Pairs of rats were housed in an experimental chamber consisting of a rotating platform and a central division beneath which there was shallow water. A *yoked-control* procedure was employed such that in each pair of rats, one was constantly sleep deprived while the other could sleep but was forced to take an identical amount of exercise at the same time (like a pair of yoked oxen). The rats were monitored continuously and when the experimental individual began to fall asleep the platform was rotated, requiring both animals to walk in order to avoid falling into the water. Eight pairs of animals were housed in the apparatus for a period of 5 to 33 days.

Results: The procedure reduced the experimental animals' sleep time by 87 per cent but that of the control animals by only 31 per cent. The control animals remained healthy but the consequences for the experimental animals were profound. They appeared to be sick, they stopped grooming themselves, became weak and uncoordinated and failed to regulate their body temperature. They ate more than usual but their elevated metabolic rate caused them to continue to lose weight. Three experimental animals died and a further four had to be killed because of the extent of their suffering. The cause of death was unclear.

Conclusion: Enforced sleep deprivation for a prolonged period of time is harmful and potentially fatal. This may be due to disruption to the immune system rather than to organ damage or the effects of stress.

Questions

1 Why were animals used in this research?

2 Why was a yoked procedure used?

3 Identify the ethical issues raised by this research.

Association for the Study of Animal Behaviour *Ethics in Research on Animal Behaviour* (1991)

The Association for the Study of Animal Behaviour (ASAB) has played a pivotal role in the ethical treatment of animals in research. The ASAB first provided guidelines for the use of animals in 1981, publishes research that justifies these recommendations and makes strategic use of the guidelines to ensure that work published in the society's journal *Animal Behaviour* is ethically sound. Its concerns include the minimising of animal suffering during experiments, issues arising from predation, aggression and infanticide and risks to habitats of wild populations.

The guidelines for the use of animals in research (1991) provide greater detail than the BPS guidelines, adding the following issues to those described above.

- *Choice of species* – The species chosen should be suited to answer the research question. Consideration should be given to the species' natural history and complexity. Knowledge of an animal's previous experience, such as whether it has been in captivity throughout its life, can be of great importance.

- *Pain or discomfort* – In fieldwork, feeding may be disrupted by observation. Adverse consequences of disruption for the animals being studied as well as other plants and animals in the ecosystem should be considered.

- *Aversive stimuli and deprivation* – Alternatives to deprivation could include the use of highly preferred foods and other rewards to motivate satiated animals.

- *Social deprivation, isolation and crowding* – The degree of stress experienced by a crowded or isolated animal will vary not only with species but also with age, sex, reproductive condition, social status, biology and previous social experience.

- *Housing and animal care* – Experimenters should be responsible for their animal's conditions of care. Caging and husbandry practices should at least meet the minimum standards set in the Universities' Federation for Animal (1987) Welfare handbook. For wild animals maintenance should incorporate where possible the aspects of the natural living conditions deemed to be important such as natural materials, refuges, perches and dust and water baths. Frequency of cleaning should represent a compromise between cleanliness and the stress created by handling, and unfamiliar surroundings, odours and bedding.

- *Final disposition of animals* – Where practical or feasible, researchers should distribute their animals to colleagues for further study unless this would result in their being exposed repeatedly to stressful or painful treatments. Field-trapped animals should be returned to the wild if this is feasible, legal and will not be detrimental to existing populations and when their ability to survive has not been impaired.

for and against

the use of animals in psychological research

+ The nervous system of non-human animals is similar to that of humans but is simpler, so they provide ideal models for testing hypotheses about behaviour.

+ Non-human animals can be used for procedures (such as isolation and surgery) that would be unethical on humans.

− The similarities between non-human animals and humans may be insufficient to justify generalisation from one to the other.

− Procedures that are deemed to be unethical for humans may cause similar but undetectable suffering for animals.

− Animals cannot readily communicate their responses, they can only be observed. This may be less informative, biased by observers and excludes access to thoughts and emotions.

Conclusions

The British Psychological Society guidelines identify consent, conduct, competence and confidentiality as central ethical issues when working with human participants. For students, the concepts of informed consent, debriefing and the right to withdraw are particularly pertinent. Non-human animals can provide excellent models for human behaviour but there are both theoretical and ethical grounds for limiting the use of animals in psychological research.

where to now?

▶ **Stamp Dawkins, M. and Gosling, M. (Eds) (1991)** *Ethics in Research on Animal Behaviour*. **London: Academic Press** – a collection of key papers on the ethics of animals in research and includes the ASAB guidelines in full

▶ **Howitt, D. and Cramer, D. (2000)** *First Steps in Research and Statistics*. **London: Routledge** – has an excellent section on the practical issues of applying ethical guidelines to student research.

what do you know?

1 Summarise the key elements of the BPS Code of Conduct for research with human participants.

2 Use one study to illustrate ways in which the issues raised in the guidelines have and have not been followed.

3 Tabulate the arguments for and against the use of non-human animals in psychological research.

4 Describe one study of non-human animals and identify the ethical issues it raises.

14

Coursework

This chapter aims to help you through each stage of your coursework from formulating an idea to presentation of the final document. References to other chapters in the text will provide the details of the techniques and procedures described but this chapter is devoted to the practical steps involved in setting up, conducting and writing up your own research.

Where to begin?

Ideas

When asked to think up an idea to research most people find that their mind goes blank. Any ideas they can generate are either impractical or unethical! How can you find an interesting topic that is not too difficult to research?

There are two options. You could think about daily life: what's interesting about the things that people do? Maybe when you look around you, you can see differences that catch your eye: do men and women use different techniques for taking off their jumpers? Do people who bite their nails also bite the ends of their pens? Which is easier, reading text presented to you upside down or reading with your head upside down but the text the right way up? Who would make more mistakes in reproducing web addresses, young people or older people? Is it okay to do your revision listening to music?

Alternatively, you could start by reading about the research conducted by other psychologists. You might be able to think up related studies or different ways to tackle the same problem. For instance, Stroop (1935) investigated the effect of using coloured ink on response time for lists of colour names (such as the word 'blue' written in blue or green ink). He found that people were slower to name the colour of ink that the words

Are there sex differences in undressing?

were written in when the words themselves were the names of colours. Similar effects have been demonstrated for time taken to read lists of colour-related words (such as sky or grass) in coloured ink and for other incongruent stimuli as illustrated below.

Variations on Stroop (1935) can produce different kinds of congruent and incongruent stimuli

Incongruent stimulus   Congruent stimulus

A project could investigate other possibilities (illustrated below). Making the shapes of numerals out of matching or different numbers, making the outlines of animals such as fish, snail, cat and mouse out of smaller illustrations or using geometric shapes could all lead to a Stroop effect.

Ideas for a Stroop effect project

245

Any project idea will have to be approved by the person supervising you and it may need to centre on a specific area of psychology. Remember not to go too far with an idea before you have had it accepted.

Finding information

If you are restricted to conducting research within an area of psychology that you have been taught, your starting point will be your textbook and other resources from your library. You will probably know what studies or theories are related to your research topic and will be able to look up key words with which you are already familiar. If, however, you have chosen a new topic to research, this task will be more difficult. You don't need to locate the exact study you are planning to conduct reported by someone else (it might not exist) but you do have to find enough related evidence to be able to justify your predictions. This information will become the basis of your *introduction*, an extended piece of text at the beginning of your write-up that sets the scene for the investigation and explains the reasoning behind your hypothesis. The evidence you describe may be provided either by studies that have focused on the same area of research but have looked at a different aspect or studies that are similar in some ways (such as the method they have used) but that have been conducted on a different topic. For example, in the case of the Stroop research with animal shapes, Stroop's original work with colour names would provide some of the basic evidence for a hypothesis that suggested we would be slower to name animals with a shape made up of different animals. Other evidence may come from research suggesting that our perception is sensitive to animal shapes, such as the effects of priming.

Perceptual priming: participants who have seen pictures of animals prior to viewing this ambiguous figure are more likely to see the rat than the man (Bugleski and Alampay, 1961)

When you are searching for information you can use both the key terms from the topic and the names of psychologists who have conducted related investigations. Remember to look through both the *index* and *contents* pages of each book you use and beware: some books may have an *author index* in addition to a *subject index*. When you find useful information, remember to record a full *reference* for its location, you will need the author, date of publication, title of the book or journal and the page numbers (also the publishers and place of publication for a book and volume number for a journal article). Looking information up using the Internet is often difficult: you may generate no matches at all or several thousand, most of which are either irrelevant or incomprehensible. The ideas opposite will help to improve the success of your Internet searches.

Using the Internet

- Compile a list of search terms before you log on.

- If you can, start from a psychology-based website.

- Choose a search engine that allows you to select 'education', 'science' or 'social science' if one is available (such as Yahoo!).

- Learn to use the selection techniques available on your search engine such as '+', putting search terms in quotation marks and the use of capital letters.

- If you get a long list that looks irrelevant, remove the summaries so that you can page through the titles more quickly.

- Find out if any of the journals that might cover the area you are researching are available online and go straight to their web address if you can.

- Navigate through links from obvious sources such as the *New Scientist* or British Psychological Society websites.

- Remember to record the exact web address for your references and the date and time you accessed the site.

Some good starting points for Internet searches are:

- www.apa.org

- www.bps.org.uk

- www.britannica.com

- www.newscientist.com

Some good websites for psychology are:

- www.biologists.com

- www.bioscience.org

- www.brain.com

- www.cogsci.soton.ac.uk

- www.illusionworks.com

- www.mentalhealth.com

- www.psych.org

- www.socialpsychology.org

- www.who.ch

Conducting research

Once you are sure that you are allowed to research your chosen topic and that you can find sufficient background information, you can start to plan your investigation. Your understanding of the subject area amassed from preparatory reading should enable you to formulate a *research question*: what is the question you are trying to answer through your investigation? From this you need to plan the best way possible to answer the question.

Design decisions

Ask yourself these questions:

- What *research method* would be best to tackle the research question I am asking?

- Is this method *ethical*?

- Is this method *practical*?

You may decide to conduct an observation, correlation, experiment, questionnaire, interview or any of the other methods described earlier in the text (Chapters 3–7). Most student projects are experiments although observations and correlations are also common. As a consequence, we will focus on the process of conducting and writing up experiments, indicating differences for other methods where they occur.

While it may be preferable for reasons of scientific rigour to use one method, you may need to settle for a less preferred technique because it is more ethically sound or achievable within the limits of time, materials or other practical constraints. Having selected an approach you then need to plan how you will conduct the investigation.

Planning a method

You are now in a position to develop your *alternative hypothesis*. This has to be testable, so you need to consider how you will collect data to support it. Work through the following steps; you may have to return to an earlier stage to reconsider your method if you cannot answer a question.

- What *variable(s)* do you want to measure?

- How will you *operationalise* the variable(s) you are measuring?

- Can you create or obtain the necessary equipment or materials to measure the variable(s)?

- Do you need to manipulate any variables?

- Can you operationalise the variable(s) you will be manipulating?

- Are the manipulations you are planning achievable?

- What controls do you need to employ (see Chapter 12)?

- Is the study you are planning achievable in the given time?

Now write your null and alternative hypotheses (see Chapter 1). Once you have fully developed your research method and started to collect data you should not change your hypothesis, regardless of your findings. Remember, if you are at all unsure about the effect one variable may have on another you can use a non-directional hypothesis (see page 7).

Having decided in principle how to collect your data, you need to create or obtain all the resources you need. This might involve producing stimuli such as pictures, lists of words, recorded sounds or videos; structured questions for interviewing; questionnaires or coding schemes for observations. Consider the factors you will need to control to minimise confounding variables and demand characteristics (see pages 197 and 204).

It is worth trying to imagine what results your investigation will generate and how you will analyse them. If the data are going to be too complex for you to analyse, change the design of the experiment to make interpretation of the results possible.

Once you have written or collected these resources you will be ready to draft the *apparatus and materials* section of the 'method' part of your write-up.

Here are some further questions to ask yourself if you are conducting an experiment:

- Are you sure you can operationalise your *independent* and *dependent* *variables* (see pages 82–85)?

- What will you call the levels of the independent variable? (Try to avoid using 1 and 2 as it will cause confusion later; give them meaningful names.)

- What *formal design* will you use: repeated measures, independent groups or matched pairs (see pages 93–99)?

- Can you justify your choice of design?

- If you are using a repeated measures design will you need to *counterbalance* or *randomise* the presentation of conditions to participants (see pages 209–210)?

- Are any other control measures necessary (see Chapter 12)?

Now you are ready to draft the *design* section for the 'method' part of your write-up.

Finding participants

The nature of your sample will depend on several factors. Consider the following questions to help you to decide:

- Does your research question dictate a particular *population* (such as children, females, people who own a pet, etc.) (see Chapter 2)?

- What *sampling* procedure would be ideal (e.g. random, quota, stratified)?

- Are you able to employ the ideal sampling method (see Chapter 2)?

- How are you going to recruit your sample (e.g. face-to-face, by advertising, by telephone)?

- Is it practical and ethical to use your chosen sample?

It is likely that you will use an *opportunity sample* of your chosen population. Even when this is the case you can take steps to gain as wide a representation as possible. Could you sample at different times of day, at different locations or on different days?

Once you have decided on your population and how you will select your sample, you have some of the information needed for your *participants* section of your method. You will also need to add information about your actual sample when you have completed your data collection, such as the *gender ratio* (the relative number of males and females), the *age range* and *attrition rate* if appropriate (see page 24).

Ethics

You need to be certain that the procedures you are planning to use conform to ethical guidelines. You are likely to need to *brief* your participants about the nature of the study to ensure that they are able to give their informed consent to participate (see page 215). This brief may be printed for them to read or you might say it to them (if so, you need to be sure that your tone does not oblige them to participate). If you are saying the brief (or standardised instructions) out loud, it is worth putting them on a card so that you remember to read them and to be certain that each participant receives the same information (see pages 205–207).

If you are taking an opportunity sample, consider whether you are treating people equally: are you likely to offend anyone by failing to ask them to participate or by excluding them?

During your study you must ensure that the participants are aware of their right to withdraw and that this is respected, even if it is expressed indirectly (such as when a child refuses to return to the test room).

At the end of the study you must fully *debrief* your participants (see page 222). They must be thanked, offered a full explanation of the purpose of the study, reminded of their right to withdraw their results and reassured. They may ask about the findings of the study so far, remember the guidelines about *competence*; you must not make claims you cannot substantiate, and *confidentiality*; do not use other participants' results as examples.

You are now ready to draft the *procedure* section of your write-up. When you have done so, you will need to check with your supervisor that your approach is ethically sound. Once this has been agreed you should not change your procedure without further consultation.

At this stage you should be able:

- To write an *introduction* with references to similar studies and relevant theories which back up your predictions.

- To state an *alternative* and a *null hypothesis*.

- To draft a *method* section with four subsections:

(a) a *design* subsection that states the hypotheses, variables and control measures including counterbalancing if appropriate;

(b) a *participants* subsection that states the population and sampling method and will later contain the gender ratio and other relevant details about the sample;

(c) an *apparatus and materials* subsection that details all the items you have used including the make and model of pieces of equipment;

(d) a *procedure* subsection that describes in detail the activities of the researchers and participants. It should include the brief, standardised instructions and debrief but should not simply consist of these. It must also include the protocol, that is, what each individual was actually required to do.

Analysing your findings

Once you have collected all your data you will need to analyse it. You may be required to use only descriptive statistics or both descriptive and inferential statistics – find out which.

Descriptive statistics

Descriptive statistics serve to illustrate your data, they provide a numerical or visual description of the measures of *central tendency* (middle) and *spread* (edges) of your data (see pages 114–121). These measures can be put into tables or displayed graphically. Remember to use the appropriate measures of central tendency and spread for your data; these are governed by the level of measurement. Work them out for each set of data (such as for levels of the independent variable or each item or group of items on a questionnaire or coding scheme). Tabulate these summary results using clear *row* and *column headings* (as we mentioned earlier, it is easier to use names for conditions and abbreviate these than to simply call them conditions 1 and 2):

	Reaction times of participants (milliseconds)	
	before chocolate (BC)	after chocolate (AC)
Mean		
Standard deviation		

Similarly, you need to select a technique for graphical representation that is appropriate to your data (see Chapter 9). In general, steer clear of pie charts and cumulative frequency graphs, and resist the urge to plot every single participant's results unless you have conducted a correlation and are drawing a scattergraph. Give each graph a *title* that explains what it shows and make sure that you have clearly labelled each axis with both the *variable* and the *units of measurement* if appropriate.

Inferential statistics

From the descriptive statistics you may well be able to guess whether the data support your alternative hypothesis. However, to be sure, you should conduct the appropriate inferential statistics (see Chapters 10 and 11). Select the correct test using the flowchart on page xii. You will need to justify your choice of test on the basis of:

- the *research method* (experiment/correlation);

- the *formal design* in an experiment (repeated measures/matched pairs/independent groups);

- the *level of measurement*;

- whether the data are *parametric* or *non-parametric*.

You may have access to statistical software on a computer that will enable you to put your data into a file and have the observed value calculated for you. Otherwise, you will need to work out the test for yourself using the instructions in Chapters 10 and 11 where there are worked examples.

When you have obtained your *observed value* you will need to compare this with a *critical value* from the table for that test (see the appendix). To look this up you will need to know:

- the name of the *test*;

- the *number of participants*, N (or the *degrees of freedom*, df, for some tests);

- whether your hypothesis was *directional* or *non-directional*;

- the *significance level (p)* you wish to use.

Remember to record all this information for your *results* section, which you should now be ready to complete.

Writing up your coursework

The details above should have led you through the steps of planning and conducting your research, recording appropriate information along the way. The aim of this section is to enable you to produce a piece of coursework that looks like an article from a scientific journal – try to see one. Your project should contain enough information for a psychologist to be able to pick it up and understand it without any other input from you. Until recently, it was conventional to write reports in the third person, avoiding the use of I, me, we, etc. This tradition is now being eroded but check with your supervisor, as many psychologists still prefer this approach. Throughout the following sections there are excerpts from students' A-level coursework.

Title

You will need to give your project a title: try to make it informative but not too long. You may want a whole title page or your supervisor may have a particular cover sheet for the front.

Project title

> *Do different types of music affect recall?*

Abstract

This is a short summary of your aims, method, results and conclusion written as a single piece of prose in the past tense. It is easier if you leave it until the end to write, although it will be the first section of the report when it is complete.

> *Abstract*
> *The aim of this experiment was to establish whether different types of music affect recall. The two-tailed hypothesis for the experiment was: "different types of music affect recall." The Ps were played an extract of pop music and a word list was shown. This was then*

repeated with classical music using a second word list. Counterbalancing was used to ensure that both levels of the IV were equally affected by order effects. On average, in the condition with pop music Ps remembered five words out of fifteen, and seven in the classical music condition. A related-t test was used and it was found that the results showed a significant difference at a 5% significance level. It would seem therefore, that recall is worse with pop music than with classical, and that different types of music do affect recall.

Abstract

Introduction

This section is an extended piece of prose, without subsections, which aims:

- to explain the research question that the project is trying to answer;

- to use evidence to predict what the outcome will be.

The 'evidence' upon which this is based can come in part from personal observations or pilot studies but should mainly consist of theories and studies that attempt to explain the phenomenon under investigation. This evidence is used to predict the responses of your participants by comparison with similar (but not necessarily identical) situations. Throughout the introduction attempts should be made to link the material quoted to the aims and hypotheses of your investigation. Explain how the hypotheses have been generated from previous research and why you are making your specific predictions. This is your rationale. Ensure that you:

- state your alternative and null hypotheses;

- explain why your alternative hypothesis is directional or non-directional;

- reference all citations fully (and keep a record of the source and page number for each one – you will need them for the *references* section and it is *much* harder to go back and look for them afterwards!);

- do not quote without referencing – this is plagiarising and constitutes cheating;

- do not copy other students' work;

- refer to studies as 'Jarvis *et al.* (2001) found/demonstrated/illustrated…' or 'it was shown by Jarvis *et al.* (2001) that…' *not* as 'In 2001

Jarvis *et al.* did such and such'; this implies they conducted the study in that year when in fact it would have been done much earlier to reach publication in 2001.

Introduction

Alternative Hypothesis: "different types of music affect recall"

Null Hypothesis: "any difference in recall of a word list between Ps listening to pop and classical music is due to chance."

In proposing this hypothesis, it is relevant to consider the interference theory. According to this theory, forgetting is simply due to the fact that new memories compete with old ones, and retrieval becomes more and more difficult. There are two ways it seems, that interference occurs. Firstly there is retroactive inhibition, or R.I which occurs when you learn A, learn B, and then try to recall A. There is also proactive inhibition which occurs when you learn A, learn B then recall B. In R.I, the list B interferes with list A, so recall of A is impaired, whilst in P.I list A interferes with the recall of B. Underwood (1957) declared that interference would be more evident in R.I after a time lapse, and more evident in P.I with more immediate recall. So it would seem that counterbalancing would be a necessary inclusion in this experiment, to try to avoid R.I and P.I effects.

One of the main studies which led to the proposal of this hypothesis is that done by McGeogh and McDonald (1931). They established that the interference task given was a main factor in recall efficiency. They presented Ps with word lists and gave them varying interference tasks. They then retested, and found that the more similar to the interference task the interference task was, the worse recall was. If differing word lists had a noticeable effect, surely types of music would show a significant difference. More precisely, it could be argued that pop music is more similar to the word list as it too has words, therefore interference in

---

this condition should be greater. However, to examine the results of the experiment more closely, there may be another reason for their findings, other than the similarity of the task to the word list. Recall with jokes as the interference task was 43%, an interference task of numbers gave 37% recall, nonsense syllables 26%, unrelated adjectives 22%, antonyms of the original list 18% and synonyms 12%. Whilst similarity to the task could affect the results, it could also be how boring the test is which causes a difference. If this were the case, perhaps pop music should result in worse recall as it is more repetitive, and therefore could be considered more boring. Or possibly classical music could be more boring to the Ps if it were less familiar.

Sokolov (1958) suggested that if the task is unstimulating mentally, i.e. produces low arousal, then noise could in fact improve recall. The word lists in the proposed experiment could not be considered to produce high arousal and therefore it is possible that music could improve recall. If Sokolov is correct in his assumptions, perhaps the pop music condition will result in higher recall, as it could be considered more stimulating and result in a higher level of arousal and therefore a more active brain process and improved memory.

Broadbent (1958) suggests that the effects of noise on memory are due to changes in attention. It seems that the brain only has a limited capacity and can only take in a part of the incoming information. Therefore the density of the music, that is how frenetic it is, how quick the beat is and the volume of it must be a highly relevant factor. It would seem that if the music is very confusing and non-sensical (i.e. does not progress in a way to which you have been accustomed) it would interfere greatly with anything you were doing simultaneously. This supports the idea that pop music would cause greater interference than classical as it is more frenetic, confusing and unpredictable. It seems likely therefore that a difference will be found between the two conditions, and the hypothesis supported. Wade and Tauris (1993) report something similar. They say that when the sensory systems are overloaded, they often cope by blocking out unimportant sights and sound and focus only those they find interesting. If this is true, surely pop music will dominate the auditory senses more than classical, causing a greater overloading. It could well be then that any other incoming information would be disregarded more readily, and could result in the second condition, that is classical music, showing better recall results.

Glass and Singer (1972) found that Ps exposed to an annoying but predictable noise were less affected in recalling words, than those given an unpredictable annoying noise. This shows that even within one type of music (e.g. pop) it is important to consider the possible variance. Some pop music is extremely repetitive and some is very changeable throughout. Glass and Singer's study implies that the type of pop music chosen in the proposed study is very important as it could affect the results considerably.

Burns and Dobson (1984) suggest that noise creates a stressful environment, which can affect recall. Surely different types of music must create differing levels of stress, which should mean that a difference should be observed. Perhaps also the direction of the effect can reasonably be predicted as surely the music with a faster beat, which is more unpredictable, i.e. the pop music, will create a more stressful environment than the classical music. Using the findings of Martin and Darbyshire (1994), it would be possible to suggest that the classical music condition will result in better recall than a condition with no noise at all. They found that Ps score in Differential Aptitude Tests (D.A.T.) actually increased in the condition where they listened to Mozart, as opposed to white noise or jazz. Perhaps classical music stimulates the brain in such a way as to improve mental processes.

Taking all these studies and theories into account, it would seem likely that different types of music do affect recall to varying extents, and that the alternative hypothesis will be accepted.

Introduction

Method

This section has four subsections. Aim to make it possible to replicate your study fully on the basis of the information in your method. Each subsection should be written as continuous prose in the past tense.

Design

State the following:

- The *research method* (experiment, correlation, interview, questionnaire, case study, observation, etc.).

- For an experiment:

  (a) state the *formal design* (repeated measures, matched pairs or independent groups);

  (b) justify this choice (consider factors such as participant and situational variables, order effects and demand characteristics);

  (c) state the independent variable giving an operational definition for each level;

  (d) state the dependent variable giving an operational definition for its measurement including any scales or units to be used.

- For a correlation state the two measured variables giving operational definitions for each.

- For all other approaches it will probably be sufficient to state the method and describe aspects of the design in the procedure section; for instance, in observations the operational definitions being used with the coding scheme.

- State all the controls you employed such as standardised instructions, random allocation of participants to conditions, counterbalancing and controlled variables. These might include features of your stimuli, times and places; all the things you did to ensure that the participant's experience was the same for each individual. In observations you may need to include how inter-observer reliability was improved.

Method

Design

The independent variable in this experiment is the different types of music.

The dependent variable is the number of words recalled from a visually presented list.

Operational Definitions: Pop Music — fast, constant volume and beat, words.

Classical music – slow, changing volumes and tempo, no words.

Repeated measures were used in this experiment to ensure that the results were not affected by variables, for instance the Ps musical preference or whether or not they usually worked with noise.

The controlled variables were:

1) The length of the word lists.

2) The machine the music was played on.

3) The volume at which the music was played.

4) The way the lists were presented.

5) The length of the two pieces of music.

Counterbalancing was used by presenting the different lists in different orders.

Group 1	Group 2
pop music, word list 1	classical music, word list 1
classical music, word list 2	pop music, word list 2

Design

Participants

State the following:

- The number of participants who started the experiment.

- The sampling method used to select them and the population they were drawn from.

- The sex ratio.

- The attrition rate (or response rate for questionnaires).

In an experiment with an independent measures design it may be appropriate to quote the ratios for each condition. In a matched pairs design the criteria used for matching should be given. Some studies may require other information about the participants. Give this only where it is directly relevant, such as whether any participants were colour-blind in a test on colour vision, were cross-lateral in a test on hand–eye coordination or were answering questions in their second language in a measure of comprehension.

> **Participants**
>
> All participants were taken from a Sixth Form College population. They were selected by opportunity sampling.
>
> Age range: 16–19 years
> Male Ps: 17
> Female Ps: 17
> Ps were placed in group 1 or 2 by random allocation
> Drop out rate = 0

Participants

Materials and apparatus

Don't panic if there appears to be very little in this section. It may be acceptable to simply list the apparatus if appropriate and to include examples (remember *not* to include ones used by your participants). This section should contain all the stimuli, questionnaires, etc., used in the study. If these are numerous put them in an appendix and indicate where they are there in this section. Include answers or solutions where relevant, such as for puzzles or anagrams. Describe or draw complex or unusual apparatus and quote the make and model of any pieces of equipment used during testing such as computers (and programs), reaction timers and cassette players. Do not worry about stopwatches or the computer you used to conduct your statistical test. You may also need to draw a sketch of the layout of the research area (for instance, in observations).

> **Apparatus**
> Word list one
> 1) title   9) music
> 2) video   10) beach
> 3) noise   11) brace
> 4) drink   12) clock
> 5) horse   13) shirt
> 6) teeth   14) table
> 7) story   15) house
> 8) metal

Word list two
1) laugh   9) brown
2) bench   10) heart
3) dress   11) puppy
4) apple   12) berry
5) price   13) media
6) cloud   14) shark
7) stand   15) paper
8) plant

Pop music – Mr. Vain by Culture Beat
Classical music – Beethoven's third symphony.
Casio tape recorder.

Materials and apparatus

Procedure

This section must clearly describe what the researcher *and* the participants did. It should almost always contain a brief, standardised instructions and a debrief, but this is generally not sufficient. In addition you need to explain how these were employed so that the reader can understand what happened during the investigation.

- **Brief**: give enough information for the participants to give their informed consent – they must have a good idea about what they will be expected to do but try to avoid saying things you do not need to about the purpose of the experiment and what you expect to happen. They must be informed of their right to withdraw.

- **Standardised instructions**: the report should quote these and say whether they are given to the participants to read or spoken to them and whether the participants asked questions (they should be allowed to). The instructions may be the same for all participants or, in experiments, there may be two almost identical versions for different conditions. If so, indicate how they were the same and different (e.g. by providing a copy of each and underlining where the differences occur).

- **Debrief**: this is usually read out to the participants after they have completed the study. It functions to thank the participants, to explain the purposes of the study and to reassure them.

Procedure

Brief: You will be shown a list of words whilst listening to either pop or classical music. After a short delay you will be asked to recall the words. You will do this twice, once for each of the conditions (pop and classical). If you want to leave the experiment at any time you may do so.

Two word lists were shown to two groups whilst they listened to either pop or classical music. They were then asked to recall the words and the results were compared.

Debrief: The aim of the experiment is to determine how recall is affected by different types of music. Feel free to ask for your score. You may withdraw your results if you wish. Thank you for taking part.

Procedure

Results

What you do here depends primarily on your *level of measurement*, that is whether your results have been measured on a nominal, ordinal, interval or ratio scale. You will probably need some descriptive statistics and perhaps an inferential test. Remember to use meaningful titles for your groups throughout.

You will need *descriptive statistics*. In an *experiment* use the following:

- For **nominal** data:

(a) table of totals and variation ratio for each group

(b) bar chart of each group total

- For **ordinal** data:

(a) table of medians and interquartile ranges

(b) bar-and-whiskers chart

- For **interval or ratio** data:

(a) table of means and standard deviations

(b) bar chart of means and standard error bars.

In a *correlation* you will also need a table summarising the data and a scattergraph plotting the relationship between the two measured variables.

If you have conducted an *observation* or *questionnaire* compile a table of totals or averages in each response or behavioural category (choose a measure of central tendency appropriate to the level of measurement). You may also be able to include a measure of spread (such as the range). The data may be presented graphically using bar charts. Lay out your columns sensibly to achieve easy comparisons, e.g. by putting opposing pairs next to one another in different colours. Resist the urge to draw stacked bar charts or pie charts. If you use a computer to draw the graphs make sure the axes are appropriately scaled and labelled.

A graph to show mean score of words recalled when words were remembered whilst listening to either pop or classical music.

A graph to show median score of words recalled and interquartile range, when words were remembered whilst listening to either pop or classical music.

Descriptive statistics

		Musical type	
		Pop	Classical
Central Tendency	Mean number of words recalled	4.76	7.3
	Median number of words recalled	5	7
Measure of spread	Standard deviation	1.28	1.44
	Inter-quartile range	4–6 : 2	6–8 : 2

You may also need to present the results of an *inferential test*. First you must describe how the test was chosen (see the flow chart on page xii), presenting the following justifications in prose form:

- The *research method* (experiment/correlation).

- The *formal design* in an experiment (repeated measures/matched pairs/independent groups).

- The *level of measurement*:

(a) nominal – named categories (the points do not lie on a linear scale);

(b) ordinal – points on a scale *without* equal intervals (say *why* the points did not all have the same value, perhaps because some items were more difficult than others or could be interpreted differently by different individuals);

(c) interval or ratio – points on a scale with equal intervals (unless they are from a mathematical scale justify *why* each point is of equal value).

- Your choice of *significance level*.

The test calculations do not need to appear in the results section but can be referred to in an appendix. You need to quote the *observed value* from this test and the appropriate *critical value* from the correct table for that test. This critical value should be quoted with the following information:

- The name of the *test*.

- The *number of participants*, N (or the *degrees of freedom*, df, for some tests).

- Whether your hypothesis was *directional* or *non-directional*.

- The *significance level* (p) you have used.

You then need to draw a conclusion with reference to your alternative and null hypotheses. Look carefully to see which figure, the observed or critical value, should be larger for the results to be significant. Then state, on the basis of the comparison between the observed and critical values, which hypothesis should be accepted and which rejected.

> The statistical test used was a related t-test, because the data was interval, and repeated measures were used. An interval scale was used as all the words used had five letters, were common, and no difficult spellings were used therefore each was equally memorable. A related t-test was also used because both conditions show an approximately

normal distribution on the graph printout, and show homogeneity of variance.

The formula for the related t-test is:

$$t = \frac{\bar{d} \times \sqrt{N-1}}{\sigma \times d}$$

This worked out to be 6.62
Observed value = 6.62
Critical value = 2.045 at degrees of freedom N-1
=34-1 =33.
P <=0.05 This was suitable as it was a novel study.
6.62> 2.045 therefore the results show a significant difference.

The alternative hypothesis was accepted: "different types of music affect recall"
The null hypothesis was rejected: "any difference found in recall of a word list between Ps listening to pop and classical music is due to chance."

Inferential statistics

Discussion

Begin your discussion by reiterating whether you have found a significant difference, correlation or association. Go on to explain this result in terms of your aims.

Relate your findings to previous research; the theories and studies mentioned in the introduction. Be specific, explain how your findings support the work of other psychologists you have described (if you found a significant effect) or how it contradicts previous findings otherwise. Discuss how your results can be explained by the models or theories discussed in the introduction or consider flaws in the models if they cannot explain what you have found. You should not need to introduce new material in the discussion (except possibly if they have accepted your null hypothesis and can find other ways of explaining the effect).

If the alternative hypothesis was accepted a *type I error* may have been made (see page 143). You need to state this and discuss the possible causes (the limitations of your study) and solutions (the modifications you could make). Make specific suggestions about problems that may have arisen, identify what kind of flaw each is and suggest ways to remedy each one. Possible limitations might include ceiling or floor effects, fatigue or practice effects, demand characteristics, participant or situational variables or any other sources of confounding variable. Where subsequent problems may arise as a result of the possible solutions (such as ethical dilemmas) discuss these too. Try to avoid criticisms that should never have arisen in the first place, such as distractions from conducting the study in a noisy place (you should have gone elsewhere unless this was an essential part of the investigation). Aim to focus on comments that relate specifically to *your* method rather than general issues that might arise in any study such as limited populations or sampling errors. If you accepted the null hypothesis, a *type II error* may have been made (see page 144). Many of the same possible flaws in the design or execution of the investigation that could have resulted in type I errors may also have been responsible for the occurrence of a type II error.

Discussion

The alternative hypothesis for the proposed experiment was: "different types of music affect recall". The results showed a significant difference and strongly suggest that pop music results in worse recall than classical. This supported the theory which relates to Broadbent's study (1958), which says that the effects of noise on memory are due to changes in attention, and that the more dense or frenetic the music, the more detrimental will be the effect on memory. It also supports Underwood's interference theory (1957), which claims that items interfere with each other in either storage or retrieval, in this case storage. Also, it supports the supposition that the more similar to the task the music is, the greater will be the interference, as the results of McGeogh's and McDonald's experiment suggest. A reasonable conclusion to make therefore, would be that it is density, and degree to which the music is confusing which so drastically affects recall, as well as its similarity to the task in hand.

There is of course a possibility of a type one error, due to inaccuracies in the experiment. The main inaccuracies in the results would be due to Ps variables. It is possible that some would have known either piece of music which could alter the amount it distracted them. The Ps were simply randomly divided into two groups and therefore the possibility of having an unequal balance of people who did and did not know the music was quite high, which may have affected the results slightly. It is also possible that some Ps often do tasks requiring concentration with a background noise, and therefore find it less distracting as they have become accustomed to it. This is particularly likely given the population, as many college students do homework etc. with music on. Had the Ps been questioned about this, their answers would have allowed them to be evenly allocated to the conditions.

The sample of Ps used was very unrepresentative of the population as a whole. The experiment would need to be repeated using Ps from other age sectors and backgrounds for the results to be deemed reliable. As a rule young people listen by choice, and are exposed to much more pop music than older people, and to determine whether or not it was this familiarity affecting the results a wider sample would have to be used. The word lists were also a problem. It was impossible to make them truly equally difficult, and also different words are more memorable to different people, which would occur purely by chance. For example, if a person had a phobia of horses according to Freud, they may subconsciously forget this word due to repression of the bad experience they may have had with horses. Admittedly this point wouldn't affect the results in any drastic way, however it should be taken into account. However, a wide variety of words were chosen, all from different subject areas, and it is likely that a few words would have had personal meaning to each of the Ps, therefore the effect throughout the sample should be fairly well balanced. More extensive counterbalancing would also have helped eliminate the problem of the two different word lists by using each list in the first or second position with each piece of music. If the experiment was repeated, it would be sensible to divide the Ps in conjunction with the points mentioned above to ensure more accurate results.

Another very important point which should have been included is a control group, where recall was tested with no noise at all, or equal volume white noise. This would have helped ensure that the difference found was actually due to the independent variable. It would also be interesting to see if the no noise condition resulted in worse recall than the classical music condition. If this were the case, it is possible that not only do different types of music result in different recall but could actually improve it depending on the type. Evidence to suggest that this is a definite possibility comes from Rauscher, Shaw and Ky (1993), who report large increases in spatial IQ after listening to Mozart as opposed to white noise or jazz.

There are also points other than participant variables which could have affected the results. To return to McGeogh and McDonald's study, who said that the interference tasks had a more detrimental effect the more similar to the actual task they were. This concept, if correct, could have swayed the results, as it could be argued that because the pop music sample had words, it was more similar to the recall task, and therefore would result in worse recall in that condition. Perhaps in a repeat experiment, pop music without words should be chosen to avoid this possibility.

The results to this experiment show that pop music results in worse recall than classical, but it would be unfair to generalise these findings and state that pop music as a whole results in worse recall as there is such a variance within the definition. For example, ambient music or a similar type is still defined as pop music, but due to its composition, probably would not have detrimental effects on recall. In further studies, it would be interesting to see if different types of pop music, or different types of classical music affect recall. It would then be easier to define exactly what it is in the music that interferes with your ability to recall. Carrying out an experiment where the music is played at different volumes could also be interesting. Perhaps a test where half the Ps know the extract well and half not at all could affect recall, although selecting the Ps could prove problematic.

The results of this experiment clearly outline that listening to pop music whilst trying to concentrate can interfere with your ability to perform the task. From the results of the experiment, it is possible to say that listening to pop music whilst working interferes with your memory and concentration, and should therefore be avoided when for example doing homework. The hypothesis was significantly supported and it can therefore be said that different types of music affect recall.

Discussion

You can then consider the value of your findings. Firstly, consider what implications they have for real life. Could they be applied to areas such as education, advertising or road safety? How? Be specific and make suggestions about what might be done, giving examples of your applications. Secondly, looking beyond the present study, where does it lead? Invent studies that follow on from the findings, that investigate related issues or that tackle the same problem in a different way. Did the study generate any new research questions? Describe further studies suggesting what could be investigated, how you would carry these out and what might be expected to happen.

Finally, state a conclusion based on the hypotheses.

Conclusion

Listening to pop music whilst performing simple memory tasks results in worse recall than if classical music is played.

Conclusion

References

Quote every citation you have made with the source (book, journal or website) using the following layout:

- **Book**: Author; initials (date) *title*, place of publication: publisher (followed by a list of citations from that book with page numbers if you are using it as a secondary source).

- **Journal article**: author; initials (date) title of article, *journal title*, volume (part number), pages.

- **Website**: state the *whole* web address and underline it. Add the date you accessed the site.

Broadbent, D. in Moray, N. (1969) *Listening and Attention*. London: Penguin.

Martin, C. and Darbyshire, J. (1995) And the band played on, *The Psychologist*, 8 (2), 55.

Rauscher, F.H., Shaw, G.L. and Ky, K.N. (1993) Music and spatial task performance, *Nature*, 365, 611

Underwood, B.J. (1957) Interference and forgetting, *Psychological Review*, 64, 49–60.

Wade, C. and Tavris, C. (1993) *Psychology*. London: WW Norton and Co.

http://www.mtsu.edu/~whuitt/psy702/cogsys/infoproc.html [Accessed 4 August 2000]

References
(extract)

Appendices

The purpose of an appendix is to hold vital information that does not need to be presented in the body of the report. This might include sample interviews, examples of stimuli, calculations from your inferential test and raw data tables. It should not contain every participant's copy of the answer sheet or questionnaire. Remember that no participant should be identifiable from their results.

Raw data sheet

number of words recalled	Pop Music		Classical Music	
	word list 1	*word list 2*	*word list 1*	*word list 2*
	4	6	9	5
	5	4	6	5
	4	4	6	7
	3	3	10	6
	7	6	8	4
	5	4	8	8
	6	3	8	8
	7	3	9	7
	7	6	7	6
	4	5	10	6
	3	3	7	7
	5	6	7	6
	4	5	9	8
	4	5	8	8
	6	6	7	9

Appendix

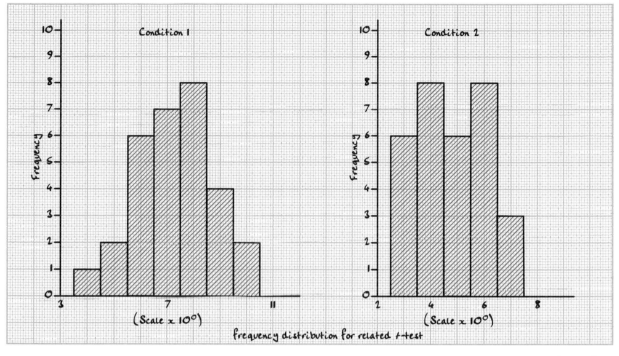

frequency distribution for related t-test

Appendix

Conclusions

Working through this chapter should have helped you to plan, conduct and write your coursework from finding information for your introduction, through designing your method to analysing your results and writing up. Remember two things: firstly, although the abstract is at the start of the report, write it last, and secondly, although the references are at the end of the report, keep a clear and thorough record of your sources from the outset!

where to now?

▶ **Fisher, D. and Hanstock, T. (1998)** *Citing References.* **Oxford: Blackwell** – this small booklet provides a thorough and understandable account of the need to reference well and how to do it

▶ **Brain, C. (2000)** *Advanced Subsidiary Psychology: Approaches and Methods.* **Cheltenham: Nelson Thornes** – has an excellent coursework checklist suitable for Edexcel AS-level students.

Appendix

Statistical tables

Table 1 Percentage points of the χ^2 distribution

	Level of significance for two-tailed test				
	0.2	0.1	0.05	0.02	0.01
	Level of significance for one-tailed test				
df	0.1	0.05	0.025	0.01	0.005
1	2.706	3.841	5.024	6.635	7 879
2	4 605	5.991	7.378	9.210	10.597
3	6.251	7.815	9.348	11.345	12.838
4	7.779	9.488	11.143	13.277	14.860
5	9.236	11.070	12.833	15.086	16.750
6	10.645	12.592	14.449	16.812	18.548
7	12.017	14.067	16.013	18.475	20.278
8	13.362	15.507	17.535	20.090	21.955
9	14.684	16.919	19.023	21.666	23.589
10	15.987	18.307	20.483	23.209	25.188
11	17.275	19.675	21.920	24.725	26 757
12	18.549	21.026	23.337	26.217	28.300
13	19.812	22.362	24.736	27.688	29.819
14	21.064	23.685	26.119	29.141	31.319
15	22.307	24.996	27.488	30.578	32.801
16	23.542	26.296	28.845	32.000	34.267
17	24.769	27.587	30.191	33.409	35.718
18	25.989	28.869	31.526	34.805	37.156
19	27.204	30.144	32 852	36.191	38.582
20	28.412	31.410	34.170	37.566	39.997
21	29.615	32.671	35.479	38.932	41.401
22	30.813	33.924	36 781	40.289	42.796
23	32.007	35.172	38.076	41.638	44.181
24	33.196	36.415	39.364	42.980	45.559
25	34.382	37.652	40.646	44.314	46.928
26	35.563	38.885	41.923	45.642	48.290
27	36.741	40.113	43.195	46.963	49.645
28	37.916	41.337	44.461	48.278	50.993
29	39.087	42.557	45.722	49.588	52.336
30	40.256	43.773	46.979	50.892	53.672
31	41.422	44.985	48 232	52.191	55.003
32	42.585	46.194	49.480	53.486	56.328
33	43.745	47.400	50.725	54.776	57.648
34	44.903	48.602	51.966	56.061	58.964
35	46.059	49.802	53.203	57.342	60.275
36	47.212	50.998	54.437	58.619	61.581
37	48.363	52.192	55.668	59.892	62.883
38	49.513	53.384	56.896	61.162	64.181
39	50.660	54.572	58.120	62.428	65.476
40	51.805	55.758	59.342	63.691	66.766
45	57.505	61.656	65.410	69.957	73.166
50	63.167	67.505	71.420	76.154	79.490
55	68.796	73.311	77.380	82.292	85.749
60	74.397	79.082	83.298	88.379	91.952
65	79.973	84.821	89.177	94.422	98.105
70	85.527	90.531	95.023	100.425	104.215
75	91.061	96.217	100.839	106.393	110.286
80	96.578	101.879	106.629	112.329	116.321
85	102.079	107.522	112.393	118.236	122.325
90	107.565	113.145	118.136	124.116	128.299
95	113.038	118.752	123.858	129.973	134.247
100	118.498	124.342	129.561	135.807	140.169

Dunstan *et al.* (1988)

Table 2 Critical values of *S* for the sign test. *S* must be *equal to or less than* the stated value to be significant

	Level of significance for one-tailed test				
	0.05	0.025	0.01	0.005	0.0005
	Level of significance for two-tailed test				
N	0.10	0.05	0.02	0.01	0.001
5	0	—	—	—	—
6	0	0	—	—	—
7	0	0	0	—	—
8	1	0	0	0	—
9	1	1	0	0	—
10	1	1	0	0	—
11	2	1	1	0	0
12	2	2	1	1	0
13	3	2	1	1	0
14	3	2	2	1	0
15	3	3	2	2	1
16	4	3	2	2	1
17	4	4	3	2	1
18	5	4	3	3	1
19	5	4	4	3	2
20	5	5	4	3	2
25	7	7	6	5	4
30	10	9	8	7	5
35	12	11	10	9	7

Clegg (1982)

Table 3A Critical values of *U* (Mann-Whitney) for a one-tailed test at 0.005; two-tailed test at 0.01*

| | n_1 | | | | | | | | | | | | | | | | | | | |
n_2	1	2	3	4	5	6	7	8	9	10	11	12	13	14	15	16	17	18	19	20
1	—	—	—	—	—	—	—	—	—	—	—	—	—	—	—	—	—	—	—	—
2	—	—	—	—	—	—	—	—	—	—	—	—	—	—	—	—	—	—	0	0
3	—	—	—	—	—	—	—	—	0	0	0	1	1	1	2	2	2	2	3	3
4	—	—	—	—	—	0	0	1	1	2	2	3	3	4	5	5	6	6	7	8
5	—	—	—	—	0	1	1	2	3	4	5	6	7	7	8	9	10	11	12	13
6	—	—	—	0	1	2	3	4	5	6	7	9	10	11	12	13	15	16	17	18
7	—	—	—	0	1	3	4	6	7	9	10	12	13	15	16	18	19	21	22	24
8	—	—	—	1	2	4	6	7	9	11	13	15	17	18	20	22	24	26	28	30
9	—	—	0	1	3	5	7	9	11	13	16	18	20	22	24	27	29	31	33	36
10	—	—	0	2	4	6	9	11	13	16	18	21	24	26	29	31	34	37	39	42
11	—	—	0	2	5	7	10	13	16	18	21	24	27	30	33	36	39	42	45	48
12	—	—	1	3	6	9	12	15	18	21	24	27	31	34	37	41	44	47	51	54
13	—	—	1	3	7	10	13	17	20	24	27	31	34	38	42	45	49	53	56	60
14	—	—	1	4	7	11	15	18	22	26	30	34	38	42	46	50	54	58	63	67
15	—	—	2	5	8	12	16	20	24	29	33	37	42	46	51	55	60	64	69	73
16	—	—	2	5	9	13	18	22	27	31	36	41	45	50	55	60	65	70	74	79
17	—	—	2	6	10	15	19	24	29	34	39	44	49	54	60	65	70	75	81	86
18	—	—	2	6	11	16	21	26	31	37	42	47	53	58	64	70	75	81	87	92
19	—	0	3	7	12	17	22	28	33	39	45	51	56	63	69	74	81	87	93	99
20	—	0	3	8	13	18	24	30	36	42	48	54	60	67	73	79	86	92	99	105

*Dashes in the body of the table indicate that no decision is possible at the stated level of significance because the numbers of subjects are too small.

Greene & D'Oliveira (1999)

Table 3B Critical values of U (Mann-Whitney) for a one-tailed test at 0.01; two-tailed test at 0.02*

n_2 \\ n_1	1	2	3	4	5	6	7	8	9	10	11	12	13	14	15	16	17	18	19	20
1	–	–	–	–	–	–	–	–	–	–	–	–	–	–	–	–	–	–	–	–
2	–	–	–	–	–	–	–	–	–	–	–	–	0	0	0	0	0	0	1	1
3	–	–	–	–	–	–	0	0	1	1	1	2	2	2	3	3	4	4	4	5
4	–	–	–	–	0	1	1	2	3	3	4	5	5	6	7	7	8	9	9	10
5	–	–	–	0	1	2	3	4	5	6	7	8	9	10	11	12	13	14	15	16
6	–	–	–	1	2	3	4	6	7	8	9	11	12	13	15	16	18	19	20	22
7	–	–	0	1	3	4	6	7	9	11	12	14	16	17	19	21	23	24	26	28
8	–	–	0	2	4	6	7	9	11	13	15	17	20	22	24	26	28	30	32	34
9	–	–	1	3	5	7	9	11	14	16	18	21	23	26	28	31	33	36	38	40
10	–	–	1	3	6	8	11	13	16	19	22	24	27	30	33	36	38	41	44	47
11	–	–	1	4	7	9	12	15	18	22	25	28	31	34	37	41	44	47	50	53
12	–	–	2	5	8	11	14	17	21	24	28	31	35	38	42	46	49	53	56	60
13	–	0	2	5	9	12	16	20	23	27	31	35	39	43	47	51	55	59	63	67
14	–	0	2	6	10	13	17	22	26	30	34	38	43	47	51	56	60	65	69	73
15	–	0	3	7	11	15	19	24	28	33	37	42	47	51	56	61	66	70	75	80
16	–	0	3	7	12	16	21	26	31	36	41	46	51	56	61	66	71	76	82	87
17	–	0	4	8	13	18	23	28	33	38	44	49	55	60	66	71	77	82	88	93
18	–	0	4	9	14	19	24	30	36	41	47	53	59	65	70	76	82	88	94	100
19	–	1	4	9	15	20	26	32	38	44	50	56	63	69	75	82	88	94	101	107
20	–	1	5	10	16	22	28	34	40	47	53	60	67	73	80	87	93	100	107	114

*Dashes in the body of the table indicate that no decision is possible at the stated level of significance because the numbers of subjects are too small.

Table 3C Critical values of U (Mann-Whitney) for a one-tailed test at 0.025; two-tailed test at 0.05*

n_2 \\ n_1	1	2	3	4	5	6	7	8	9	10	11	12	13	14	15	16	17	18	19	20
1	–	–	–	–	–	–	–	–	–	–	–	–	–	–	–	–	–	–	–	–
2	–	–	–	–	–	–	–	0	0	0	0	1	1	1	1	1	2	2	2	2
3	–	–	–	–	0	1	1	2	2	3	3	4	4	5	5	6	6	7	7	8
4	–	–	–	0	1	2	3	4	4	5	6	7	8	9	10	11	11	12	13	13
5	–	–	0	1	2	3	5	6	7	8	9	11	12	13	14	15	17	18	19	20
6	–	–	1	2	3	5	6	8	10	11	13	14	16	17	19	21	22	24	25	27
7	–	–	1	3	5	6	8	10	12	14	16	18	20	22	24	26	28	30	32	34
8	–	0	2	4	6	8	10	13	15	17	19	22	24	26	29	31	34	36	38	41
9	–	0	2	4	7	10	12	15	17	20	23	26	28	31	34	37	39	42	45	48
10	–	0	3	5	8	11	14	17	20	23	26	29	33	36	39	42	45	48	52	55
11	–	0	3	6	9	13	16	19	23	26	30	33	37	40	44	47	51	55	58	62
12	–	1	4	7	11	14	18	22	26	29	33	37	41	45	49	53	57	61	65	69
13	–	1	4	8	12	16	20	24	28	33	37	41	45	50	54	59	63	67	72	76
14	–	1	5	9	13	17	22	26	31	36	40	45	50	55	59	64	67	74	78	83
15	–	1	5	10	14	19	24	29	34	39	44	49	54	59	64	70	75	80	85	90
16	–	1	6	11	15	21	26	31	37	42	47	53	59	64	70	75	81	86	92	98
17	–	2	6	11	17	22	28	34	39	45	51	57	63	67	75	81	87	93	99	105
18	–	2	7	12	18	24	30	36	42	48	55	61	67	74	80	86	93	99	106	112
19	–	2	7	13	19	25	32	38	45	52	58	65	72	78	85	92	99	106	113	119
20	–	2	8	13	20	27	34	41	48	55	62	69	76	83	90	98	105	112	119	127

*Dashes in the body of the table indicate that no decision is possible at the stated level of significance because the numbers of subjects are too small.

Greene & D'Oliveira (1999)

Table 3D Critical values of U (Mann-Whitney) for a one-tailed test at 0.05; two-tailed test at 0.10*

n_2	n_1 1	2	3	4	5	6	7	8	9	10	11	12	13	14	15	16	17	18	19	20
1	–	–	–	–	–	–	–	–	–	–	–	–	–	–	–	–	–	–	0	0
2	–	–	–	–	0	0	0	1	1	1	1	2	2	2	3	3	3	4	4	4
3	–	–	0	0	1	2	2	3	3	4	5	5	6	7	7	8	9	9	10	11
4	–	–	0	1	2	3	4	5	6	7	8	9	10	11	12	14	15	16	17	18
5	–	0	1	2	4	5	6	8	9	11	12	13	15	16	18	19	20	22	23	25
6	–	0	2	3	5	7	8	10	12	14	16	17	19	21	23	25	26	28	30	32
7	–	0	2	4	6	8	11	13	15	17	19	21	24	26	28	30	33	35	37	39
8	–	1	3	5	8	10	13	15	18	20	23	26	28	31	33	36	39	41	44	47
9	–	1	3	6	9	12	15	18	21	24	27	30	33	36	39	42	45	48	51	54
10	–	1	4	7	11	14	17	20	24	27	31	34	37	41	44	48	51	55	58	62
11	–	1	5	8	12	16	19	23	27	31	34	38	42	46	50	54	57	61	65	69
12	–	2	5	9	13	17	21	26	30	34	38	42	47	51	55	60	64	68	72	77
13	–	2	6	10	15	19	24	28	33	37	42	47	51	56	61	65	70	75	80	84
14	–	2	7	11	16	21	26	31	36	41	46	51	56	61	66	71	77	82	87	92
15	–	3	7	12	18	23	28	33	39	44	50	55	61	66	72	77	83	88	94	100
16	–	3	8	14	19	25	30	36	42	48	54	60	65	71	77	83	89	95	101	107
17	–	3	9	15	20	26	33	39	45	51	57	64	70	77	83	89	96	102	109	115
18	–	4	9	16	22	28	35	41	48	55	61	68	75	82	88	95	102	109	116	123
19	0	4	10	17	23	30	37	44	51	58	65	72	80	87	94	101	109	116	123	130
20	0	4	11	18	25	32	39	47	54	62	69	77	84	92	100	107	115	123	130	138

*Dashes in the body of the table indicate that no decision is possible at the stated level of significance because the numbers of subjects are too small.

Greene & D'Oliveira (1999)

Table 4 Critical values of *T* at various levels of probability (Wilcoxon)

	Level of significance for one-tailed test					Level of significance for one-tailed test			
	0.05	0.025	0.01	0.005		0.05	0.025	0.01	0.005
	Level of significance for two-tailed test					Level of significance for two-tailed test			
N	*0.10*	*0.05*	*0.02*	*0.01*	*N*	*0.10*	*0.05*	*0.02*	*0.01*
5	1	–	–	–	28	130	117	102	92
6	2	1	–	–	29	141	127	111	100
7	4	2	0	–	30	152	137	120	109
8	6	4	2	0	31	163	148	130	118
9	8	6	3	2	32	175	159	141	128
10	11	8	5	3	33	188	171	151	138
11	14	11	7	5	34	201	183	162	149
12	17	14	10	7	35	214	195	174	160
13	21	17	13	10	36	228	208	186	171
14	26	21	16	13	37	242	222	198	183
15	30	25	20	16	38	256	235	211	195
16	36	30	24	19	39	271	250	224	208
17	41	35	28	23	40	287	264	238	221
18	47	40	33	28	41	303	279	252	234
19	54	46	38	32	42	319	295	267	248
20	60	52	43	37	43	336	311	281	262
21	68	59	49	43	44	353	327	297	277
22	75	66	56	49	45	371	344	313	292
23	83	73	62	55	46	389	361	329	307
24	92	81	69	61	47	408	379	345	323
25	101	90	77	68	48	427	397	362	339
26	110	98	85	76	49	446	415	380	356
27	120	107	93	84	50	466	434	398	373

*Dashes in the body of the table indicate that no decision is possible at the stated level of significance because the numbers of subjects are too small.

Greene & D'Oliveira (1999)

Table 5 Critical values of the Spearman rank correlation coefficient

One tailed Two tailed *n*	0.1 0.2	0.05 0.1	0.025 0.05	0.01 0.02	0.005 0.01
4	1.0000	1.0000	1.0000	1.0000	1.0000
5	0.7000	0.9000	0.9000	1.0000	1.0000
6	0.6571	0.7714	0.8286	0.9429	0.9429
7	0.5714	0.6786	0.7857	0.8571	0.8929
8	0.5476	0.6429	0.7381	0.8095	0.8571
9	0.4833	0.6000	0.6833	0.7667	0.8167
10	0.4424	0.5636	0.6485	0.7333	0.7818
11	0.4182	0.5273	0.6091	0.7000	0.7545
12	0.3986	0.5035	0.5874	0.6713	0.7273
13	0.3791	0.4780	0.5604	0.6484	0.6978
14	0.3670	0.4593	0.5385	0.6220	0.6747
15	0.3500	0.4429	0.5179	0.6000	0.6536
16	0.3382	0.4265	0.5029	0.5824	0.6324
17	0.3271	0.4124	0.4821	0.5577	0.6055
18	0.3170	0.4000	0.4683	0.5425	0.5897
19	0.3077	0.3887	0.4555	0.5285	0.5751
20	0.2992	0.3783	0.4438	0.5155	0.5614
21	0.2914	0.3687	0.4329	0.5034	0.5487
22	0.2841	0.3598	0.4227	0.4921	0.5368
23	0.2774	0.3515	0.4132	0.4815	0.5256
24	0.2711	0.3438	0.4044	0.4716	0.5151
25	0.2653	0.3365	0.3961	0.4622	0.5052
26	0.2598	0.3297	0.3882	0.4534	0.4958
27	0.2546	0.3233	0.3809	0.4451	0.4869
28	0.2497	0.3172	0.3739	0.4372	0.4785
29	0.2451	0.3115	0.3673	0.4297	0.4705
30	0.2407	0.3061	0.3610	0.4226	0.4629
31	0.2366	0.3009	0.3550	0.4158	0.4556
32	0.2327	0.2960	0.3494	0.4093	0.4487
33	0.2289	0.2913	0.3440	0.4032	0.4421
34	0.2254	0.2869	0.3388	0.3972	0.4357
35	0.2220	0.2826	0.3338	0.3916	0.4296
36	0.2187	0.2785	0.3291	0.3862	0.4238
37	0.2156	0.2746	0.3246	0.3810	0.4182
38	0.2126	0.2709	0.3202	0.3760	0.4128
39	0.2097	0.2673	0.3160	0.3712	0.4076
40	0.2070	0.2638	0.3120	0.3665	0.4026
41	0.2043	0.2605	0.3081	0.3621	0.3978
42	0.2018	0.2573	0.3044	0.3578	0.3932
43	0.1993	0.2542	0.3008	0.3536	0.3887
44	0.1970	0.2512	0.2973	0.3496	0.3843
45	0.1947	0.2483	0.2940	0.3457	0.3801
46	0.1925	0.2455	0.2907	0.3420	0.3761
47	0.1903	0.2429	0.2876	0.3384	0.3721
48	0.1883	0.2403	0.2845	0.3348	0.3683
49	0.1863	0.2377	0.2816	0.3314	0.3646
50	0.1843	0.2353	0.2787	0.3281	0.3610
60	0.1678	0.2144	0.2542	0.2997	0.3301
70	0.1550	0.1982	0.2352	0.2776	0.3060
80	0.1448	0.1852	0.2199	0.2597	0.2864
90	0.1364	0.1745	0.2072	0.2449	0.2702
100	0.1292	0.1654	0.1966	0.2324	0.2565

Dunstan *et al.* (1988)

Table 6 Percentage points of Student's *t*-distribution (independent and related)

Two-tailed 0.2 One-tailed 0.1	0.1 0.05	0.05 0.025	0.02 0.01	0.01 0.005	Two-tailed 0.2 One-tailed 0.1	0.1 0.05	0.05 0.025	0.02 0.01	0.01 0.005
df					**df**				
1 3.078	6.314	12.706	31.821	63.657	29 1.311	1.699	2.045	2.462	2.756
2 1.886	2.920	4.303	6.965	9.925	30 1.310	1.697	2.042	2.457	2.750
3 1.638	2.353	3.182	4.541	5.841	31 1.309	1.696	2.040	2.453	2.744
4 1.533	2.132	2.776	3.747	4.604	32 1.309	1.694	2.037	2.449	2.738
5 1.476	2.015	2.571	3.365	4.032	33 1.308	1.692	2.035	2.445	2.733
6 1.440	1.943	2.447	3.143	3.707	34 1.307	1.691	2.032	2.441	2.728
7 1.415	1.895	2.365	2.998	3.499	35 1.306	1.690	2.030	2.438	2.724
8 1.397	1.860	2.306	2.896	3.355	36 1.306	1.688	2.028	2.434	2.719
9 1.383	1.833	2.262	2.821	3.250	37 1.305	1.687	2.026	2.431	2.715
10 1.372	1.812	2.228	2.764	3.169	38 1.304	1.686	2.024	2.429	2.712
11 1.363	1.796	2.201	2.718	3.106	39 1.304	1.685	2.023	2.426	2.708
12 1.356	1.782	2.179	2.681	3.055	40 1.303	1.684	2.021	2.423	2.704
13 1.350	1.771	2.160	2.650	3.012	45 1.301	1.679	2.014	2.412	2.690
14 1.345	1.761	2.145	2.624	2.977	50 1.299	1.676	2.009	2.403	2.678
15 1.341	1.753	2.131	2.602	2.947	55 1.297	1.673	2.004	2.396	2.668
16 1.337	1.746	2.120	2.583	2.921	60 1.296	1.671	2.000	2.390	2.660
17 1.333	1.740	2.110	2.567	2.898	65 1.295	1.669	1.997	2.385	2.654
18 1.330	1.734	2.101	2.552	2.878	70 1.294	1.667	1.994	2.381	2.648
19 1.328	1.729	2.093	2.539	2.861	75 1.293	1.665	1.992	2.377	2.643
20 1.325	1.725	2.086	2.528	2.845	80 1.292	1.664	1.990	2.374	2.639
21 1.323	1.721	2.080	2.518	2.831	85 1.292	1.663	1.988	2.371	2.635
22 1.321	1.717	2.074	2.508	2.819	90 1.291	1.662	1.987	2.368	2.632
23 1.319	1.714	2.069	2.500	2.807	95 1.291	1.661	1.985	2.366	2.629
24 1.318	1.711	2.064	2.492	2.797	100 1.290	1.660	1.984	2.364	2.626
25 1.316	1.708	2.060	2.485	2.787	125 1.288	1.657	1.979	2.357	2.616
26 1.315	1.706	2.056	2.479	2.779	150 1.287	1.655	1.976	2.351	2.609
27 1.314	1.703	2.052	2.473	2.771	200 1.286	1.653	1.972	2.345	2.601
28 1.313	1.701	2.048	2.467	2.763	∞ 1.282	1.645	1.960	2.326	2.576

Dunstan *et al.* (1988)

Table 7 Critical values of the Pearson's product moment correlation coefficient

n	Level of significance for one-tailed test				
	0.1	0.05	0.025	0.01	0.005
	Level of significance for two-tailed test				
	0.2	0.1	0.05	0.02	0.01
4	0.8000	0.9000	0.9500	0.9800	0.9900
5	0.6870	0.8054	0.8783	0.9343	0.9587
6	0.6084	0 7293	0.8114	0.8822	0.9172
7	0.5509	0.6694	0.7545	0.8329	0.8745
8	0.5067	0.6215	0.7067	0.7887	0.8343
9	0.4716	0.5822	0.6664	0.7498	0.7977
10	0.4428	0.5494	0.6319	0.7155	0.7646
11	0.4187	0.5214	0.6021	0.6851	0.7348
12	0.3981	0.4973	0.5760	0.6581	0 7079
13	0.3802	0.4762	0.5529	0.6339	0.6835
14	0.3646	0.4575	0.5324	0.6120	0.6614
15	0.3507	0.4409	0.5140	0.5923	0.6411
16	0.3383	0.4259	0.4973	0.5742	0.6226
17	0.3271	0.4124	0.4821	0.5577	0.6055
18	0.3170	0.4000	0.4683	0.5425	0.5897
19	0.3077	0.3887	0.4555	0.5285	0.5751
20	0.2992	0.3783	0.4438	0.5155	0.5614
21	0.2914	0.3687	0.4329	0.5034	0.5487
22	0.2841	0.3598	0.4227	0.4921	0.5368
23	0.2774	0.3515	0.4132	0.4815	0.5256
24	0.2711	0.3438	0.4044	0.4716	0.5151
25	0.2653	0.3365	0.3961	0.4622	0.5052
26	0.2598	0.3297	0.3882	0.4534	0.4958
27	0.2546	0.3233	0.3809	0.4451	0.4869
28	0.2497	0.3172	0.3739	0.4372	0.4785
29	0.2451	0.3115	0.3673	0.4297	0.4705
30	0.2407	0.3061	0.3610	0.4226	0.4629
31	0.2366	0.3009	0.3550	0.4158	0.4556
32	0.2327	0.2960	0.3494	0.4093	0.4487
33	0.2289	0.2913	0.3440	0.4032	0.4421
34	0.2254	0.2869	0.3388	0.3972	0.4357
35	0.2220	0.2826	0.3338	0.3916	0.4296
36	0.2187	0.2785	0.3291	0.3862	0.4238
37	0.2156	0.2746	0.3246	0.3810	0.4182
38	0.2126	0.2709	0.3202	0.3760	0.4128
39	0.2097	0.2673	0.3160	0.3712	0.4076
40	0.2070	0.2638	0.3120	0.3665	0.4026
41	0.2043	0.2605	0.3081	0.3621	0.3978
42	0.2018	0.2573	0.3044	0.3578	0.3932
43	0.1993	0.2542	0.3008	0.3536	0.3887
44	0.1970	0.2512	0.2973	0.3496	0.3843
45	0.1947	0.2483	0.2940	0.3457	0.3801
46	0.1925	0.2455	0.2907	0.3420	0.3761
47	0.1903	0.2429	0.2876	0.3384	0.3721
48	0.1883	0.2403	0.2845	0.3348	0.3683
49	0.1863	0.2377	0.2816	0.3314	0.3646
50	0.1843	0.2353	0.2787	0.3281	0.3610
60	0.1678	0.2144	0.2542	0.2997	0.3301
70	0.1550	0.1982	0.2352	0.2776	0.3060
80	0.1448	0.1852	0.2199	0.2597	0.2864
90	0.1364	0.1745	0.2072	0.2449	0.2702
100	0.1292	0.1654	0.1966	0.2324	0.2565

Dunstan *et al.* (1988)

Appendix

Table 8 Random digits
The table gives 2500 random digits, from 0 to 9, arranged for convenience in blocks of 5

87024	74221	69721	44518	58804	04860	18127	16855	61558	15430
04852	03436	72753	99836	37513	91341	53517	92094	54386	44563
33592	45845	52015	72030	23071	92933	84219	39455	57792	14216
68121	53688	56812	34869	28573	51079	94677	23993	88241	97735
25062	10428	43930	69033	73395	83469	25990	12971	73728	03856
78183	44396	11064	92153	96293	00825	21079	78337	19739	13684
70209	23316	32828	00927	61841	64754	91125	01206	06691	50868
94342	91040	94035	02650	36284	91162	07950	36178	42536	49869
92503	29854	24116	61149	49266	82303	54924	58251	23928	20703
71646	57503	82416	22657	72359	30085	13037	39608	77439	49318
51809	70780	41544	27828	84321	07714	25865	97896	01924	62028
88504	21620	07292	71021	80929	45042	08703	45894	24521	49942
33186	49273	87542	41086	29615	81101	43707	87031	36101	15137
40068	35043	05280	62921	30122	65119	40512	26855	40842	83244
76401	68461	20711	12007	19209	28259	49820	76415	51534	63574
47014	93729	74235	47808	52473	03145	92563	05837	70023	33169
67147	48017	90741	53647	55007	36607	29360	83163	79024	26155
86987	62924	93157	70947	07336	49541	81386	26968	38311	99885
58973	47026	78574	08804	22960	32850	67944	92303	61216	72948
71635	86749	40369	94639	40731	54012	03972	98581	45604	34885
60971	54212	32596	03052	84150	36798	62635	26210	95685	87089
06599	60910	66315	96690	19039	39878	44688	65146	02482	73130
89960	27162	66264	71024	18708	77974	40473	87155	35834	03114
03930	56898	61900	44036	90012	17673	54167	82396	39468	49566
31338	28729	02095	07429	35718	86882	37513	51560	08872	33717
29782	33287	27400	42915	49914	68221	56088	06112	95481	30094
68493	88796	94771	89418	62045	40681	15941	05962	44378	64349
42534	31925	94158	90197	62874	53659	33433	48610	14698	54761
76126	41049	43363	52461	00552	93352	58497	16347	87145	73668
80434	73037	69008	36801	25520	14161	32300	04187	80668	07499
81301	39731	53857	19690	39998	49829	12399	70867	44498	17385
54521	42350	82908	51212	70208	39891	64871	67448	42988	32600
82530	22869	87276	06678	36873	61198	87748	07531	29592	39612
81338	64309	45798	42954	95565	02789	83017	82936	67117	17709
58264	60374	32610	17879	96900	68029	06993	84288	35401	56317
77023	46829	21332	77383	15547	29332	77698	89878	20489	71800
29750	59902	78110	59018	87548	10225	15774	70778	56086	08117
08288	38411	69886	64918	29055	87607	37452	38174	31431	46173
93908	94810	22057	94240	89918	16561	92716	66461	22337	64718
06341	25883	42574	80202	57287	95120	69332	19036	43326	98697
23240	94741	55622	79479	34606	51079	09476	10695	49618	63037
96370	19171	40441	05002	33165	28693	45027	73791	23047	32976
97050	16194	61095	26533	81738	77032	60551	31605	95212	81078
40833	12169	10712	78345	48236	45086	61654	94929	69169	70561
95676	13582	25664	60838	88071	50052	63188	50346	65618	17517
28030	14185	13226	99566	45483	10079	22945	23903	11695	10694
60202	32586	87466	83357	95516	31258	66309	40615	30572	60842
46530	48755	02308	79508	53422	50805	08896	06963	93922	99423
53151	95839	01745	46462	81463	28669	60179	17880	75875	34562
80272	64398	88249	06792	98424	66842	49129	98939	34173	49883

Dunstan *et al.* (1988)

glossary

Abstract A short summary of the aims, method, results and conclusions of a study that appears at the beginning of a published journal article or piece of coursework.

Aim Having decided upon the question to be answered, this needs to be stated as an achievable goal for a piece of research, this is the *aim*. Each study a psychologist conducts arises from a **research question**, the aim of the study is to answer the research question posed.

Alternative hypothesis, H_1 or H_A A testable statement that proposes the expected outcome of the study, it is a prediction based on the researcher's knowledge from observations, related studies and previous investigations.

Appendices Separate sections at the end of a journal article or piece of coursework holding supplementary items such as examples of test materials.

Attitude object The topic that you have chosen to design a questionnaire about (e.g. drugs, Christmas, pets).

Attrition rate (drop-out rate) The loss of participants during the study. It is expressed as the percentage retention of those who complete the study and uses the formula:

$$\frac{\text{Total initial number of participants } - \text{ remaining number of participants}}{\text{Total initial number of participants}} \times 100$$

Author index An alphabetical list of the authors cited in a book. It can be used to look up specific studies if you know the name of the researcher(s).

Bar-and-whisker plot This is used to display the median and interquartile range in the form of a graph. The bar represents the median while the whiskers show the upper and lower quartiles.

Bar chart This is used to display nominal data and average scores in the form of a graph. There are gaps between each bar that is plotted on the graph.

Between subjects design see **Independent groups design**.

Binomial sign test A non-parametric inferential statistical test. Used when you have nominal data, the research is repeated measures (or matched pairs) and you are looking for a difference in the effect each level of the independent variable has on the dependent variable.

Bi-polar adjectives These are used as part of the Semantic Differential question-naire design. These are pairs of words with opposite meaning (e.g. good–bad, ugly–beautiful).

Blocked randomisation Can be used to avoid the problem of truly randomised allocation, that several subsequent participants may experience the same order of conditions. Instead of true randomisation, pairs of participants are allocated to each randomly generated order, one of whom performs the conditions as indicated, the other in reverse order.

Brief A description given to participants to indicate what will be expected of them during a study and to describe its general purpose so that they can give their informed consent to participate. It should also state their right to withdraw at any time.

Case study An in-depth analysis of an individual or a 'unit' of individuals (e.g. a family).

Checklist A simple list of all the behaviours being recorded. On every occurrence of a behaviour on the list, a single tally is recorded. At the end of the observation period, the observer has a record of the number of occurrences of each of the behaviours being investigated.

Chi-squared (χ^2) test of association A non-parametric inferential statistical test. Used when you have nominal data, the research is independent groups and you are looking for an association between the independent variable and the dependent variable.

Closed questions Questions that have set answers for participants to choose from.

Coding scheme A set of statements that operationally define the behaviours to be observed. This ensures that they are measurable, i.e. that the observers can recognise the behaviours from the definitions and accurately record the behaviours exhibited.

Concurrent validity An indicator of **validity** which compares measures of the same phenomenon to determine whether they produce similar results in the same circumstances.

Confounding variables Uncontrolled variables that could disrupt the effect of the phenomenon under investigation.

Constant errors Uncontrolled variables that act on only one level of the **independent variable**. Their action may either be in the same direction as a predicted difference, exaggerating the apparent effect of the IV or in the opposite direction, obscuring the effect of the IV.

Construct validity An indicator of **validity** which aims to demonstrate that the phenomenon being measured actually exists, for example, by justifying it in relation to a model or theory.

Content analysis Examination of certain types of media (e.g. books, TV, magazines, the Internet) to see what effect they may be having on our percep-tions and/or behaviour. It involves the analysis of language, certain words or certain activities that appear in the chosen media.

Control condition In some situations an experimenter does not want to compare two alternative levels of the IV but instead wishes to observe the effect of the presence or absence of a variable. In this instance there is an experimental condition and a *control condition*, the latter being a situation in which the variable under consideration is absent.

Controls The steps taken to limit factors that could distort the collection of valid and reliable data.

Correlation A relationship between two measured variables.

Counterbalancing The systematic variation of the order of presentation of the levels of the IV in a **repeated measures design**.

Critical value The value that is compared with the observed (calculated) value in an inferential statistical test. Each inferential statistical test has a table or tables of critical values. The comparison with the observed (calculated) allows you to conclude if you have found a significant result.

Debrief A procedure that follows participation in a study. It ensures that participants are aware that they have taken part and are offered the opportunity to discuss their experience, withdraw their consent retrospectively or ask for their data to be destroyed. It also allows the researcher to ensure that the participants fully understand the purpose and expected outcome of the research and to monitor any unforeseen negative effects or misconceptions.

Demand characteristics The features of an experiment that inform participants about the aim and influence their behaviour independently of the experimental objectives and thereby confound the results.

Dependent variable (DV) The measurable outcome in an experiment. It is called the *dependent* variable because the alternative hypothesis predicts that any changes in this variable are caused by (i.e. dependent upon) changes in the **independent variable**.

Design An experiment aims to investigate whether the **independent variable** produces a change in the **dependent variable**. We therefore need either to compare the effects of the independent variable for participants in different conditions or to observe differences in the dependent variable for the same participants experiencing each of the different levels of the IV. These alternatives are essentially the different formal designs used in experiments.

Design section A part of the methods section of a journal article or piece of coursework that describes the formal design, variables and control measures employed in a study.

Directional hypotheses (one-tailed hypotheses) These indicate the nature of an effect, for instance stating which condition in an experiment will affect the results the most or in a particular way (making them 'better' or 'worse'). In a correlation, a directional hypothesis predicts whether the relationship will be positive or negative.

Discussion A section of a journal article or piece of coursework that considers the results in terms of the context of other research and future directions. It may also explore possible flaws with the research and propose modifications to overcome these.

Disproportionate strata sampling A technique for selecting participants from a population that does not result in the relative incidence of subgroups being reflected in the sample. This may be deliberate in order to ensure that there is some representation for particularly 'rare' groups or unequal weighting may be given to subgroups which are known to be more variable.

Drop-out rate see **Attrition rate**.

Dual bar chart Used to display nominal data where more than one category can be plotted on the same axis.

Ecological (external) validity The extent to which a test measures a real-world phenomenon.

Equivalent forms May be used to establish **reliability** by using different but comparable versions of the same test. These are used with a single group of participants whose results on each version should correlate strongly if the tests are reliable.

Event sampling An observational recording method in which observation, timing and recording are continuous. The onset and end of each behavioural event is recorded along a single time base.

Experimenter expectancy effect see **Investigator effect**.

Experiments These serve to investigate a causal relationship; whether one factor affects another. This is achieved by systematically varying one factor, the **independent variable**, while observing the effect of that change on another factor, the **dependent variable**. So, in an experiment, the independent variable is manipulated to create two or more levels and consequent changes in the dependent variable are measured. In addition, other factors that might affect the dependent variable should be controlled, that is kept constant across different conditions of the independent variable. This ensures that any difference in the dependent variable between conditions is the result of the IV and not due to other, chance, variations.

External validity see **Ecological validity**.

Face validity An indicator of **validity** based on whether the measure *appears* (at *face value*) to test what it claims to.

Fatigue effects Arise when participants become tired or bored if they repeat a repetitive or demanding task, so their performance worsens in later conditions.

Field experiments Studies with an experimental design (they have an IV and DV) that take place using participants in their normal surroundings.

Focused observations Direct the observers' attention to a limited number of behavioural events.

Frequency polygon Used to display the distribution of scores for two groups or more on the same graph. Sometimes called a line graph.

Generalisability The extent to which findings based on the investigation of a sample of participants are representative of the whole of the original population or of other populations.

Histogram Used to display the distribution of scores for one set of data. The data must be numerical and there should be no gaps between the bars.

Hypothesis A testable statement, expressing the **aims** of a study, which can be accepted or rejected to indicate the outcome of the research. It must be possible to gather evidence that will demonstrate that a hypothesis is either supported or refuted.

Independent groups designs Used in experiments when separate groups of individuals participate in the different levels of the IV, that is the data sets relating to each level of the IV are *independent* of each other. This is also referred to as a *between subjects* or *unrelated design* since comparisons are being made *between* groups rather than within them and the data points in one level of the IV are *unrelated* in any specific way to the data points for other levels.

Independent t-test A parametric inferential statistical test. Used when you have interval or ratio data, the research is independent groups and you are looking for a difference in the effect each level of the independent variable has on the dependent variable.

Independent variable (IV) The factor that is manipulated in an experiment. By controlling either the nature of the participants, their experiences or the way data are selected for analysis, the experimenter generates levels of the IV. These levels or 'conditions' are used to compare the effects of the variable under investigation.

Instantaneous scan sampling (I/S) A **time sampling** technique in which no records are made until the end of the time interval. At this *instant* a record is made of any behaviours which are occurring.

Internal validity The validity of test items themselves in relation to the objective.

Inter-observer reliability A measure of the extent to which different individuals generate the same records when they observe the same sequence of behaviour. By correlating the scores of observers we can measure inter-observer reliability: individuals (or groups) with highly correlated scores are demonstrating good inter-observer reliability.

Interquartile range The spread of scores for the middle 50 per cent of scores.

Interval data Data where the gaps between one point and the next are equivalent.

Interview Usually a verbal research method where the participant answers a series of questions.

Introduction A section of a journal article or piece of coursework that serves to set the study in the context of previous research and to explain the rationale behind the aims and/or hypotheses.

Investigator effect (experimenter expectancy effect) A bias resulting from a prejudgement by the researcher that subsequently affects the way in which the participants behave. It is sometimes called the experimenter expectancy effect because it is the effect of the experimenter's expectations that affect the behaviour of the participants.

Items analysis A technique used to make a questionnaire more reliable. It eliminates questions or items that do not discriminate between a high and low score on your questionnaire.

Laboratory experiments These are conducted in a laboratory or other contrived setting away from the participants' normal environment. The experimenter is able to manipulate the levels of the independent variable and accurately record changes in the dependent variable. In addition, considerable control can be exercised over potential confounding variables.

Level of measurement This describes the type of scale against which a variable is being assessed. In any study it must be possible to measure the observed effect of the variable being investigated. The data collected about a variable may be used in many different ways. In any situation, the data generated by the study can be classified into one of four types: **nominal**, **ordinal**, **interval** or **ratio**.

Level of significance The probability we set (*p*-value) that makes us believe the results are due to the independent variable and not due to chance. This is usually $p \leq 0.05$.

Likert scale A common form of questionnaire design. It is a series of statements usually with a choice of answers ranging from strongly agree to strongly disagree.

Lower quartile The data point that is at the 25 per cent point of your data set when in rank order.

Mann–Whitney U-test A non-parametric inferential statistical test. Used when you have ordinal data, the research is independent groups and you are looking for a difference in the effect each level of the independent variable has on the dependent variable.

Matched pairs design In this experimental design, scores are obtained for each level of the IV from different participants (as in an independent groups design). However, for each member of one group there exists in the other group an individual with certain characteristics in common. The groups are created by ensuring that every participant is part of a *matched pair*; two individuals who have been selected because they share features of importance to the experiment.

Materials and apparatus section A section of a journal article or piece of coursework that lists, describes or contains examples of the resources used by researchers during a study.

Mean A measure of average where you add up all of the scores and divide by the number of scores you have. It is best used on data that are interval or ratio. Can be affected by extreme scores.

Median A measure of average where you rank the data from smallest to largest and find the mid-point of the ranked data. It is best used on data that are ordinal and where there are extreme scores (the median is unaffected by extreme scores).

Method section A section of a journal article or piece of coursework that details the **design**, **participants**, **materials and apparatus** and **procedure** employed in a study.

Mode A measure of average where you find out which is the most common category. It is best used on nominal data.

Natural experiments **Quasi-experiments** in which the researcher cannot control the IV at all: the levels are derived from pre-existing and naturally occurring differences. The researcher can neither control allocation of participants to conditions nor when or how those conditions arise.

Naturalistic observation A study in which the researcher gathers data by watching participants (people or non-human animals) in their normal environment which may not, necessarily, be their 'natural' situation.

Negative correlation A relationship between two measured variables where as one measure increases the other measure decreases.

Nominal data Data that are in categories.

Non-directional hypotheses (two-tailed hypotheses) These are used when researchers can only predict that the variable(s) under investigation *will* affect the outcome rather making a more precise judgement about *how* the results will be affected. A non-directional hypothesis simply states that there will be a difference between conditions or a link between variables.

Non-parametric tests Inferential statistical tests where there is no assumption about the data collected. Usually used on data that are nominal or ordinal.

Non-participant observation This requires that the observer is unseen so that they cannot affect the behaviour of the participants. This might be achieved by being a long way away or by being hidden from the observed.

Non-representative sampling A technique for selecting participants from a population which cannot guarantee that the full range of diversity that exists within that population will be accessed when a sample is obtained. Those individuals who are unavailable may share an important criterion that will, as a consequence, be under-represented in the sample.

Normal distribution A distribution that is represented on a graph by a 'bell-shaped' curve.

Null hypothesis In any study, it must be possible for the alternative hypothesis to be contradicted by the findings. When this is the case, the H_1 is rejected but we still need a conclusion. This conclusion must be that our findings are not the consequence of the predicted effect but, instead, are due to chance. This possibility is expressed by the null hypothesis.

Observed (calculated) value The value that your collected data creates after an inferential statistical test. It is compared to the critical value to see if the result is significant.

One-tailed hypothesis see **Directional hypothesis**.

One-zero sampling (1/0) A **time sampling** technique in which a record is made during each time interval if the chosen behaviour occurs at all. No further record is made if that behaviour occurs again within that interval.

Open questions Questions where there are no set answers so the participant can write an answer in or reply freely in an interview.

Operational definition A description that serves to put a variable into *operation*, that is, to make it usable. It identifies variables by factors that can be manipulated or measured, for instance because they are observable. It provides a framework for improving reliability both within and between observers.

Operationalisation The process of systematically changing a variable or making a variable measurable using an operational definition.

Opportunity sampling A technique for selecting participants based on the section of the population available at a given time. It is non-representative because the full diversity of people within the population may not be available.

Order effects **Constant errors** that arise as a result of the order in which levels of the independent variable are presented to participants.

Ordinal data Data that can be ranked in order, but it is uncertain whether the gap between one data point and the next is equivalent (e.g. questionnaire scores from a Likert scale).

Parametric tests Inferential statistical tests that make assumptions about the data collected. These assumptions are (1) that the data are normally distributed for the population(s) used in the research from which you have drawn your sample, (2) data from both levels of the independent variable have equal variance, and (3) the data are from interval or ratio scales.

Participant observation Ensures that the participants are unaware of the presence of an observer by their being disguised as a legitimate member of the situation.

Participant reactivity see **Responder bias**.

Participants section A section of a journal article or piece of coursework that details the number of individuals (human or animal) participating in a study and indicates their source, such as the **population** from which they were drawn and the **sampling method** used.

Participant variables Confounding effects that arise from the characteristics of the people performing in a study, such as their age, gender, state of hunger or level of arousal.

Pearson's product moment correlation coefficient A parametric inferential statistical test. Used when you have interval or ratio data, the research is correlational and you are looking for a linear relationship between the two measured variables.

Pilot study A scaled-down pre-run of an experiment used to test the method and identify any uncontrolled variables. The results obtained from these participants do not contribute to the final analysis.

Placebo An inert substance administered in place of a drug to 'blind' participants, that is, ones who are unaware that they are not receiving a real drug. A placebo can thus act as a control.

Point sampling A technique similar to time sampling which allows the observer to record the behaviour of each member of a group during each time interval.

Population (or target population) The group to which the results of the study are intended to relate and from which those individuals selected to participate in the study will be drawn. A population consists of all of the cases within a given definition from which the sample is selected and it thus includes only those individuals who it was possible to access.

Positive correlation A relationship between two measured variables where as one measure increases the other measured variable increases too.

Practice effects These arise if participants become more skilled in familiar tasks, so their performance improves in later conditions.

Predictive validity An indicator of **validity** based on whether a test can accurately predict future performance on the measure in question.

Predominant activity sampling (P/A) A time sampling technique in which observation is continuous and an estimate is made in relation to the activity that occupied most of the preceding time interval.

Procedure section A section of a journal article or piece of coursework that explains how the study was conducted. It may contain a brief, standardised instructions and debrief and will describe a protocol providing sufficient information for replication.

Proportionate strata sampling A technique for selecting individuals from different strata within a population according to the incidence of each subgroup within the population.

Publication bias A tendency for some research findings, particularly positive ones, to be selected for publication in journals whereas others are not.

p-value Represents the probability of something happening by chance. *p*-values range from 0 to 1, with 0 representing no influence of chance and 1 representing a complete influence of chance. They are written as proportions, e.g. $p \leq 0.05$.

Quasi-experiment An experimental design in which control cannot be exercised over the allocation of participants to levels of the IV or over any aspect of the IV.

Questionnaire A research method that is usually written. There are many types of questionnaire design, for example the Likert scale, semantic differentials, Thurstone method and open and closed questions.

Quota sampling A technique for obtaining participants by selecting individuals from each chosen stratum of a population by questioning any available individuals. As time progresses, individuals are encountered who fulfil the requirements. When the target sample size for a subgroup has been met, further similar individuals are rejected. Sampling continues until sufficient numbers in each category have been obtained. It is essentially a **proportionate strata sample** obtained by opportunity and is, as a consequence, less rigorously representative than a strata sample.

Random errors These are caused by uncontrolled variables which act in unsystematic ways.

Randomisation A technique used to minimise the effects of practice and fatigue by allocating participants to randomised orders for participation in each condition (see also **Blocked randomisation**).

Random sampling A technique for selecting participants such that each member of the population has an equal chance of being chosen.

Range The spread of scores from the highest score to the lowest score plus one.

Ratio data Data taken from a universal scale that has a true zero point (e.g. Kelvin measurement for temperature).

References An alphabetical list of the citations made in a journal article or piece of coursework. It should include electronic sources as well as those from books or journals.

Related design see **Repeated measures design**.

Related t-test A parametric inferential statistical test. Used when you have interval or ratio data, the research is repeated measures (or matched pairs) and you are looking for a difference in the effect each level of the independent variable has on the dependent variable.

Reliability A measure of whether replications of a test or technique would produce similar results, if so then the measure is reliable.

Repeated measures design (within-subjects or related design) This is an experimental design in which each individual participates in every level of the IV, that is, the levels of the IV are compared by each participant *repeating* their performance under different conditions.

Representative sampling A method of selecting a group of participants that contains all the important characteristics of the parent population.

Research question The general question that a study intends to answer.

Researcher bias The tendency of experimenters or observers to record the response they expect from the participants in different conditions, either because of subjective observation and recording or through acting differently towards participants in different conditions causing systematic variations in their behaviour.

Responder bias (participant reactivity) The tendency of a participant to produce responses that are socially desirable, are what the experimenter wants or are biased.

Results section A section of a journal article or piece of coursework that contains descriptive statistics that summarise the findings and, if appropriate, the results of inferential statistics.

Sample The group of individuals selected from the **population** to participate in a study so that the researcher can make generalisations about the whole of the original population.

Sampling method A technique by which a sample of participants is taken from a population.

Scattergraph Used to display a correlation in the form of a graph.

Semantic differentials A form of questionnaire design where participants rate either pictures or pieces of text on a bi-polar adjective scale.

Simulations A situation that is set up (artificial) to examine how people behave in it. For example, setting up a courtroom to examine how jurors act as a group.

Situational variables Confounding effects arising from the influence of the environment on the behaviour of participants, such as lighting, noise levels and temperature.

Snowball effect A sampling technique used with an **opportunity sample** to increase availability of participants. The recruitment base is expanded by asking existing participants to ask other people whether they would consider participating. This increases the absolute number of participants and may provide a means to recruit from within otherwise inaccessible groups.

Spearman's rank order correlation coefficient A non-parametric inferential statistical test. Used when you have ordinal data, the research is correlational and you are looking for a relationship between the two measured variables.

Split-half reliability A measure of the internal reliability of the test. It indicates whether all the items on the test are measuring the same phenomenon by correlating participants' scores on one half of the test with their scores on the other half. These should correlate highly if the test is internally reliable.

Standard deviation A measure of dispersion (spread) based around the mean score of your results.

Standard error bar This is used to display the mean and standard deviation in the form of a graph. The bar represents the mean and the whisker shows the standard deviation.

Standardised instructions Guidance given to participants in a study to ensure that each one receives the same information about the requirements of the task to minimise variation between their experiences.

Stratified sampling A method for obtaining participants in which individuals are taken from each major strata or layer represented within the population. Such subdivisions might include socio-economic groups, ages, geographical locations and racial origin.

Structured observation A systematic approach to recording behaviours in which target actions are categorised, selected and defined prior to observation.

Subject index An alphabetical list of the topics and ideas discussed in a book. It can be used to look up areas of research rather than specific studies.

Systematic sample This is a technique for obtaining participants which generates a sample that is representative of the population variety of characteristics exhibited within the population. The basis of systematic sampling is very simple: we select every *n*th person on a list. By dividing the total population by the size of the sample we require we find the basis for sampling. For example, if we have a population of 100 and wish to select a sample of 20, we would include every fifth person (100/20 = 5, hence every fifth). However, this technique does not necessarily result in a representative sample.

Test–retest reliability An assessment of the **reliability** of a measure in which a group of participants completes the test twice, at different times. If their first and second scores are highly correlated, then the test is reliable.

Thurstone method A questionnaire design where an 'expert panel' rate each question before participants fill the questionnaire in. Each item is weighted depending on what the judges believe.

Time sampling A technique that enables the observer to record some information about *when* behaviours occur. There are three recording schedules each providing only an indication of the frequency and duration of behaviours rather than the sequential relationship between behaviours. The observation period is divided into predetermined intervals and records of behaviours are related to these.

Two-tailed hypothesis see **Non-directional hypotheses**.

Type I error Rejecting the null hypothesis when in fact we should accept it. If we set our level of significance less stringently, e.g. $p \leq 0.1$, it is easier to reject the null hypothesis and we may commit a Type I error as the null hypothesis may well be correct.

Type II error Accepting the null hypothesis when in fact we should reject it in favour of the alternative/experimental hypothesis. If we set our level of significance too stringently, e.g. $p \leq 0.001$, it is easier to accept the null hypothesis and we may commit a Type II error as the experimental/alternative hypothesis may well be correct.

Upper quartile The data point that is at the 75 per cent point of your data set when the data is ranked in order.

Validity The extent to which a technique achieves the purpose for which it was designed. A valid test would measure what it claims to measure.

Variance A measure of spread based around the mean. It is the square of the standard deviation.

Variation ratio A measure of spread that is the proportion (usually a percentage) of scores that are not the mode.

Volunteer sample In most cases, those individuals who participate in a study do so voluntarily, so they thus constitute a *volunteer sample*.

Wilcoxon's signed rank matched pairs test A non-parametric inferential statistical test. Used when you have ordinal data, the research is repeated measures (or matched pairs) and you are looking for a difference in the effect each level of the independent variable has on the dependent variable.

Within subjects design see **Repeated measures design**.

references

Abernethy, E.M. (1940) The effect of changed environmental conditions on the results of college examinations. *Journal of Psychology*, 10, 293–301

Ackerman, A.M., McMahon, P.M. and Fehr, L.A. (1984) Mock trial jury as a function of adolescent juror guilt and hostility. *Journal of Genetic Psychology*, 144 (2), 195–201

Allen, K. and Blascovich, J. (1996) The value of service dogs for people with severe ambulatory disorders. *Journal of the American Medical Association*, 275, 1001–6

Andersson, B. (1992) Effects of day-care on cognitive and socioemotional competence of thirteen-year-old Swedish schoolchildren. *Child Development*, 63, 20–36

Angbratt, M. and Moller, M. (1999) Questionnaire about calcium intake: can we trust the answers? *Osteoporosis International*, 9 (3), 220–5

Arey, D. (1992) Straw and food as reinforcers for preparatural sows. *Applied Animal Behaviour Science*, 33, 205–35

Asch, S.E. (1955) Opinions and social pressure. *Scientific American*, 193, 31–5

Baenninger, R., Dengelmaier, R., Navarette, J. and Sezov, D. (2000) What's in a name? Uncovering connotative meanings of animal names. *Anthrozoös*, 13 (2), 113–17

Bandura, A., Ross, D. and Ross, S.A. (1961) Transmission of aggression through imitation of aggressive models. *Journal of Abnormal and Social Psychology*, 63, 575–82

Baron-Cohen, S., Leslie, A.M. and Frith, U. (1985) Does the autistic child have a theory of mind? *Cognition*, 21, 37–46

Bartholomew, R.E., Basterfield, K. and Howard, G.F. (1991) UFO abductees and contactees: psychopathology or fantasy-proneness? *Professional Psychology: Research and Practice*, 22 (3), 215–22

Bateson, P. (1986) When to experiment on animals. *New Scientist*, 1496, 30–2

Baydar, N. and Brooks-Gunn, J. (1991) Effects of maternal employment and child-care arrangements on preschoolers' cognitive and behavioral outcomes:

evidence from the children of the National Longitudinal Survey of Youth. *Developmental Psychology*, 27, 932–45

Bjork, J.M., Dougherty, D.M. and Moeller, F.G. (1997) A positive correlation between self-ratings of depression and laboratory measured aggression. *Psychiatry Research*, 69 (1), 33–8

Bluedorn, A.C., Turban, D.B. and Love, M.S. (1999) The effects of stand-up and sit down meeting formats on meeting outcomes. *Journal of Applied Psychology*, 84, 277–85

Breakwell, G.M. (1995) Interviewing. In Breakwell, G.M., Hammond S. and Fife-Shaw, C. (eds) *Research Methods in Psychology*, Chapter 15, pp. 230–42. London: Sage Publications

British Psychological Society (1978) *Ethical Principles*. Leicester: British Psychological Society

British Psychological Society (1985) *Guidelines for the Use of Animals in Research*. Leicester: British Psychological Society

British Psychological Society (1998) *Code of Conduct, Ethical Principles and Guidelines*. Leicester: British Psychological Society

Bugleski, B.R. and Alampay, D.A. (1961) The role of frequency in developing perceptual sets. *Canadian Journal of Psychology*, 15, 205–11

Cabe, P.A. and Pittenger, J.B. (2000) Human sensitivity to acoustic information from vessel filling. *Journal of Experimental Psychology: Human Perception and Performance*, 26, 313–24

Canterino, J.C., VanHorn, L.G., Harrigan, J.T., Ananth, C.V. and Vintzileos, A.M. (1999) Domestic abuse in pregnancy: A comparison of a self-completed domestic abuse questionnaire with a directed interview. *American Journal of Obstetric Gynecology*, 181 (5, pt 1), 1049–51

Carey, M. (1978) Does civil inattention exist in pedestrian passing? *Journal of Personality & Social Psychology*, 36, 1185–93

Chantome, M., Perruchet, P., Hasboun, D., Dormont, D., Sahel, M., Sourour, N., Zouaoui, A., Marsault, C. and Duyme, M. (1999) Is there a negative correlation between explicit memory and hippocampal volume. *Neuroimage*, 10 (5), 589–95

Chawarski, M.C. and Sternberg, R.J. (1993) Negative priming in word recognition: a context effect. *Journal of Experimental Psychology: General*, 122, 195–206

Cho, K., Ennaceur, A., Cole, J.C. and Suh, C.K. (2000) Chronic jet lag produces cognitive deficits. *Journal of Neuroscience*, 20 (RC66), 1–5

Clark, W.M. and Serovich, J.M. (1997) Twenty years and still in the dark? Content analysis of articles pertaining to gay, lesbian and bisexual issues in marriage and family therapy journals. *Journal of Marriage and Family Therapy*, 23 (3), 239–53

Clarke-Stewart, K.A., Gruber, C.P. and Fitzgerald, L.M. (1994) *Children at Home and in Day Care*. Hillsdale, NJ: Erlbaum

Clegg, F. (1982) *Simple Statistics*. Cambridge: Cambridge University Press

Colpaert, F.C., de Witte, P.C., Maroli, A.N., Awouters, F., Niemgeens, C.A. and Janssen, P.A.J. (1980) Chronic pain. *Life Science*, 27, 921–8

Colwell, J., Schroder, S. and Sladen, D. (2000) The ability to detect unseen staring: a literature review and empirical tests. *British Journal of Psychology*, 91, 71–85

Corkin, S. (1984) Lasting consequences of bilateral medial temporal lobectomy: clinical course and experimental findings in H.M. *Seminars in Neurology*, 4, 249–59

Dawkins, M. (1980) *Animal Suffering: The Science of Animal Welfare*. London: Chapman & Hall

Dawkins, M.S. (1983) Battery hens name their price: consumer demand theory and the measurement of ecological 'needs'. *Animal Behaviour*, 31, 1195–205

DeMello, L.R. (1999) The effect of the presence of a companion-animal on physiological changes following the termination of cognitive stressors. *Psychology and Health*, 14, 859–68

Dement, W. and Kleitman, N. (1957) The relation of eye movements during sleep to dream activity: an objective method for the study of dreaming. *Journal of Experimental Psychology*, 53 (5), 339–46

Derȩgowski, J.B., McGeorge, P. and Wynn, V. (2000) The role of left–right symmetry in the encodement of spatial orientations. *British Journal of Psychology*, 91, 241–57

Donovan, R.J., Holman, C.D., Corti, B. and Jalleh, G. (1997) Face-to-face household interviews versus telephone interviews for health surveys. *Australian and New Zealand Journal of Public Health*, 21 (2), 134–40

Driscoll, J.W. and Bateson, P. (1988) Animals in behavioural research. *Animal Behaviour*, 36, 1569–74

Duncan, L.G. and Seymour, P.H.K. (2000) Socio-economic differences in foundation-level literacy. *British Journal of Psychology*, 91, 145–66

Dunstan, F.D.J. (1988) *Elementary Statistical Tables 2nd edition*. Cardiff: RND Publications

Dupuy, H.J. (1985) The Psychological General Well-Being (PGWB) Scale. Part II: Assessment Methodologies and Assessment, 170–83

DuRant, R.H., Rome, E.S., Rich, M., Allred, E., Emans, S.J. and Woods, E.R. (1997) Tobacco and alcohol use behaviours portrayed in music videos: a content analysis. *American Journal of Public Health*, 87 (7), 1131–5

Dutton, D.C. and Aron, A.P. (1974) Some evidence for heightened sexual attraction under conditions of high anxiety. *Journal of Personality and Social Psychology*, 30, 510–17

Escamilla, G., Cradock, A.L. and Kawachi, I. (2000) Women and smoking in Hollywood movies: a content analysis. *American Journal of Public Health*, 90 (3), 412–14

Féry, Y.-A. and Vom Hofe, A. (2000) When will the ball rebound? Evidence for the usefulness of mental analogues in appraising the duration of motions. *British Journal of Psychology*, 91, 259–73

Fick, K.M. (1993) The influence of an animal on social interactions of nursing home residents in a group setting. *American Journal of Occupational Therapy*, 47, 529–34

Fife-Shaw, C. (1995) Questionnaire design. In Breakwell, G.M., Hammond, S. and Fife-Shaw, C. (eds) *Research Methods in Psychology*, Chapter 12, 174–93. London: Sage

Fride, E. *et al.* (2000) reported in *New Scientist* 8 July 2000, 9

Fritz, C.L., Farver, T.B., Kass, P.H. and Hart, L.A. (1995) Association with companion animals and the expression of noncognitive symptoms in Alzheimer's Disease. *The Journal of Nervous and Mental Disease*, 183 (7), 459–63

Graham, C.A., Janssen, E. and Sanders, S.A. (2000) Effects of fragrance on female arousal and mood across the menstrual cycle. *Psychophysiology*, 37, 76–84

Greene, J. and D'Oliveira, M. (1999) *Learning to Use Statistical Tests in Psychology 2nd edition*. Buckingham: Open University Press.

Grubb, N.R., Fox, K.A., Smith, K., Blane, A., Ebmeier, K.P., Glabus, M.F. and O'Carroll, R.E. (2000) Memory impairment in out-of-hospital cardiac arrest survivors is associated with global reduction in brain volume, not focal hippocampal injury. *Stroke*, 31 (7), 1509–14

Halligan, P.W., Athwal, B.S., Oakley, D.A. and Frackowiak, R.S. (2000) Imaging hypnotic paralysis: implications for conversion hysteria. *The Lancet*, 355, 18 March, 986–7

Hara, T.J. (1986) Role of olfaction in fish behaviour. In Pitcher, T.J. (ed.) *The Behaviour of Teleost Fishes*. London: Croom Helm

Harlow, H.F. (1965) Love in infant monkeys. *Scientific American*, 200, 68–74

Harrell, A.W., Bowlby, J.W. and Hall-Hoffarth, D. (2000) Directing wayfinders with maps: the effects of age, route complexity and familiarity with the environment. *The Journal of Social Psychology*, 140, 169–78

Havens, B. and Swenson, I. (1989) A content analysis of educational media about menstruation. *Adolescence*, 24 (6), 901–7

Haverkate, I., Muller, M.T., Cappetti, M., Jonkers, F.J. and van der Wal, G. (2000) Prevalence and content analysis of guidelines on handling requests for euthanasia or assisted suicide in Dutch nursing homes. *Archives of International Medicine*, 160(3), 317–22

Hayashi, M., Iwanaga, T., Mitoku, K. and Minowa, M. (1999) Getting a high response rate of sexual behaviour survey among the general population in Japan: three different methods of survey on sexual behaviour. *Journal of Epidemiology*, 9 (2), 107–13

Hemmings, B., Smith, M., Graydon, J. and Dyson, R. (2000) Effect of massage on physiological restoration, perceived recovery and repeated sports performance. *British Journal of Sports Medicine*, 34, 109–15

Hofling, K.C., Brotzman, E., Dalrymple, S., Graves, N. and Pierce, C.M. (1966) An experimental study in the nurse–physician relationship. *Journal of Nervous and Mental Disorders*, 143, 171–80

Hollien, H., Bennett, G. and Gelfer, M.P. (1983) Criminal identification comparison: aural versus visual identifications resulting from a simulated crime. *Journal of Forensic Science*, 28 (1), 208–21

Howell, F. (1996) Smoking in Irish journals: a content analysis 1960–1994. *Irish Medical Journal*, 89 (2), 18–20

Hoyt, W.T. (2000) Rater bias in psychological research: when is it a problem and what can we do about it? *Psychological Methods*, 5, 64–86

Humphreys, L. (1970) *Tearoom Trade*. London: Gerald Duckworth & Co.

Ireland, M.C. (1990) The behaviour and ecology of the American mink *Mustela vison* (Schreber) in a coastal habitat. Unpublished PhD thesis. University of Durham

Jacob, S. and McClintock, M.K. (2000) Psychological state and mood effects of steroidal chemosignals in women and men. *Hormones and Behaviour*, 37, 57–78

Jang, K.L., Lam, R.W., Harris, J.A., Vernon, P.A. and Livesley, W.J. (1998a) Seasonal mood change and personality: an investigation of genetic co-morbidity. *Psychiatry Research*, 78, 1–7

Jang, K.L., Livesley, W.J. and Vernon, P.A. (1998b) A twin study of genetic and environmental contributions to gender differences in traits delineating personality disorder. *European Journal of Personality*, 12, 331–44

Jang, K.L., Livesely, W.J. and Vernon, P.A. (1999) The relationship between Eysenck's P-E-N model of personality and traits delineating personality disorder. *Personality and Individual Differences*, 26, 121–8

Jones, F., Harris, P. and Chrispin, C. (2000) Catching the sun: an investigation of sun-exposure and skin protective behaviour. *Psychology Health and Medicine*, 5, 131–41

de Jong-Gierveld, J. and van Tilburg, W. (1991) *Manual of the Loneliness Scale*. Amsterdam: Department of Social Research Methodology, Vrije Universiteit

Kirk, J.M. and de Wit, H. (2000) Individual differences in the priming effect of ethanol in social drinkers. *Journal for the Study of Alcohol*, 61 (1), 64–71

Kissinger, P., Rice, J., Farley, T., Trim, S., Jewitt, K., Margavio, V. and Martin, D.H. (1999) Application of computer-assisted interviews to sexual behaviour research. *American Journal of Epidemiology*, 149 (10), 950–4

Kohler, W. (1925) *The Mentality of Apes*. New York: Harcourt, Brace

Koivisto, M., Revonsuo, A., Krause, C., Haarala, C., Sillanmaki, L., Laine, M. and Hamalainen, H. (2000) Effects of 902 MHz electromagnetic field emitted by cellular telephones on response times in humans. *Neuroreport*, 11, 413–15

Leaper, C. (2000) Gender, affiliation, assertion, and the interactive context of parent–child play. *Developmental Psychology*, 36, 381–93

Lewis, M.K. and Hill, A.J. (1998) Food advertising on British children's television: a content analysis and experimental study with nine-year olds. *International Journal of Obesity and Related Metabolic Disorders*, 22 (3), 206–14

Likert, R.A. (1932) A technique for the measurement of attitudes. *Archives of Psychology*, 140, 55

Low, J. and Durkin, K. (2000) Event knowledge and children's recall of television based narratives. *British Journal of Developmental Psychology*, 18, 247–67

Lukoff, D., Edwards, D. and Miller, M. (1998) The case study as a scientific method for researching alternative therapies. *Alternative Therapy, Health and Medicine*, 4 (2), 44–52

Lund, E. and Gram, I.T. (1998) Response rate according to title and length of questionnaire. *Scandinavian Journal of Social Medicine*, 26 (2), 154–60

MacDonald, T.K., Fong, G.T., Zanna, M.P. and Martineau, A.M. (2000) Alcohol myopia and condom use: can alcohol intoxication be associated with more prudent behaviour? *Journal of Personality and Social Psychology*, 78, 605–19

MacRae, A.W. (1994) Common misconceptions about statistics. In Hatcher, D. (ed.) *Proceedings of the Association for the Teaching of Psychology*. Birmingham: Birmingham University

Magai, C., Kennedy, G., Cohen, C.I. and Gomberg, D. (2000) A controlled clinical trial of sertraline in the treatment of depression in nursing home patients with late-stage Alzheimer's disease. *American Journal of Geriatric Psychiatry*, 8 (1), 66–74

Maguire, E.A., Gadian, D.G., Johnsrude, I.S., Good, C.D., Ashburner, J., Frackowiak, R.S. and Frith, C.D. (2000) Navigation-related structural changes in the hippocampi of taxi drivers. *Proceedings of the National Academy of Sciences USA*, 97 (8), 4398–403

Marsh, P., Rosser, E. and Harré, R. (1978) *The Rules of Disorder*. London: Routledge, Kegan, Paul

Martin, N. (1999) The social psychology of sitting. *The Psychologist*, 12, 563

Matthies, E. and Krömker, D. (2000) Participatory planning – a heuristic for adjusting interventions to the context. *Journal of Environmental Psychology*, 20, 1–10

McCann, S.E., Marshall, J.R., Trevisan, M., Russell, M., Muti, P., Markovic, N., Chan, A.W. and Freudenheim, J.L. (1999) Recent alcohol intake as estimated by the Health Habits and History Questionnaire, the Harvard Semiquantitative Food Frequency Questionnaire and a more detailed alcohol intake questionnaires. *American Journal of Epidemiology*, 150 (4), 334–40

McConway, K. (1991) The number of subjects in animal behaviour experiments: is Still still right? In Stamp Dawkins, M. and Gosling, M. (eds) *Ethics in Research on Animal Behaviour*. London: Academic Press/Association for the Study of Animal Behaviour

McNicholas, J. and Collis, G.M. (2000) Dogs as catalysts for social interactions: robustness of the effect. *British Journal of Psychology*, 91, 61–70

Melhuish, E.C., Mooney, A., Martin, S. and Lloyd, E. (1990a) Type of childcare at 18 months I. Differences in interactional experience. *Journal of Child Psychology and Psychiatry*, 31, 849–59

Melhuish, E.C., Lloyd, E., Martin, S. and Mooney, A. (1990b) Type of childcare at 18 months II. Relations with cognitive and language development. *Journal of Child Psychology and Psychiatry*, 31, 861–70

Metzler, C.W., Biglan, A., Noell, J., Ary, D.V. and Ochs, L. (2000) A randomised controlled trial of a behavioural intervention to reduce high-risk sexual behaviour among adolescents in STD clinics. *Behavior Therapy*, 31, 27–54

Milgram, S. (1963) Behavioural study of obedience. *Journal of Abnormal and Social Psychology*, 67, 371–8

Millings Monk, E. (1999) Student Well-being. *The Psychologist*, 12, 67

Morrison, C.M., and Ellis, A.W. (2000) Real age of acquisition of effects in word naming and lexical decision. *British Journal of Psychology*, 91, 167–80

Morrongiello, B.A. and Dawber, T. (2000) Mothers' responses to sons and daughters engaging in injury-risk behaviors on a playground: implications for sex differences in injury rates. *Journal of Experimental Child Psychology*, 76, 89–103

Neer, C.A., Dorn, C.R. and Grayson, I. (1987) Dog interaction with persons receiving institutional geriatric care. *Journal of the American Veterinary Medical Association*, 191, 300–4

Neumayer, L., McNamara, R.M., Dayton, M. and Kim, B. (1998) Does volume of patients seen in an outpatient setting impact test scores? *American Journal of Surgery*, 175 (6), 511–14

North, A.C. and Hargreaves, D.J. (2000) Musical preference during and after relaxation and exercise. *American Journal of Psychology*, 113, 43–67

Orne, M.T. (1962) On the social psychology of the psychological experiment: with particular reference to demand characteristics and their implications. *American Psychologist*, 17, 776–83

Ory, M.G. and Goldberg, E.L. (1983) Pet possession and well-being in elderly women. *Research on Aging*, 5 (3), 389–409

Osgood, C.E., Suci, G.J. and Tannenbaum, P.H. (1957) *The Measurement of Meaning*. Urbana: University of Illinois

Parker, H.J. (1974) *View from the Boys*. Newton Abbott: David and Charles

Parnell, J.O. and Sprinkle, R.L. (1990) Personality characteristics of persons who claim UFO experiences. *Journal of UFO Studies*, 2, 48–58

Patrick, J. (1973) *A Glasgow Gang Observed*. London: Methuen

Perrig-Chiello, P., Perrig, W.J. and Stähelin, H.B. (1999) Health control beliefs in old age - relationship with subjective and objective health, and health behaviour. *Psychology, Health and Medicine*, 4, 83–94

Poppe, E. and Linssen, H. (1999) In-group favouritism and the reflection of realistic dimensions of difference between national states in Central and Eastern European nationality stereotypes. *British Journal of Social Psychology*, 38, 85–102

Rajecki, D.W., Rasmussen, J.L. and Conner, T.J. (2000) Relinquish the dog? Movie messages about misbehaviour. *Antrozoös*, 13 (3), 140–9

Rechtschaffen, A., Gilliland, M.A., Bergmann, B.M. and Winter, J.B. (1983) Physiological correlates of prolonged sleep deprivation in rats. *Science*, 221, 182–4

Roberts, C. (2000a) Pet ownership, social support and psychological health in community-dwelling older adults in the United Kingdom. *Hunden på 2000-talet: Om hundens roll i dagens samhälle, dess medicinska och sociala betydelse*, 52–4. Spånga: Svenska Kennelklubben

Roberts, C.A. (2000b) UK UFO organisations: what do they have knowledge of and what do they investigate? *European Journal of UFO and Abduction Studies*, 1 (1), 26–32

Roberts, C.A., McBride, E.A., Rosenvinge, H.P., Stevenage, S.V. and Bradshaw, J.W.S. (1996) The pleasure of a pet: the effect of pet ownership and social support on loneliness and depression in a population of elderly people living in their own homes. In Nicholoson, J. and Podberscek, A. (eds) *Proceedings of Further Issues in Research in Companion Animal Studies*, September 1996, University of Cambridge, 64. SCAS: Callender

Roberts, C.A., McBride, E.A., Horn, S., Rosenvinge, H. and Bradshaw, J.W.S. (1998) Pet ownership, social support and psychological health in community older adults. *Proceedings of the 8th International Conference on Human–Animal Interactions: The changing roles of animals in society*, 77. Praha: Ceska Republika

Roberts, C.A., Russell, J. and Chandler, E. (in press) What do children produce when asked to draw how an alien would travel to Earth? *European Journal of UFO and Abduction Studies*, 2 (1), published March 2001

Roberts, R.D. and Kyllonen, P.C. (1999) Morningness–eveningness and intelligence: early to bed, early to rise will make you anything but wise! *Personality and Individual Differences*, 27, 1123–33

Robson, C. (1993) *Real World Research*. Oxford: Blackwell

Rosenblum, L.D., Yahal, D.A. and Green, K.P. (2000) Face and mouth inversion effects and audiovisual speech perception. *Journal of Experimental Pscyhology: Human Perception and Performance*, 26, 806–19

Rosenbluth, R., Grossman, E.S. and Kaitz, M. (2000) Performance of early-blind and sighted children on olfactory tasks. *Perception*, 29, 101–10

Russell, J. (1990) Is object play in young carnivores practice for predation? Unpublished PhD thesis. University College London

Scholey, A., Chandler, C. and Wesnes, K. (2000) Interactions between actual and informed caffeine content on subsequent cognitive performance. *Proceedings of the British Psychological Society*, 8, 45

Schooler, J.W., Ohlsson, S. and Brooks, K. (1993) Thoughts beyond words: when language overshadows insight. *Journal of Experimental Psychology: General*, 122, 166–83

Serpell, J.A. (1996) Evidence for an association between pet behaviour and owner attachment levels. *Applied Animal Behaviour Science*, 47, 49–60

Seyfarth, R.M. and Cheney, D.L. (1986) Vocal development in vervet monkeys. *Animal Behaviour*, 34, 1640–58

Shaughnessy, J.J. and Zechmeister, Z. (1997) *Research Methods in Psychology*. New York: McGraw-Hill

Spanos, N.P., Cross, P.A., Dockson, K. and DuBreuil, S.C. (1993) Close encounters: an examination of UFO experiences. *Journal of Abnormal Psychology*, 102 (4), 624–32

Stamp Dawkins, M. and Gosling, M. (Eds) (1991) *Association for the Study of Animal Behaviour Ethics in Research on Animal Behaviour*. London: Academic Press/Association for the Study of Animal Behaviour

Still, A.W. (1982) On the number of animals used in animal behaviour experiments. *Animal Behaviour*, 30, 873–80

Stone-Carmen, J. (1992) Personality characteristics and self-identified experiences of individuals reporting possible abduction by Unidentified Flying Objects (UFOs). Dissertation as part fulfilment of a Doctorate in Philosophy and Psychology, San Diego, USA, 10–59

Stroop, J.R. (1935) Studies of interference in serial verbal reactions. *Journal of Experimental Psychology*, 18, 643–62

Tajfel, H. (1970) Experiments in intergroup discrimination. *Scientific American*, 223, 96–102

Thornton, A. and Lee, P. (2000) Publication bias in meta-analysis: its causes and consequences. *Journal of Clinical Epidemiology*, 53, 207–16

Thurstone, L.L. (1931) The measurement of social attitudes. *Journal of Abnormal and Social Psychology*, 26, 249–69

Universities Federation for Animal Welfare (1987) *The UFAW Handbook on the Care and Management of Laboratory Animals*. Edinburgh: Churchill

Vachon, C.M., Sellers, T.A., Kushi, L.H. and Folsom, A.R. (1998) Familial correlations of dietary intakes among postmenopausal women. *Genetic Epidemiology*, 15 (6), 553–63

Wareing, M., Fisk, J.E. and Murphy, P.N. (2000) Working memory deficits in current and previous users of MDMA ('ecstasy'). *British Journal of Psychology*, 91, 181–8

Wells, M.J. (1978) *Octopus*. London: Chapman & Hall

Williamon, A. and Valentine, E. (2000) Quantity and quality of musical practice as predictors of performance quality. *British Journal of Psychology*, 91, 353–76

Williams, R.G.A., Johnson, M., Willis, L. and Bennett, A.E. (1976) Disability: a model and a measurement technique. *British Journal of Preventative and Social Medicine*, 30, 71–8

Williamson, J., Raynard, R. and Cuthbert, L. (2000) A conversation-based process tracing method for use with naturalistic decisions: an evaluation study. *British Journal of Psychology*, 91, 203–21

Wright, D.B., Self, G. and Justice, C. (2000) Memory conformity: exploring misinformation effects when presented by another person. *British Journal of Psychology*, 91, 189–202

Zaleski, E.H. and Schiaffino, K.M. (2000) Religiosity and sexual risk-taking during the transition to college. *Journal of Adolescence*, 23, 223–7

Zigmond, A.S. and Snaith, R.P. (1983) The Hospital Anxiety and Depression Scale. *Acta Psychologica Scandinavica*, 67, 361–70

Index

Figures in **bold** indicate where these terms are defined or, in the case of some statistical tests, where the relevant formula can be found.